VLADIMIR NABOKOV

Other studies by G. M. Hyde

*How are Verses Made?* by Vladimir Mayakovsky,
translated and edited by G. M. Hyde
(Jonathan Cape, 1970, reprinted 1974)
*D. H. Lawrence as Translator*, in *Delos* 4
(University of Texas, 1970)
*The Poetry of the City* and *Russian Futurism*
in the Penguin *Modernism* volume (1976)

CRITICAL APPRAISALS SERIES

General Editor: John Fletcher

# VLADIMIR NABOKOV

## America's Russian Novelist

G. M. HYDE

Marion Boyars
London

A MARION BOYARS BOOK
distributed by
Calder & Boyars Ltd
18 Brewer Street, London W1R 4AS

First published in Great Britain in 1977 by
Marion Boyars Publishers Ltd
18 Brewer Street, London W1R 4AS



ISBN 0 7145 2573 1

Printed in Great Britain by
Villiers Publications Ltd.,
London NW5

# CONTENTS

# GENERAL EDITOR'S FOREWORD

Since about the turn of the century, and more so than at any other time previously in our history, we in the West have been preoccupied with the question of the 'modernity' of our culture. The 'modern' has for some while now been a term of praise or blame, depending on your point of view; and as an object of active investigation it has preoccupied, and continues to preoccupy, anyone trying to keep abreast of the frequently disturbing and disorientating achievements of our age.

This is particularly true of the writers, artists and thinkers who are the subject of this series, which is concerned first and foremost with the phenomenon variously known as 'neo-modernism' or 'post-modernism', i.e. work produced roughly since the Second World War which explores media in a more or less radical way. The series concentrates on present-day innovators of one kind or another working in the tradition of earlier great moderns who are now dead, such as Joyce, Proust and Thomas Mann. It does not concern itself with the ups and downs of the volatile avant-garde, but only with such contemporary writers, artists, works, genres and movements as can be said to satisfy at least one of the following criteria:

1 that they have affected in a perceptible way current styles or attitudes;

2 that they already have produced an appreciable opus or corpus of creativity;

3 that they are demonstrably 'masterly' in the sense of having made a real impact on the contemporary arts and stayed in the forefront of cultural endeavour.

This series aims to offer a fresh and original way of approaching the work of our contemporaries and render accessible what is challenging and often difficult. Although the stress falls mainly on creative writing, there is also a place for artists working in other media and in fields generally considered peripheral to literature proper. All forms of contemporary art hang so much together that none can be scrutinized in isolation, and the series overall stresses the organic nature of art in a period of rapid and often disconcerting change.

For many people Vladimir Nabokov is coming to be recognized as one of the greatest contemporary novelists; it is therefore particularly opportune to have this sympathetic but not uncritical study by George Hyde, who lectures in Comparative Literature at the University of East Anglia and who combines two essential qualifications for writing about this author: a knowledge of Russian and of the Russian literary tradition on the one hand, and on the other a thorough acquaintance with the English, American and French sources of so much of Nabokov's work. It is this broad comparatist's background which enables Mr. Hyde to relate *Laughter in the Dark* to Tolstoy and *Ada* to Proust, to see in Nabokov the 'bearer of a whole wasteland of cultural fragments', and at the same time to stress his essential contribution to neo-modernism in his undertaking to 'make art from the aching void of an endless sense of loss'.

John Fletcher
General Editor

## ACKNOWLEDGEMENTS

For permission to make quotations from the works of Vladimir Nabokov acknowledgement is gratefully made to Messrs. Weidenfeld & Nicolson Ltd. For quotations from all other works acknowledgement is made to copyright holders as listed in the Bibliography on pp. 221-25 below.

# INTRODUCTION

Yet another study of Nabokov demands a brief apology. Since the publication of *Lolita* (to which Nabokov himself subsequently appended a nervously insouciant critique[1]) Nabokov criticism has gone up like a rocket, carrying its great originals, Andrew Field, L. S. Dembo, Page Stegner and Alfred Appel, Jr., into dazzling orbit.[2] If my own study refers only rather sparsely to these critics, or to many others, this should not be interpreted as disrespect. I have inevitably drawn on their work, and I hope I will be forgiven for not footnoting all the borrowings and partial assimilations. But my own approach to Nabokov is a little different from theirs, and the scope of my work is smaller than (for example) Field's.

It may have been prompted by my eye falling on a sentence of Donald Davie's, printed on the cover of my Panther edition of *The Gift*, which runs:

> *The Gift* seems to me not just brilliant (Nabokov is always that), but also profound and persuasive.[3]

This seemed to me when I read it (and the impression has subsequently been strengthened) to strike a true note in the midst of a nervous exegetical jangle. Nabokov is, indeed, a brilliant writer, and his ease and mastery, which rarely degenerates into flashiness, are a constant source of pleasure. Moreover, this pleasure is (as Julia Bader has stressed in her book, *Crystal Land*[4]) not incidental, but central to the themes of the novels. Yet, in spite of this, his work seems often to have been overread by critics whose whole delight has been to work out the intricacies that Nabokov has carefully worked in. There seems to have been a tendency to have the meaning (lots of meaning, all at one go) and miss the experience.

Nabokov has himself assimilated more completely than his critics the modernist devices which afford them such pleasure. His novels are, on the one hand, parodies of realism as well as parodies of themselves; but on the other they reveal Nabokov's continuity with classic Russian literature (with its unshakeable moral concern[5]), effect a scrupulous, witty, and original revaluation of the Russian literary tradition (by way of those European modernists whose innovations, as Nabokov likes to remind us, were often anticipated in the Russian nineteenth century[6]), and aim at their moral ends by a route of great formal dexterity, as in the work of Nabokov's beloved Pushkin.[7] They are more human than the fictions of Borges, I think, or those modern American novelists with whom Nabokov is perhaps too patly compared,[8] and evidently have proved difficult for the critic to handle, since so many get lost in the semantic wood while admiring the stylistic trees. Since some knowledge of Russian literature seems to me indispensable for an understanding of his English as well as his Russian novels, I have tried to refer to it without, I hope, becoming mandarin or irrelevant. On the other hand, I have necessarily omitted not only the writer's poems, plays, and short stories, but also his translations and auto-translations, except where they enter my discussion of his novels, all of which I have treated as if they were first written in English: an unscholarly procedure, of course.[9] There follows a brief biography, happily not yet 'bound in moss'.[10]

## NOTES

1. 'On a book entitled Lolita', appended to *Lolita* (London: Weidenfeld and Nicolson, 1959), p. 301.
2. Andrew Field, *Nabokov: His Life in Art* (London: Hodder and Stoughton, 1967); L. S. Dembo (ed.), *Nabokov: The Man and his Work* (University of Wisconsin Press, 1967); Alfred Appel and Charles Newman, *Nabokov: Criticism, reminiscences, translations and tributes* (London: Weidenfeld and Nicolson, 1971). Better than these is Page Stegner's misleadingly entitled book *Escape into Aesthetics: The Art of Vladimir Nabokov* (London: Eyre and Spottiswoode, 1967).
3. Each cover of *The Gift* (London: Panther Books, 1966).
4. Julia Bader, *Crystal Land* (University of California, 1972).
5. Fyodor's father reads Horace, Montaigne, and Pushkin on his travels (*The Gift*, p. 116). Morality and didacticism are not, of course, synonymous.

6. See, for example, his introduction to *King Queen Knave* (London: Weidenfeld and Nicolson, 1968), p. viii.
7. cf. Nabokov's comments on the purity of Pushkin's diction, his 'meaningful and noble music', and the 'impression' he gives 'of noble sense': A. S. Pushkin, *Eugene Onegin*, translated by V. Nabokov (London: Routledge and Kegan Paul, 1964, vol. 2), pp. 36 and 313.
8. See, for instance, the comments on his work by American novelists in *The Saturday Review*, January 1973.
9. For illuminating analysis of the revisions incorporated in the translations of his novels, see Andrew Field, op. cit.
10. cf. the second paragraph of *Laughter in the Dark* (Harmondsworth, Penguin Books, 1963).

## BIOGRAPHICAL NOTES

1899 (April 10th, Old Style; April 22nd, New Style): Vladimir Vladimirovich Nabokov born in St. Petersburg. Both his parents were rich and well-connected, his father being in addition a distinguished liberal politician who spent three months in solitary confinement for subversive activities. Key themes already sounded: relativity, iconoclasm, exile.

1913 -1916 Attended the liberal Tenishev School in St. Petersburg, where Mandelshtam and Zhirmunsky were later pupils. Accused by teachers of 'showing off'.

1917 While his father remained in St. Petersburg, the rest of the family moved to the Crimea. By 1918, the Whites held gay Yalta, and the author's father was a member of the Simferopol Regional Government.

1919 Red breakthrough. Flight of Nabokov family to Turkey on a Greek fruit boat.

1919-1922 Fluent in English since childhood, Nabokov took a degree in French and Russian at Cambridge, which he writes of archly in *Glory* and more soberly in *Speak, Memory*: 'Not once in my three years of Cambridge did I visit the University Library.'

1922 Father assassinated in Berlin, where he edited a liberal newspaper, by a Russian rightist who later became Hitler's administrator of emigré Russian affairs.

1923 Published two books of poems, some of which (along with reviews and stories) had already appeared in his father's paper in Berlin, where he was now living. Used the pen-name 'Sirin', and discusses this writer in *Speak, Memory* as if he was someone else: 'Among the young writers produced in exile he was the loneliest and most arrogant one.' cf. *Look at the Harlequins*.

1925 Married Vera Evseevna Slonim.

1977 Died July 2 in Montreux, Switzerland.

1926 Published his first novel, *Mashenka,* translated into German two years later, but not into English until 1970. As subsequent novels followed, they provoked 'an acute and morbid interest on the part of the critics', his opponents condemning his immorality, his admirers making 'perhaps too much of his unusual style, brilliant precision, functional imagery and that sort of thing.' (*Speak, Memory.*)

1928 Second novel: *King, Queen, Knave.* Tries to get away from emigré topics, though actually they are just driven underground. Translated into English in 1968.

1929 Third novel: *The Luzhin Defence,* translated into English in 1964 as *The Defence.* In all his later introductions Nabokov points out resentfully just how long each novel had to wait for its translator (often the author himself).

1930 *The Spy* (translated in 1965 as *The Eye*), stories, poems.

1931 *The Exploit* (translated 1971 as *Glory*). This patchy *Bildungsroman* seems as if it is taking on those emigré critics who accused Nabokov of trifling.

1932 *Kamera Obskura* (translated 1938, revised 1961, as *Laughter in the Dark*). Generally considered his nastiest book.

1934 Birth of Nabokov's only child, Dmitri. *Despair* published (translated 1966).

1935 *Invitation to a Beheading* (translated 1959).

1937 *The Gift* serialised in censored form (full version 1952; translated 1963). The Nabokovs were now living in Paris, in considerable poverty.

1949 Abandoned still unfinished novel, *Solus Rex,* and left France for America.

1941 First English novel, *The Real Life of Sebastian Knight* (written in France) published. Lecturer in literature and resident writer at Wellesley College until 1948. Simultaneously Fellow of Harvard Museum of Comparative Zoology.

1944 Vivid elliptical study of Gogol published.

1945 Death of his eldest brother Sergey ("Sebastian Knight") in Nazi prison camp.

1948 Appointed professor in the literature department of Cornell University. Engaged in autobiographical writings later systematised in the spirals of *Speak, Memory,* and with translations and the composition of *Lolita* and *Pnin*. *Bend Sinister* published.

1957 *Pnin* published, bringing Nabokov real popularity with English readers.

1959 'Now I am kept by a little girl named Lolita'. If *Pnin* brought popularity, *Lolita* brought notoriety and wealth. Gave up teaching, moved to Montreux.

1962 *Pale Fire* published. Little understood, and for this reason received as self-evidently a work of genius. Critics rival each other in brilliance.

1964 *Eugene Onegin* published in Nabokov's controversial translation, with massive scholarly apparatus and a clutch of fine essays.

1969 *Ada or Ardor: A Family Chronicle* published. More like current American novels than his other books, it was received with irritation in many quarters and criticized for self-indulgence and sentimentality.

1972 *Transparent Things* shocks by a concentration as extreme as *Ada's* diffuseness. It reads like a disenchanted afterword to that novel. Nabokov still living in Montreux with his wife, Vera, to be near their son, an opera singer in Italy.

1974 *Look at the Harlequins* published. Somewhat reminiscent of this biographical survey. The 'only real identity papers' of the novelist are his novels: but the whole literary career seems as if it were someone else's.

# I

## Tradition and Innovation: **The Gift** (1952, 1963: written 1935-7)

Criticism of Nabokov has customarily paid tribute to his brilliance and originality, often with a reference to lepidoptera (eg 'the shimmer of colours on a butterfly's wing'[1]). His power of conjuring fictional worlds into being, of excluding all normative appeals to 'reality' (as Tony Tanner says admiringly of *Pale Fire*, 'it is nearly all foreground'[2]), has commonly been seen as a retreat into protective word-games analogous to the procedures of some modern American novelists, or of the labyrinth-maker Borges (with whom in fact Nabokov has less in common than is sometimes supposed). The erection of verbal citadels is felt to be related to the predicament of the writer in the modern world, and the critical response to this activity has tended to be an extreme exegetical ingenuity, by means of which the critic bids for admission to the citadel of the fiction. While not for the moment suggesting that it is wrong to see Nabokov in these terms, I am struck by the fact that the demands Nabokov makes of his reader, involving him in the creative process and then laying traps and false clues for him (his texts are all, to use Barthes' categories, 'scriptible' rather than 'lisible'[3]) has tended to blind some professional readers to the fact that the aim of his endeavour is not so much to transcend the world as to give it back to us afresh, to make us see things as they are. Since this can only be accomplished through an existential process in which we actively participate, which for Nabokov necessarily entails the deformation of a habitually accepted 'reality', his novels are formally strange and ingenious. But his deformations have the same function as the optician's lens has when it distorts the image in order to compensate for the distorting effect of our myopic eye: the end of Nabokov's art is to make us see more clearly what is really there, and this could be described quite properly as a moral end.

Games, pastiche, butterfly-chases of one kind or another, in other words, are for Nabokov not just ways of being clever, or asserting a superiority over the reader or the work (though they have been taken as such by some professional readers whose dissipated ingenuities far outdo Nabokov's own); they are rather devices organized towards the creation of an art which, in Nabokov's own words, merges 'the precision of poetry and the excitement of pure science'. The paradox built into this formula hopefully effects an inextricable conjunction. In the same interview[4] — Nabokov's most illuminating — from which this comes, he adds:

> A lily is more real to a naturalist than it is to an ordinary person. But it is still more real to a botanist. And any further stage of reality is reached with that botanist who is a specialist in lilies.

Nabokov's art is shaped by a nostalgia for the exact correspondence of the word and the thing, a literary taxonomy as watertight as the scientist's. To call it a love of craftsmanship would be to pitifully understate the case; it is a passion for truth, and a search for a mechanism of sensibility, both analytic and synthetic, adequate to the perception and communication of this truth. The favourite language of classification, the appeal to the 'specialist' whose trained eye observes the minute deviation within the established norm (an art, like his, which values surprise, is *ipso facto* an art which relies on convention and tradition — see, for instance, the detective story[5]) can appear cold; but in fact the impersonality of the scientist is prized mainly for its power of resisting the unhelpful mystical ecstasy which tempts those Romantic writers who, like Nabokov, interpret the hidden meanings of the world. To abandon the actuality of the world for an artificial paradise of myth and miracle is to court comic disaster: you begin by walking on the water and end up (like Dostoevsky or Thomas Mann, perhaps) 'descending upright among staring fish'.[6] The greatest art therefore fuses profundity with urbanity, passion with objectivity. The desiderata are not so far from those of Eliot, when he wrote:

> When a poet's mind is perfectly equipped for its work, it is constantly amalgamating disparate experience; the ordinary man's experience is chaotic, irregular, fragmentary . . . Those who object to the 'artificiality' of Milton or Dryden sometimes tell us to 'look into our hearts and write'. But that is not looking deep enough; Racine or Donne looked into a good deal more than the heart. One must look into the cerebral cortex, the nervous system, and the digestive tracts.[7]

The Bergsonian quasi-scientific language of this reminds us that the 'synthesis' both Eliot and Nabokov desire has an extreme perceptual complexity in its fusion of time past and present. The revaluation and renewal of the literary tradition is undertaken, for Russian literature, by Nabokov in *The Gift* (where the relative judgements, as first-hand and idiosyncratic as Eliot's, gave as much offence as Eliot's did). His search for new bearings among the great works of the past (an essentially creative effort safeguarding living continuity) posits a Bergsonian interpenetration of memory and perception enacted on the cultural as well as the personal plane, Pushkin and Gogol serving Nabokov as examples of that admirable 'mechanism of sensibility'[8] which Eliot finds in the English poets of the seventeenth century. The analogy should perhaps not be pressed much farther than this, since Nabokov has found occasion for profound disagreement with Eliot's work and thought; suffice it to say that if Eliot saw the mid-nineteenth century as 'an age of bustle, programmes, platforms, scientific progress, humanitarianism and revolutions which improved nothing',[9] accompanied by a coarsening of language and sensibility which threatened serious literature, Nabokov (though Eliot's polemical pathos is a mode altogether alien to him) seems to agree:

> The fifties are now in full fan. It is permitted to smoke on the streets. One may wear a beard. The overture to *William Tell* is thundered out on every musical occasion. Rumours spread that the capital is being moved to Moscow; that the old calendar is going to be replaced by the new. Under this cover Russia is busily gathering material for Saltikov's primitive but juicy satire.[10]

It was because of this 'modern' freedom with the great social-reforming tradition of the Russian nineteenth century that the crucial fourth chapter of *The Gift* was turned down by the leading Liberal emigré journal.[11]

Fyodor, the hero of *The Gift*, sets out to write an exploratory biography of his dead explorer father in order to define his relationship with him and by doing so to grasp his own identity. Adrift, when the novel opens, in an impressionistic world of surfaces without a centre, he dreams of literary success, but cannot connect the fantasy world in which he is a great poet with the shadowy Berlin in which he lives as a rootless outsider. His fantasies entail that schizoid condition (seeing his 'real' self reflected in the mirror of his fame) which in other Nabokov heroes becomes a pathological condition, but is here no more than a Prufrockian impotence punctuated (and punctured) by real embarrassments, as, for instance, when the 'other' Chernyshevsky — not the nineteenth century radical whom he later writes about, but the emigré of the same name who has lost his hold on reality, and whose son kills himself in a romantic-literary fit of melancholia — fools him into believing that his poems have been enthusiastically reviewed.[12] The stream of Fyodor's consciousness keeps dissolving into imaginary literary dialogue with the emigré writer he most admires, artfully presented by Nabokov in such a way that the reader follows him into passionate debate without realizing that it is actually Laforguian monodrama. In his impermanent world of ephemeral bedsitters (from which he is constantly locking himself out) Fyodor builds a compensatory inner world. But if this were all he did, he might follow Chernyshevsky into sheer insanity or, like Yasha, take his life. This does not happen; instead, Fyodor finds the key to the chamber containing his 'gift', and he does so by a process whereby he recognizes the connections betwen his own talent (one meaning of 'gift') and the heritage (another meaning of 'gift') of Russian literature, together with the knowledge that the two are indissolubly linked (inasmuch as his talent is genuine and not, like Busch's, a fit of literary nostalgia[13]). He also discovers that his very awareness of his own being in the world can be morally defined and strengthened through a sense of cultural continuity: 'tradition' sustains the 'individual talent'. For, as Bergson tells us, as long as we regard the past as *merely* past we impoverish our present:

> We shall never reach the past unless we frankly place ourselves within it. Essentially virtual, it cannot be known as something past unless we follow and adopt the movement by which it expands into a present image, thus emerging from obscurity into the light of day.[14]

Fyodor's quest for his father, which has the larger cultural overtones of that archetypal search of a mazed artificer, Stephen Dedalus's in *Ulysses*,[15] leads him out of the ivory tower of self-conscious lyricism into plain prose. Already in Chapter Two, entering the base of the rainbow (as he heard his father had once done on his travels), Fyodor passes through the looking-glass of art (which hitherto had mocked him with his own futile reflection) into a landscape of memory which at the same time offers a crystal precision of detail (it is by no means a delusion of nostalgia). Initially, his vision fades too easily back into the tramcars of the Berlin street; but accompanied by his mother on his 'silent walk performed by two minds, using according to the rules of the game the rate of a human footstep',[16] he pitches his melody of art and memory according to what he calls 'the purest sound from Pushkin's tuning fork' — the marvellous *Journey to Arzrum*.

Pushkin, having impulsively left Petersburg in March 1830, headed for the Caucasus to see his brother and some friends who were serving with the Russian Army there. On the way he stopped in Moscow to pay court to his future wife, Natalya Goncharova. He received General Paskevich's permission to join the army, and proceeded from Tiflis to meet up with Paskevich at the citadel of Kars, whence he was planning an assault on the Turkish city of Erzerum (or Arzrum, as Pushkin spells it). He enjoyed army life, and took part in the conquest of Erzerum, whereupon he made his way back to Moscow via the romantic garrison towns and spas that map out the wanderings of Pechorin in *A Hero of Our Time*. But Pushkin's *Journey* is not romantic in the Lermontov style; although it is pervaded by a sense of wonder, it is notable for its objectivity, coherence, and disinterestedness, and for a prose which combines imagination and urbanity in the manner which is wholly characteristic of its author. E. J. Simmons remarks that:

> Everybody knew that the famous poet had been with the army, and upon his return they expected thrilling verse on Russia's victories and heroes. Pushkin published nothing, and his silence was severely criticized, especially by Bulgarin. His Caucasian experiences inspired a few short pieces, however, and several years later (1836) he wrote his prose *Journey to Erzerum*.[17]

Pointed and laconic observation of scenery and fauna in a spirit of scientific curiosity reveals a strangeness the equal, as Pushkin himself says, of any 'Spanish novel'. His meticulously timed prose creates a sense of the mere fact or event being its own adequate symbolization (as in the well-known account of coming upon a party of Georgians carrying the coffin of Griboedov, murdered in Teheran). The notion of the 'podvig' or glorious exploit (*Podvig* is the title of the Nabokov novel translated as *Glory*) is quietly deflated, and, in general, there is no spilt poetry. Indeed, in his preface to the *Journey*, Pushkin quotes a French account of the expedition in which he finds himself named —

> M. Pouchkine . . . avait quitté la capitale pour chanter les exploits de ses compatriotes

— an account which, he says, angered him much more than the censures of Russian critics. 'Seeking inspiration,' he writes,

> 'has always seemed to me a ludicrous and absurd fancy: inspiration will not be sought; it must itself find the poet. To join in a war in order to sing of the great deeds (*podvig*) to come would seem to me on the one hand altogether egocentric, and on the other hand quite indecent.'[18]

With these words (and with the whole conduct of his narrative) Pushkin asserts the disinterestedness of the artist, and it is the 'accuracy of the words and the absolute purity of their conjunction' of this work and of Pushkin's *History of the Pugachov Rebellion* that Fyodor takes as his model in order to, as he puts it, 'enlarge his lungs'.[19] Trying the door of his cell, he finds he can unlock it after all. Stepping into the fresh air, he finds that Nature and Pushkin (like Nature and Homer, in Pope's *Essay on Criticism*) are the same.

The naturalness of Pushkin's art was of course a great synthetic achievement, bringing together native Russian and foreign (especially French) material, civilizing the one (and thereby establishing the foundations of the Russian literary language) and Russianizing the other: Pushkin is the Russian Shakespeare. Modern Russian criticism has had to feel its way back to this source, like English criticism in the case of Shakespeare and the seventeenth century, across the rockfalls and false trails of literary history. If the Russian path is shorter, the undergrowth is denser on account of the relative newness and instability of the Russian literary language. Yet this approach to the great Pushkin (and the light it throws on the culture which his father stood for) is only the beginning of Fyodor's journey. His designated way is ultimately more circuitous, and he must negotiate a massive mountain range altogether less alluring than the misty Caucasus: the socially committed literature which dominates the nineteenth century in Russia, and the ideological polemics which shape the historicist criticism which accompanies it. One might have thought, at first sight, that Fyodor (and Nabokov) could have circumvented this obstacle as easily as Eliot negotiates the ethical and utilitarian literature of the English nineteenth century — but this was impossible. The Belinsky-Chernyshevsky-Dobrolyubov[20] line of literary criticism, historicist and increasingly materialist, not only dominates Russian literature to such an extent that exasperated social debate swings back and forth in the work of *all* the major novelists (and bystanders whose minds were on quite different matters get caught up in it — Gogol, for instance), but also represents a stand against autocracy and the tyranny of literary censorship, and an opposition to the obscurantist Slavophilism of, for example, Dostoevsky, which is Nabokov's special bête noire. And here is a fine paradox: while this 'progressive' school of criticism has been institutionalized in the Soviet Union, the Russian emigration (which, as Nabokov never tires of pointing out, did not consist entirely of monocled White officers and Parisian taxi-driving princes) considered itself entrusted with the responsibility for safeguarding the ideals of liberty enshrined in this tradition and betrayed, as they saw it, by the Bolsheviks. When Koncheyev reviews Fyodor's life of Chernyshevsky, he begins:

> by drawing a picture of flight during an invasion or an earthquake, when the escapers carry away with them everything that they can lay hands on, someone being sure to burden himself with a large, framed portrait of some long-forgotten relative. 'Just such a portrait' (wrote Koncheyev) 'is for the Russian intelligentsia the image of Chernyshevsky, which was spontaneously but accidentally carried away abroad by the emigrés, together with other, more useful things.'[21]

and he ends up (by way of explaining the hostility to Fyodor's book, echoed in the hostility to Nabokov's): 'Somebody suddenly confiscated the portrait.'

Actually this is an overstatement, for if Fyodor *does* deprive the emigration of their familiar image of Chernyshevsky, he gives them in its place a new picture, one in which art breathes life into dry bones. His father combined a love of lepidoptera with a love of freedom, and in order for Fyodor to apprehend him fully, to reach the point at which his father will walk in the door and present Fyodor with all the cultural and personal riches of his 'gift', he must pass beyond Pushkin's libertarian idealism and broaden the basis of a revaluation of the tradition of Russian literature conceived symbolically as free consciousness pitted against the autocracy of time and space. In order to return to the fullness of his father's being and his own (and thus to make possible his marriage to Zina, the intensely personal culmination to the whole process) he must extend his conception of patrimony —

> In order to arrive at what you are not
> You must go through the way in which you are not.[22]

He abandons the unfinished biography of his father, noting in a letter to his mother that

> When I read his . . . books and I hear their entrancing rhythm, when I study the position of the words that can neither be replaced nor rearranged, it seems to me a sacrilege to take all this and dilute it with myself.[23]

He moves to new lodgings (attracted by a premonition of Zina) — about as far away from the old, says Nabokov, as Gogol Street is from Pushkin Avenue — and his quest enters a decisive new phase. The presiding genius is no longer Pushkin but Gogol, the theme not Fyodor's father but a father-figure of Russian liberalism, Chernyshevsky. The style of the novel at once becomes more comic and devious, more fanciful and 'metaphysical', yet at the same time more grotesquely involved with the minutiae of Berlin life. Pushkin, the forefather, has brought him to this point, and can take him no further; Gogol must now be his guide, and the resources of baroque Gogolian wit will be stretched to the utmost by being applied to such an apparently unsuitable subject as Chernyshevsky, thereby enabling Nabokov to exact at the same time a sweet revenge for the misappropriation of Gogol by materialist criticism.[24] In the Pushkin commentary Nabokov remarks of a cancelled stanza that it

> affords an admirable example of Pushkin's genius for extracting meaningful and noble music out of the most trivial words; in fact, it is exactly the contrast between their humdrum, subservient nature and the sonorities they develop within the acoustical paradise of Pushkin's tetrameter that produces the impression of noble sense . . . This is exactly opposite to the technique that Gogol employed when introducing dummy words, adverbial weeds, and prepositional debris into the stumbling patter of his automatons and larval homunculi, as, for instance, in his *The Carrick* (or *Greatcoat*).[25]

At this point the debt to Bergson already hinted at takes on a new form.

Nabokov is of course a comic writer, and the renewal of the tradition which takes place in his work is inseparable from a process of parodic defamiliarization. Critics talk of his flair for pastiche; but while it is true that he has a Joycean ear for the idiolects of other writers, it should be clear that pastiche and parody are in his work essentially comic versions of the *ostranenie*, or defamiliarization, which Russian critics promoted to the status of the principal device of modern art (and of the art of the past alive in the present).[26] If both Eliot and Nabokov owe to Bergson their conception of the indissoluble interrelatedness of tradition and the individual talent, Nabokov (whose later work contains highly critical references to 'wastelandism' — Spenglerian cultural pessimism — and to those who, like Chaadaev, find 'a cure for . . . spleen in the Roman Catholic Faith'[27]) differs from Eliot in giving pride of place not to *Matter and Memory* but to *Laughter* (*Le Rire*, 1900). In this Nabokov is in step with Russian criticism of the modernist period (which, characteristically, he hardly refers to, though he does admit to admiring Tomashevski's edition of *Eugene Onegin*). The scope of Bergson's short book is, of course, larger than its title suggests; it studies, in his own words, 'the general relation that art bears to life',[28] and the theory of comedy advanced in it presents comedy as a phenomenon situated *between* art and life. In his own words:

> Comedy lies midway between art and life. It is not disinterested as genuine art is. By organizing laughter, comedy accepts social life as a natural environment; it even obeys an impulse of social life, and in this respect it turns its back upon art, which is a breaking away from society and a return to pure nature.[29]

It is therefore altogether appropriate that Fyodor should ultimately feel his way towards a social persona (and towards the reincarnation of his father) by way of comedy.

Life in Schyogolev's flat is presented comically. We find here all the devices that Bergson lists as conducive to laughter: an abundance of strictly human, and merely human, detail; a delimited and strictly *social* environment; habitual and automated acts on the part of the comic protagonists (Schyogolev's vulgar gestures and mechanically reiterated catch-phrases, and Fyodor's chronic absent-mindedness, both of which contrast with what Bergson calls 'the living pliableness of a human being',[30] the property which his vitalist philosophy considers crucial to human survival). The value of comedy, as Bergson sees it, is defined by evolution; by its means, society mocks at and rejects rigid, inflexible behaviour patterns which are inimical to the adaptability required of the organism which is to survive. But Bergson goes further than this utilitarian argument: the deformities and grimaces presented by comedy — in caricature, for instance — not only call attention to the 'deep-seated recalcitrance of matter'[31] they also imply an ideal of vital movement, the shaping lightness of the soul, and

> The originality of a comic artist is thus expressed in the special kind of life he imparts to a mere puppet.[32]

Evidently we have drawn close to the imaginative world of Fyodor's biography of Chernyshevsky. If comedy turns upon 'a mechanical element introduced into nature and an automatic regulation of society',[33] Chernyshevsky is a 'gift' to the comic writer, since he devoted his life to the automatic regulation of society, was a rigorous materialist, and wrote with a mechanical logic suggestive of an automaton. Fyodor need do no more than set his puppet in motion.

In fact, of course, he *does* do more. As Bergson pursues his argument, his terms of reference become wider. Comedy is also sport, 'a game that imitates life',[34] such as children play, and one which draws on our memories in order to activate the fullness of our being in the face of the inertia of matter. The foregrounding of mechanical patterns of action and rigidities of language (cf. Nabokov's comment on Gogol above) is a parodic device tending towards the defamiliarization of concepts, the breaking of habits; because, in Bergson's words,

> A comic effect is always obtainable by transposing the natural expression of an idea into another key.[35]

This is precisely what Fyodor does. Laughter has taken us (as it takes Fyodor) from the framed portrait valued from a habit of deference to institutionalized values to the sensation of life itself as a dynamic continuum.

> The rigid, the ready-made, the mechanical, in contrast with the supple, the ever-changing, and the living, absent-mindedness in contrast with attention, in a word, automatism in contrast with free activity, such are the defects that laughter singles out and would fain correct.[36]

Laughter, in other words, born of a very serious kind of parody and pastiche, helps Fyodor out of the emigré wasteland of inactivity and compensatory fantasy in which the heroes of *Mary* and *The Exploit* are marooned.

And if we look closely at his biography of Chernyshevsky, we find that it is not derisive, but an act of homage. Chernyshevsky's theories of art [37] evidently cannot be taken seriously, since they are shaped by the materialist fallacy that the mind has unmediated access to reality. This is as untrue as the contention that consciousness has direct access to the past. There must be some mediating agent. Bergson elsewhere calls it memory, giving to the word a very wide meaning; here he calls it art, and his theory of art is Nabokov's.

> What is the object of art? Could reality come into direct contact with sense and consciousness, could we enter into immediate communion with things and with ourselves, probably art would be useless, or rather we should all be artists, for then our soul would continually vibrate in perfect accord with nature . . . Between nature and ourselves, nay, between ourselves and our own consciousness a veil is interposed: a veil that is dense and opaque for the common herd — thin, almost transparent, for the artist and the poet . . . The *individuality* of things or of beings escapes us . . . we confine ourselves to reading the labels affixed to them . . . Art is certainly only a more direct vision of reality. But this purity of perception implies a break with utilitarian convention, an innate and specially localized disinterestedness of sense or consciousness, in short, a certain immateriality of life, which is what has always been called idealism . . . Realism is in the work when idealism is in the soul . . . it is only through ideality that we can resume contact with reality.[38]

I have quoted this passage at length because it seems to me to provide the terms with which to answer those critics who accuse Nabokov of trifling, or of retreating into a world of pure aesthetics; art is for him, as for Bergson, our most translucent window on the world (though to the casual observer it looks like a mirror). Likewise, Fyodor's biography of Chernyshevsky, apparently a witty and narcissistic display piece, is actually the precipitate and synthesis of his musings on art and his encounters with society. While two critics, extreme representatives of the idealist and the materialist approaches to their author, pass contradictory and irreconcilable judgements, Fyodor, who contains and controls both of them, writes the biography suggested to him (appropriately enough) by a chess problem in a Soviet magazine (wherein chess games are presented as 'tasks' rather than as problems). With scraps of Bely and Gogol drifting through his head, helping him to overcome the automatized vulgarity of Berlin life, and to find a proper language, he comes to reflect on the scrap of Chernyshevsky's diary printed in the chess magazine. The style fascinates him.

> The drolly circumstantial style, the meticulously inserted adverbs, the passion for semicolons, the clogging down of thought in midsentence and the clumsy attempts to extricate it (whereupon it got stuck at once elsewhere, and the author had to start worrying it out all over again), the drubbing-in, rubbing-in tone of each word, the knight-moves of sense in the trivial commentary on his minutest actions, the viscid ineptitude of these actions (as if some workshop glue had got onto the man's hands, and both were left), the seriousness, the limpness, the honesty, the poverty — all this pleased Fyodor so much, he was so amazed and tickled by the fact that an author with such a mental and verbal style was considered to have influenced the literary destiny of Russia, that on the very next morning he signed out the complete works of Chernyshevsky from the state library. And as he read, his astonishment grew, and this feeling contained a peculiar kind of bliss.[30]

A string of comic devices of the kind described by Bergson initiates Fyodor's attempt to penetrate the living reality of his subject. 'Firing practice,' he calls it; but his biography, 'on the very brink of parody' (his words to Zina), leads him deep into the utilitarian tradition of Russian literature, and at every turn he fishes out of these muddy waters some strange missing link between reality and fantasy, as if a Bergsonian muse had exacted revenge on those who maintained that matter can be directly grasped by consciousness. Strange little gremlins mock rationality at its most solemn moments, language wriggles away from the nets of intellect, the rigid teleology imposed on life by materialist historicism is pitifully (and splendidly) negated by the quirks of life itself which seem to reveal not a Hegelian purpose but a pattern of spiralling recurrences like the rhyme scheme of a poem. Indeed, Fyodor's biography will be set within a sonnet, so that he can end with Chernyshevsky's birth (which he does literally and in the sense that the last line of a poem, like that of Shade's *Pale Fire*, points to its first); and so that the finiteness of a book 'which . . . is opposed to the circular nature of everything in existence' is subsumed by 'a continuously curving, and thus infinite, sentence',[40] Joyce's dream realized in *Finnigan's Wake*.

Fyodor's biography was rejected, as was Nabokov's novel in its complete form. But it would be wrong to interpret this as evidence of Wilde's contention that nature imitates art, a theory as inadequate as the utilitarian belief that art imitates nature. It is even more beside the point to suppose that Nabokov endorses Wilde's easy aphorism. Art is nature's handmaid, serving to reveal truth by means of a complex assault on habit. It does not aim to be freakish, though parodic distortion is one of its weapons. It does not try to evade reality, and nothing could be more real than the image of Chernyshevsky that emerges from Fyodor's pages, which frankly lay bare the devices they employ in order to isolate the 'themes' of his life (conceived as quasi-biological patterns in the behaviour of an organism of a given genetic mix: thoroughly Bergsonian). Fate mocked him: Fyodor does not. There is, after all, a queer kind of kinship between an author and his creation, and, as in Bergson's analysis of the child playing with the Jack-in-the-Box (always pressed down, always springing up again — like Pnin), 'comic fancy gradually converts a material mechanism into a moral one'.[41] He has the jerky energy of a Gogol character — 'his love for materiality was not reciprocated';[42] he is known in official circles as a buffoon, and for this reason dangerous, whereas he was in fact the most humourless of men, and so theoretical as to be altogether safe (Fyodor's wit, however, restores his radical strangeness). A life dedicated to freedom was passed in the small cell of his own limited imagination and in prison and exile. Even in Siberia he lived pressed between the pages of his books, oblivious to the natural riches around him which softened many a political exile. Fyodor, far from deriding this amazingly original and honest man who is conventionally honoured not as a human being but as a social institution, would like to help him to escape the bonds of necessity (as Nabokov helps Krug in *Bend Sinister*). If only, for example, he had been executed when his fame was at its height, instead of dragging on in obscure exile to a lonely and embittered death! But the false ending Fyodor provides cannot be allowed to stand, and the best he can do is salvage from a futile exile (one grows more and more conscious of how salutary a tale Chernyshevsky's life is for Fyodor) a handful of striking images: Chernyshevsky standing for hours in a Siberian stream with his trousers rolled up, or hearing at last the news of his pardon; or Chernyshevsky translating 'with machinelike steadiness' (one 'theme' of his life is the perpetual motion machine he invented as a boy) Georg Weber's *Universal History*, into which he smuggles ideas of his own.

The eventual publication of Fyodor's book gives Nabokov the chance to write a sequence of deft pastiches of emigré reviewers. One is intelligent (Koncheyev, of course, with whom Fyodor is to have a last imaginary conversation); and a nice Prague professor takes him to task for using an imaginary source, the scholar Strannolubsky, a name which translates into English as 'Strangelove' (the professor does not realize that this pseudonym is a code masking Fyodor's strange love for Chernyshevsky). But matter of greater moment is still to come. The publication of the book coincides with the death of the 'other' Chernyshevsky, Fyodor's half-demented emigré friend, father of Yasha, the suicide. The father and son theme echoes Fyodor's biography, for the historical Chernyshevsky, too, had an unbalanced and to him incomprehensible son, whose mad detachment from the world seemed like a thematic counterpoint to his father's rigorous materialism (the emigré Chernyshevsky dies sure that there is nothing after death; this is 'as clear as the fact that it is raining', he says, hearing the upstairs tenant watering her flowers on this dry spring day[43]). And Gogol attends his funeral (the 'prim gentleman with a blond little beard and unusually red lips'[44] who haunts Fyodor's biography). Art reveals its purpose: to tell the truth, to strip off the dead husk that encloses 'the other world' which, as Nabokov's favourite fictional philosopher Delalande remarks, 'surrounds us always and is not at all at the end of some pilgrimage.'[45] Practically naked in the Berlin woods, close to the place where Yasha killed himself, Fyodor recalls his father's expeditions and the Pushkinesque prose in which he had imagined them described. Nabokov does not deal openly in ritual and myth, but it is clear that this glade by a lake (echoed in *Despair* and *Lolita*) is the culmination of a process of spiritual growth.

Fyodor feels the interrelatedness of his life and Yasha's, and consequently of the two Chernyshevskys, of all fathers and all sons (Joyce's *Ulysses* seems close at hand, but so, of course, is Turgenev's novel *Fathers and Sons*, the most disinterested witness to this nineteenth century debate). Salvation is personal, but cannot be merely personal. The imaginary dialogue with Koncheyev is more self-critical than the earlier one, and Fyodor is more aware of how much he has borrowed 'on the strength of the legacy' — the riches he has been left by his father, all his fathers. It is appropriate that he should be naked — stripped of his camouflage of fantasy — and that he should have to run the gauntlet of the Berlin streets thus (previously, he had cultivated a distance which permitted him a sort of superiority to the boorish aliens around him). Now he is fit to confront his father.

He has gone a long way to come back to where he started from, but now he does indeed, in Eliot's phrase, 'know the place for the first time'.[46] The dream of his father, a magnificent sequence in which the streets of Berlin melt into those of Petersburg, dissolves his 'icy' heart in 'paradisal' warmth. He wakes (like Proust's Marcel) into a 'dungeon of dingy non-being', but now he has the key — and knows where to use it, and what it will disclose. Amid allusions to 'lost keys', a theme of the novel just as spectacles and perpetual motion machines were themes of the Chernyshevsky biography, Fyodor opens the door on life with Zina, and a music sounds that resonates beyond the last paragraph, where the author arbitrarily sets the magic formula 'The End'. It is Nabokov's warmest and happiest conclusion, evidently prompted by a sense of personal fulfilment at this stage of his own life. Things will not, of course, stay like that, and the wide terrain covered by Fyodor will have to be fought for and repossessed piecemeal, over and over again. But the powerful normative impulse which shapes *The Gift* persists in Nabokov's work. The interlingual Joycean games of his English novels are an exile's dream of the only free world than can accommodate him — but they are not evasions of moral problems, except in the case of those of his protagonists whose hypertrophied language is a device to set them 'above' the common herd. If they have an appeal and interest which goes far beyond the literal theme of exile, this is because exile (as *Speak, Memory* reveals) is a representative condition insofar as we are exiled from our pasts, and thus from part of ourselves, unless art can restore the wholeness we have lost. Nabokov's hostility to materialist interpretations of human life (each novel or preface contains an obligatory derisive reference to Freudianism) by no means entails an aesthete's religion of art. He has a holy dread of religion's claim to know the unknowable, and the religion of art is to him as misguided as the dogmatic faith of those who have fled from exile into the church. He is instead a born translator, in the way the modern writer has to be, and has learned to accept that his life shall be spent shifting his cultural belongings from one lodging to another, from one language to another (a process culminating in his masterly edition of *Eugene Onegin* and the more abstract assault on the divisiveness of space and time in *Ada* and — with more than a hint of despair — *Transparent Things*). His work is all of a piece, even if it does not have quite the artistic shape imposed on it with the benefit of authorial hindsight in the frequently misleading prefaces he has supplied to English versions of his Russian works (in themselves a striking if not quite honest Bergsonian fusion of matter and memory). He defies criticism by anticipating it and weaving it into the texture of his work, but this lepidopteral camouflage has not prevented his being torn apart and digested by hungry exegetes. His curious maskings and disguises have actually proved highly attractive. Criticism enjoys nothing so much as a juicy butterfly. Yet the shadow of the butterfly flies on, like the waxwing of Shade's poem.[47]

## Notes to Chapter One

1. Julian Mitchell, back cover of *The Gift*.
2. Tony Tanner, *City of Words: American Fiction 1950-70* (London: Jonathan Cape, 1971), p. 33.
3. This distinction is set out, for example, in Roland Barthes, S/Z, (Paris: Edition du Seuil, 1970). It hinges on the proposition that some texts can be 'read' in the sense of passively consumed, while others demand a creative effort on the part of the reader, who as it were 'writes' the book as he reads it.
4. 'Vladimir Nabokov on His Life and Work', an interview with Peter Duval Smith in *The Listener*, LXVIII (Nov. 22nd, 1962), pp. 856-858.
5. Modern French structural criticism, following Russian formalist critics like Shklovsky, has devoted serious attention to the detective story as a genre in which plot devices are foregrounded — thus providing a simplified model on which generalizations about novel form can be based. See Tsvetan Todorov, *Théorie de la Littérature* (Paris: Editions du Seuil, 1965) and, for example, *Teksty sovetskogo literaturovedcheskogo strukturalizma*, ed. Karl Eimermacher (München: Fink Verlag, 1971), pp. 65-68, 119-123.
6. Nabokov, *Transparent Things* (London: Weidenfeld and Nicolson, 1973). The book is concerned with the fragility of the surface tension maintaining the world of human experience.
7. T. S. Eliot, *Selected Essays* (London: Faber, 1958) p. 287.
8. *Ibid.*
9. *Ibid*, p. 427.
10. Nabokov, *The Gift*, p. 227.
11. Nabokov himself gives an account of how *Sovremmenye Zapiski* published the novel with the omission of Chapter Four in his 'Foreword' to *The Gift*.
12. Nabokov, *The Gift*, p. 15.
13. Busch's ridiculous verse-drama, with its musty odour of Petersburg in the '90s and the symbolist plays of Blok, is a derivative exercise in a spent convention (*The Gift*, p. 68). It was tempting for emigrés to live through this moment of literary history over and over again.
14. Henri Bergson, *Matter and Memory* (London: Allen and Unwin, 1950) p. 173. Bergson's book was first published in English in 1911, this being a translation of the fifth French edi-

tion (*Matière et Mémoire*) of 1908. It was first published in 1896.

15. James Joyce, *Ulysses* (Paris, 1922) gives a mythic ordering to the quest for continuity, and this of course distinguishes his novel sharply from Nabokov's, where myth is chastely eschewed. Nabokov has expressed his admiration for Joyce, and his reservations, in an interview with Alfred Appel Jr. See *Nabokov: The Man and his Work*, ed. Dembo, p. 26ff.
16. Nabokov, *The Gift*, p. 86.
17. E. J. Simmons, *Pushkin* (New York: Vintage Books, 1964), p. 305.
18. A. S. Pushkin, *Sochineniya*, vol. 3 (Moscow: State Publishing House for Literature, 1962), pp. 501-2. My translation.
19. Nabokov, *The Gift*, p. 94.
20. A footnote is hardly the place to characterize and distinguish these giants. I refer the reader to Ralph Matlaw, *Belinsky, Chernyshevsky and Dobrolyubov: Selected Criticism* (New York: E. P. Dutton, 1962), a paperback collection of their seminal essays.
21. Nabokov, *The Gift*, p. 281.
22. T. S. Eliot, 'East Coker', in *Four Quartets* (London: Faber and Faber, 1944).
23. Nabokov, *The Gift*, p. 131.
24. See, for instance, V. G. Belinsky, *Thoughts and Notes on Russian Literature*, in Simmons, Pushkin, p. 3.
25. Pushkin, *Eugene Onegin*, tr. Nabokov, vol. 2, p. 313. The analogy Nabokov draws between the two writers rests on the word 'opposite', which implies 'the other side of the coin' rather than divergence.
26. See, for example, Viktor Shklovsky, *Art as Technique* (elsewhere referred to as *Art as Device*), in L. T. Lemon and M. J. Reis, *Russian Formalist Criticism: Four Essays* (University of Nebraska Press, 1965).
27. Pushkin/Nabokov, *Eugene Onegin*, vol. 2, p. 46.
28. Henri Bergson, 'Laughter', in Wylie Sypher (ed.), *Comedy* (New York, Doubleday Anchor, 1956), p. 145.
29. *Ibid.*, p. 170.
30. This phrase, or a variant of it, is used a dozen times by Bergson to characterize the positive implicit in the negatives and distortions of comedy.
31. Taken in the largest sense, of course, Chernyshevsky is a highly suitable comic subject. Moreover the perpetual motion

machine he was obsessed with as a boy seems to be ticking on in Bergson's reference (op. cit.) to the comic attention to 'processes that consist in looking upon life as a repeating mechanism' (p. 126).

32. *Ibid.*, p. 80.
33. *Ibid.*, p. 90.
34. Bergson defines 'imitation' with care, and means mime rather than mimesis (cf. Bergson, 'Laughter', p. 127).
35. Bergson, 'Laughter', p. 140.
36. It is evident here that Bergson's concern with comic devices is at the same time moral. The 'rigidity' of which he talks is a moral fault as well as an artistic technique. This is made explicit on p. 156.
37. Chernyshevsky's master's dissertation, oddly described by Fyodor in a dismissive aside as 'disingenuous', was on *The Aesthetic Relations of Art to Reality* (*The Gift*, p. 205).
38. Bergson, 'Laughter', p. 157.
39. Nabokov, *The Gift*, p. 179.
40. *Ibid.*, p. 188.
41. Bergson, 'Laughter', p. 110. There is more on this process on p. 69.
42. Nabokov, *The Gift*, p. 207.
43. *Ibid.*, p. 285. This beautiful passage finely illustrates the seriousness underlying Nabokov's mirror-play, as well as exemplifying his Bergsonian talent for making poetic imagination 'but a full view of reality' (*Laughter*).
44. *Ibid.*, pp. 285 and 258.
45. *Ibid.*, p. 283.
46. T. S. Eliot, 'Little Gidding', in *Four Quartets*.
47. 'I was the shadow of the waxwing slain
    By the false azure in the windowpane;
    I was the smudge of ashen fluff — and I
    Lived on, flew on, in the reflected sky.'
    (*Pale Fire*, the opening of the poem)

# II

## Three early novels: **Mary** (1926, 1970) **King, Queen, Knave** (1928, 1968) and **Glory** (1932, 1971)

*Mary* (Mashenka) and *King, Queen, Knave* (*Korol, Dama, Valet*) are Nabokov's first two novels; *Glory* (*Podvig*) is actually his fifth, but I bracket it here with the other two because, although it follows the more mature *The Defense*[1] (*Zashchita Luzhina*), it is unmistakably 'early' by virtue of the fact that its material is autobiographical (much of it appears again in *Speak, Memory*) and is presented with very little distance. In this respect it is analogous to Joyce's *Portrait of the Artist* (1917), which was published later than the more completely achieved *Dubliners* (1914) and marred by the author's reluctance to be objective about Stephen, or even Lawrence's *Sons and Lovers*, in which the author is so involved with the destiny of the hero that the surface coherence of his earlier novels, *The White Peacock* and *The Trespasser*, is lost. *Glory* does not have a comparable importance in Nabokov's *oeuvre*, and most of the material later drawn from it and reworked is improved in the process; but it keeps, as we shall see, considerable diagnostic value, and contains some fine episodes.

Nabokov's first novel, *Mary*, opens with a virtuoso piece the effect of which depends upon the witholding of one crucial piece of information, or 'clue'. It thus anticipates Nabokov's subsequent interest in the mechanics of plot in the thriller and detective story (an interest that long predates the current interest in analysing and parodying literary structures of this type). Moreover it originates in all probability where structuralist plot-analyses do: in Russian Formalist criticism, and especially Shklovsky's concept of *ostranenie*, the defamiliarization of the world, the suspension of the conceptual framework that shapes experience, which (following Flaubert, who made surprise of key aesthetic effect, and Bergson in 'Laughter') he considers the main end of art's 'devices'. The virtuosity is of course not gratuitous; Ganin's encounter with Alfyorov in the darkness of a stationary lift, just by the omission of that specification of locale, acquires a larger significance within the careful and conspicuous symbolic design of this novel. There is a chilling little vignette in *Bend Sinister* of an aristocrat who takes refuge from Paduk's dictatorship by making his temporary home in a broken-down lift, which he turns into a microcosm of what Soviet critics used to call 'inner emigration'. In *Mary*, emigration is represented as a perpetual waiting, an interrupted journey, an endless frustrating sense of being stuck in a little cubicle of time and space, dreaming of the infinity of Russia, love, and childhood. Lest the device should appear too neat, Nabokov adopts the Chekhovian strategy (and this is perhaps the most Chekhovian of his works, in theme, mood, and method) of calling attention to the symbol in the last line of the first chapter — like the magician revealing that it is all done with mirrors, but not, for that reason, any the less worth doing, let alone that it could be done any other way.[2] We are allowed to discover only gradually that Alfyorov's wife, the Mary of the title, is Ganin's former love, the unattainable embodiment of his yearning who takes on the shape of his whole past before (and the process represents some kind of maturing) leading him towards the future and the new start that as a young man he feels is always possible (though *Glory* suggests that rootlessness is a more desperate condition, that the exile has no future).

The cramped lift of Chapter One opens into the equally

cramped corridor of Chapter Two, with its suggestion of a prison in which the inhabitants of this emigré boarding house are 'doing time'. The economy of the device (room numbers are pages torn from an old calendar, so that the inmates are trapped in the perpetually recurring same six days of the preceding April — Eliot's 'cruellest month'[3]) is admirable, supported as it is by concrete details of the sad day-to-day lives of these people, all drawn, except for Ganin, with a few deft Chekhovian lines. Alfyorov lives only for the arrival of Mary, Podtyagin for the day when he will be given permission to move to Paris, and Klara for the love of Ganin which she will never win, and which is intended to save her from her dreary secretarial routine (evoked through the 'mauve-coloured line of type' and the 'tattered book' propped on the 'black Remington' with a vividness that invites comparison with the vignette of the typist in *The Waste Land*). The ballet-dancers, too, with their sad mockery of love and precarious shunting from one engagement to the next, are creatures of the 'waste sad time stretching before and after',[4] relics of that great international manifestation of Russian culture, the Ballet Russes. The boarding house is thus a dusty variant of Mann's Magic Mountain, an impossible little society held together as much by hostility as by affection, and presided over by the ghost of Russia; in Klara's room ('April 5th') hangs Böcklin's *Isle of the Dead*, a classic of German kitsch much admired by the Russian bourgeoisie and the inspiration of one of Rachmaninov's best-known works.

The ghostly parody of family and society, whose figurehead is Lydia Nicolaevna (her late husband's furniture, distributed among her lodger's rooms, takes on 'the inept, dejected look of a dismembered skeleton's bones'[5]) is the spiritual desert in which Ganin's memories of Mary (who of course makes no personal appearance in the deadlocked present of the novel) acquire such totemic significance. His despair is treated in part humorously (he has become so gloomy that he has lost his ability to walk on his hands; a stunt foreshadowing Van's Mascodagama act in *Ada*, though without the symbolic overtones it acquires in the later novel). Dressing in the morning, he likens himself to a circus poodle in human clothes — clothes having a meaning, in addition to their function, only in a social context. But at the same time the comedy becomes the vehicle for the expression of deep spiritual anguish. His work as a film extra, for example — an extension of these circus images — is seen in terms that go beyond satire, since for Nabokov films are quite commonly illusions which travesty art (cf. *Laughter in the Dark, King, Queen, Knave,* etc.) as well as confirmations of the emigré condition: ghostly shadow-play. To act in a film is to sell one's shadow (oddly akin to selling one's soul); it is a favourite occupation for Russian emigrés because nowhere else can film directors find distinguished-looking people who are so desperately short of money that they will gladly ape, say, a crowd at the opera (the 'striking-looking man with the black beard and the ribbon across his chest' puts on his tattered coat when shooting ends, and goes back to his humble job and lodgings[6]). Cinema images are lost souls trapped in the illusions of the film's realism — illusions which entail the reduction of the human actor to the status of a thing (Nabokov vividly evokes the total subjection of the actor to the director, and in *Lolita* extends this theme[7]).

As Ganin watches his 'doppelgänger' acting in the film, we are aware of the tragic split that emigration induces (to be explored to the bitter end in *The Eye* and *Despair,* where it is associated with the aesthetic self-division attendant upon the act of writing, where one both is and is not the tale one tells and the characters one creates). Unlike Albinus (*Laughter in the Dark*) he has the moral awareness to connect the illusions of the screen with his own life, and in particular his false love affair with Lyudmilla, in which he is deceiving himself even more than he is deceiving her. It is at this critical point that he discovers that Alfyorov's wife is his own beloved Mary, the one 'sure' thing in his world (though now reduced to a photograph in another man's desk drawer that he has to furtively sneak a look at — this intensifies the taboo that gives her so vast and improbable a significance). The third chapter of the novel, following this discovery, is straight from the symbolist world of Blok or Bely. But its ecstatic skywriting has an ironic twist, since in addition to the fact that the old tramp recalls the blind beggar of *Madame Bovary* (hubris) we see that it is the vision which confirms the prison: the gleam of transcendence illuminates only the hopelessness of the quest. Ganin, as he traces his images of Mary back through memories of his adolescence, sees himself as a god, 're-creating a world that had perished'.[8] But the material of his memories is not penetrated by present consciousness as it is (and much of it is the same material) in *Speak, Memory* or in *The Gift*; it is a consoling fantasy and little more, and it is sustained only by a photograph which is surrounded by guilt.

This is not to deny the intrinsic charm of the autobiographical material; Podtyagin at one point says that 'without the love of us emigrés, Russia is finished',[9] and indeed Ganin's loving evocation of Russian landscape and mores (the rural theatre, the boating expedition) is as vivid, and as artful, as Turgenev's. Moreover, Ganin's courtship of Mary at one point is cast in the classic mould of Kitty and Levin's love in *Anna Karenina*, except that (and there is a sad irony in it) instead of the lovers spelling out a declaration of love on a table top, they rub out the letters that some 'village rowdy' had scrawled there, linking their names 'by a short, crude verb, which moreover he had misspelled'. In this episode (very like one in *Speak, Memory*) the strongest impressions are of transience, and self-deception, and the last image in this sequence, that of Mary running along with her bow 'looking in flight like a huge Camberwell Beauty', turns her into Nabokov's classic symbol of memory and desire. We suspect already that no reality could give substance to this dream except the reality of art, which for Ganin (and for Edelweiss in *Glory*) is not a possibility.

The tacit recognition that first love is what it is because fated to pass, that the sweet sorrow of separation is all part of the saga and even desired, is clear in this novel as it is in the stories of Chekhov and Turgenev from which it derives. The train that carries Ganin finally away from Mary, the train that will bring her back to Alfyorov, the train that Ganin leaves Berlin by, the trains that run through *Glory* (railways are as hard worked in these early novels as they are in *Anna Karenina*) — all these and the ghostly trains which seem to run right through the boarding house are not purposeful instruments of communication (like the arrow-like Bolshevik trains in *Dr. Zhivago*) but rumblings and coruscations of an inner space which permit (as in *Glory*) a glimpse of twinkling lights in the distance which may or may not have an actual geographical location. The ballet dancers' party, inaugurated by the roaring of a train which turns the house into 'a spectre you could put your hand through'[10] (such passages presage the virtuoso evocations of mad subjectivity in *King, Queen, Knave*) is the *Walpurgisnacht* in which Ganin first adopts, then discards the role of Mephistopheles. The clearly marked time of expectation measured by Alfyorov's watch is intersected by Ganin's memories and his plot to get Alfyorov drunk and meet Mary himself. Podtyagin's fatal heart attack is a mere distraction interrupting the obsessive sequence ('She's coming, coming, coming, he — Alfyorov — said to himself in time with the ticking').[11] He has pencilled a mark on the watch-face to indicate the apocalyptic moment when Mary will arrive and the unredeemable present of those endlessly recurring six April days will stop; but as he falls asleep, the way 'drunken tramps used to sleep in Russian villages',[12] Ganin sets Alfyorov's alarm clock for the wrong time — bending time to his own purposes — and goes to meet Mary. On the way he passes 'the thick, heavy hands on the huge white clockface that projected sideways from a watchmaker's sign',[13] time massively reified in such a way as to bring home to him the fact that the past cannot so easily be pressed into his service, bent to the whim of a fantasist. The light is ambiguous, yet one can still see that this is early morning, not sunset, for him a departure, not an arrival — and his future cannot be founded on the image of Mary, which belongs to the past. This represents a moment of moral insight, beautifully rendered:

> As Ganin looked up at the skeletal roof in the ethereal sky he realized with merciless clarity that his affair with Mary was ended forever. It had lasted no more than four days — four days which were perhaps the happiest days of his life. But now he had exhausted his memories, was sated by them, and the image of Mary, together with that of the old dying poet, now remained in the house

> of ghosts, which itself was already a memory.
>
> Other than that image no Mary existed, nor could exist.[14]

One suspects, of course, that the 'pleasurable excitement' with which the novel ends will last no longer than the youthful euphoria concluding Joyce's *Portrait* ('Welcome, o life!') or Lawrence's *Sons and Lovers* (Paul walking romantically alone towards the lights of Nottingham); but this is an inescapable formal problem for the youthful autobiographer — a problem which might be said to constitute the very theme of *Glory*.

*King, Queen, Knave*, Nabokov's second novel, seems at first radically different from *Mary*, yet the harder one looks at it (and the extreme brilliance of the writing seems made to invite the most accusing scrutiny) the more it seems to be, at bottom, again worrying away at the problem of rootlessness. *Mary* was steeped in Russianness; now, as if to show that his talent did not, like that of so many emigré writers, depend upon the 'portable Petersburg' (a phrase from *Glory*) of remembered Russian life and letters, Nabokov writes what he later called a 'bright brute'[15] of a novel: toughly modern (in an expressionistic mode), sexually explicit (as *Mary* was sentimentally reticent — and indeed Russian literature has characteristically shown reserve in such matters) and fiercely satirical, heartlessly extending the possibilities of Bergson's analysis of automatism as the basis of comedy, while recognizing that 'automatic' behaviour may also bear witness to desperate psychic disorder. Skolimovsky's film of the novel, though less obtuse than other filmed Nabokov has been, made of it a blend of slapstick and sexual romp. In fact it is founded on a moral fable as sharp (though not as deliberately stark) as the Tolstoyan *Laughter in the Dark* of five years later.

The brilliant opening of *King, Queen, Knave*, like that of *Mary*, seems at first gratuitous, then at once falls into place among the thematic elements of the whole — not so much as part of a pattern of motifs (though the railway journey is never a neutral component in Nabokov's world), but rather as an index of the psychic processes of Nabokov's hero, Franz. In his later introduction, the author notes his use of the 'monologue intérieur', derived, he claims, from Tolstoy rather than from Joyce; but this (like so much else in these prefaces) is a little misleading. The terms 'monologue intérieur' or 'stream of consciousness' have a limited usefulness at the best of times; here they scarcely begin to describe the way that the world of this novel is distorted and fragmented through the consciousness of Franz, which initially strikes us as the overheated fantasy of a naïve provincial adolescent and gradually (when Franz is goaded beyond endurance) takes on the psychopathic but prophetic dimensions of Moosbrugger's solipsistic broodings in Musil's *Man without Qualities*,[16] or Nabokov's own Hermann in *Despair*, published eight years later. One thinks inevitably of Nazism's exploitation of adolescence.

The novel is, as its title suggests, a struggle for power as unfeeling as a card game, with the part of the Knave played by a poor provincial boy adopted by his rich uncle and spirited off to the city (the opening passages suggest that Franz has no control over his fate) where he is seduced by his aunt (of course he sees it differently). He is forced to become not only her lover but her accomplice in a Macbeth-like plot to kill the rightful King (her husband, Dreyer, whose unquestioning assumption of supreme authority is superbly caught) and inherit his fortune. Franz's adolescent lust (and his secret vice) are accompanied by a hatred of physical contact and horror of deformity that go beyond normal adolescent fastidiousness, but which seem connected with the sense of sin that accompanies his pleasure at travelling second class instead of third and staring hungrily at the elegant lady opposite (who turns out to be his aunt). Religious images are associated with the village he comes from, evoking a dark and oddly primitive gothic Christianity which has shaped his consciousness and scarcely equipped him to deal with the big city or the glossy milieu of the Dreyers. We are told of the 'pious popular prints that had frightened him in childhood',[17] with which he associates the deformed man in the third class carriage (whom Dreyer casually sees as possible advertising material); we hear also of the 'dark grove of pines and oaks and that old dungeon on its wooded hill where cobolds had haunted his childhood',[18] confirming Franz's regression to a state of paralysed superstition fed by ghosts and gremlins from his childhood, and making possible his lapse, under Martha's influence, into a condition where 'human speech, unless representing a command, was meaningless'.[19]

Waking in Berlin, Franz at once breaks his glasses, exposing his myopic soul nakedly to the kaleidoscopic lure of the sinful city (and Martha, far more dangerous in her 'madonna-like' beauty than the prostitutes who excite his sense of sin). His journey, half-blind, to the Dreyer household is a tour de force: already he is helpless, acting by instinct rather than by reason, practically smelling his way, mole-like, to the villa; he is, as Martha coldly reflects, 'warm, healthy young wax that one can manipulate and mould till its shape suits your pleasure'.[20] This anticipates, in its clear sexual allusion, her prostituting of herself to Franz as well as the tale of the mad inventor and his mannequins made of a new manipulable substance called 'voskin' (*vosk* is Russian for 'wax') which runs parallel to the development of the main plot and underlines its themes. When Dreyer, bouncy as one of his own tennis-balls, plies Franz with drink, his intoxication, marvellously described, puts him more helplessly than ever at the mercy of his obscure sensations, more incapable of discerning the intricate comedy of manners into which he has blundered. It seems a brutal microcosm of society, this expensive unloved villa in which the nearest thing to a human being is Tom, the dog (a 'character' with a significant moral function in a tale in which humans behave worse than brutes). Despite Nabokov's eschewal of overt social criticism, something akin to Musil's plot inescapably asserts itself: an inarticulate, brutalized peasant-cum-proletarian, with homicidal tendencies, is pitted against a shallow and corrupt high society which in its artificial refinement and emotional sterility is morbidly fascinated by primitivism and animalism. The roles of all the protagonists are apparently as immutable as those of playing cards, or like the chess pieces in the second section of Eliot's *Waste Land*.

This world of moral automatism (the cold queen caught in her own machinery with blind, primitive Franz, who stays initially at the same hotel as the mad inventor, the Montevideo, or Video for short, where his crushed glasses doubtless crunch still under the washstand — his blindness strips him of logic and language) spins faster and faster, like an overheated engine, till it seizes solid: Martha dies and Franz is 'free', though there is a strong hint of insanity in the 'frenzy of young mirth' which bursts out of him on the last page of the novel. Nabokov and his wife stroll innocently in and out carrying butterfly nets but seem to see nothing worth catching (the author is hidden in the guest list of the hotel as 'Blavdak Vinomori'); they serve largely as objects, in their serene enjoyment of life, of Franz's bitter envy. The whole process is counterpointed with the inventor's scheme to make mannequins of 'voskin' which will be indistinguishable from human beings. Nobody troubles to explain *why*, or pause to object that only God can create living beings; except, of course, Nabokov himself, who by linking the charlatan and blasphemer with Dreyer highlights the real nastiness of the King, a nastiness hidden by his amiable urbanity. The end of Chapter Five brings this out well:

> The inventor continued to talk. Dreyer threw down the pencil, reclined limply in his armchair and surrendered to the fascination.
>
> 'What was that?' he interrupted. 'The noble slowness of a sleepwalker's progress?'
>
> 'Yes, if desired,' said the inventor. 'Or at the other extreme, the restrained agility of a convalescent.'
>
> 'Go on, go on,' said Dreyer, closing his eyes. 'This is pure witchcraft.'

Although Nabokov frequently represents himself as the god of his fictional world, he checks his Hoffmanesque urge to murder and create; or rather, in this, his most Hoffmanesque novel, represents such an urge as the work of the devil, in the guise of Big Business.[21] There is no overt political allegorizing, though one cannot help supplying some.

Inevitably, there is a predominance of images of dressing, and the mirrors which, as Nabokov kindly points out, are working overtime are not passageways to looking-glass worlds so much as satirical glasses held up to deformed nature.[22] Cruel artifice, the black magic of the King and Queen, usurps the creative robes of art in order to enslave nature: this is the moral schema of the novel, more transparent than in Nabokov's other works. If Franz is natural man, blindly at the mercy of primitive fears and superstitions, he is natural man stripped of the culture that controls the passions of even the most primitive savage. Instead he has only the materialist 'civilization' that the Dreyers stand for. His work is the peddling of expensive disguises, as well as an apprenticeship in manipulation. As an efficient salesman he must make an automaton of the customer, fooling him into buying things he doesn't need at inflated prices. But he is the automaton. The dummies that stand silently around the Dreyer emporium — one of them associated with the deformed man Franz met in the train, and thus symbolic of poor unglamorous and unredeemed Man, constant under all his disguises — are objective correlatives of Franz's state of soul. Martha literally undresses him and dresses him like a dummy, Dreyer will rig him out in sporting gear (despite his evident ineptitude) like a dummy, and on the tennis court he stands as helpless and motionless as a dummy. It is a bitter little allegory, and for a bonus we are invited to consider the possibility that Franz is only a figment of the heated imagination of his landlord, who is also practising the black arts. A motif of the cinema, as so often in Nabokov's work, accompanies this analysis of the tyranny of fantasy and a destructive ritual of sado-masochism (note the naked slave-girl on Franz's wall, with whom Martha willingly identifies herself). A cinema is being built near Franz's lodging-house, and the drama of these dead souls (Dreyer, in Chapter Two, is reading *Die Toten Seelen* by a Russian author) is intercut with progress reports on the construction of this huge fantasy-palace (and the film that is to run there, oddly enough, is called *King, Queen, Knave*). The first time the cinema is mentioned, it is linked with another cheap erotic painting, in a room Franz doesn't take:

> A palace-like affair that the landlord said would be a movie house was being built on the corner, and this gave life to the surroundings. A picture above the bed showed a naked girl leaning forward to wash her breasts in a misty pond.[23]

The implications of 'this gave life' are clear. Martha, a movie addict, identifies Franz with a favourite star (killed, moreover, in a car accident on his way to his sick wife's bedside: an instance of imperfect congruence typical of Nabokov's method). The camera habitually lies. Dreyer is snapped skiing by another ghost of the author (Mr. Vivian Badlook, a teacher of English): suave in the photo, he in fact fell ignominiously a moment later. Art is concerned with truth; however deviously; the ghastly mockeries of it perpetrated by photographers, mad conjurors, kitschy painters, commercial film directors, and owners of fashionable (if mass-market) emporia outrage not only the author's aesthetic fastidiousness, but also some deeper quasi-religious sense of the blasphemy of naturalistic illusion passing itself off as reality. The two-dimensional Russian ikon flouted the laws of human time and perspective. Representationalism marked its secularization and decline. Dreyer had always wanted to be an artist, and although 'his commercial ventures during the inflation' had given him great artistic satisfaction, he longs for an opportunity to create 'real' art. The art-form he chooses (voskin men) turns out to be a grotesque parody of realism, the art which apes God's creatures. This warped creative urge is explored in other Nabokov novels: Smurov suffers from it (*The Eye*), as well as Hermann (*Despair*) and Humbert (*Lolita*), and in each case it is seen as a compensatory fantasy and distinguished from the real artist's disciplined pursuit of truth. All its facets are combined in *Pale Fire*.

*Glory* returns to autobiographical material, tracing the genesis of that fiery phoenix which Nabokov illegally sent up the chimney of his Trinity rooms;[24] though his hero, Martin Edelweiss, is not himself a writer, Nabokov's family chronicles early entered the preserve of Mnemosyne (mother of the muses) rather than recollection pure and simple, Russia having disappeared from all maps known and unknown. Martin, however, dreams of a material end to his quest for his lost homeland, a dream realized in *Look at the Harlequins*. This is a delusion which sustained — if that is the word — many emigrés in the period immediately following the Revolution. Gruzinov, the sympathetic radical emigré who seems to know that his intelligence work in Russia is futile, tries to dissuade

Martin. Pointing to the latter's sorry little plan of his secret route into the Soviet Union, he indicates — and one is not sure on what level the fiction works — landmarks: 'Here's Carnogore, here's Torturovka . . . a very dense wood, called Rogozhin' (names redolent of *Ada's* Tartary, the last, of course, drawn from Dostoevsky's *Idiot* and symbolizing the madness of Martin's scheme). *Glory*, then, like so many of Nabokov's other novels, is the record of a delusion, ironically presented in the form of a displaced person's dream of forging an identity by means of his 'podvig'.[25] Nabokov has translated the title as he has (rather than as 'exploit', literally closer) because 'podvig' is a highly emotive concept in which all Martin's adolescent longings can be accommodated. The enterprise is doomed, Martin disappears; but the internalization of the emigré's loss holds out no surer promise of equilibrium, as the schizoid fantasies of other Nabokov protagonists make clear. As Nabokov himself says in his later preface to the novel, 'nothing much happens at the very end'; yet it is clear that the novel had an importance disproportionate to its slight merits in helping Nabokov evaluate some possible strategies open to the emigré, and for this reason alone deserves attention.

The easiest course for Martin is to take refuge in nostalgia, to enter the comfortable past and there lapse dreamily away. *Mary* had already raised this possibility in order to dismiss it, though perhaps there was not enough of the enchanted stuff of Nabokov's own memories in it for all the magic to be contained. Here, where there is much more, it is countered by Martin's determination not to succumb. The neutral territory of Switzerland, predictive of *Ada* and *Transparent Things*, could at a pinch, serve Martin as a microcosmic Russia. Full of Russian exiles, as it was in the nineteenth century too, its snows evoke Russia for Martin, who has a too obviously Swiss-sounding name and who certainly cannot feel in any way at home in Cambridge. In fact he merely makes use of convenient local mountains as a testing-ground for his 'podvig',[26] which he comes to feel can only take the form of a return to Russia — his exploit. To settle in Switzerland would be death; Oblomovian paralysis holds this little emigré group in its magic grip. Uncle Henry, who presides over it, spends his time lamenting the mad flurry of modern life while bucolic provincial Switzerland pursues its imperturbable and unchanging course. Nabokov, conscious of his liberal-reforming forebears, has consistently shown little sympathy for those followers of Spengler who proclaim the apocalyptic end of civilization and lament the lost totality of the past, thereby fixing it under its little glass dome like one of those paperweight ornaments that crop up in his novels and enshrine a fabulous Zembla. If his later development has at times suggested that he has been forced to make too much from too little, to depend too exclusively on the resources of his 'portable world' (*Pnin*), which must not betray the fact that it is resting on nothing,[27] he has, as early as *Glory*, impressively diagnosed and rejected the alternative course of regarding Russia as a lost land which the present cannot touch and delighting in its hermetic containedness. This is a fatal kind of compensation for an ineffectual life, and Martin is made to turn decisively away from it as embodied in his teacher, Archibald Moon, whose faultlessly dead Russian is 'like chewing thick elastic Turkish Delight powdered with confectioner's sugar'[28] and whose habit of 'treating Russia as an inanimate article of luxury'[29] becomes offensive (he is balanced by Vadim, whose stock-in-trade is a conventionally colourful, Esenin-like Russianness). It was a happy stroke to give this antiquarian and aesthetic Russia to an Englishman rather than to one of the emigrés: it emphasizes the irrelevance of it to the actual predicament of emigration, which is an urgent and troubling question for Martin. Moreover, it is clear that Moon's homosexuality, like Kinbote's in *Pale Fire*, indicates that this Russia, like Kinbote's Zembla, can have no progeny.

If the final impression left by this novel is a certain thinness, it is, I think, because the most substantial part of it is set in a Cambridge which doesn't go much beyond Rupert Brooke and picture postcards. It is, of course, all part of Martin's predicament that he cannot 'belong' in Cambridge; yet the anecdotal material — amusing though it is, and doubtless much appreciated by Nabokov's Russian readers — obscures any more serious attempts to elucidate Martin's rootlessness in relation to a cultural continuum which is certainly nothing if not rooted

(*Speak, Memory* goes over some of the Cambridge material again, with the benefit of hindsight and deeper understanding).

It is clear that Nabokov is too close to his hero, and because of this lacks a consistent attitude towards him. This matters more than it otherwise might have because Martin, like Paul Morel, comes close to crossing that fine borderline in his own make-up which separates the romantic adolescent, steeped in literature and burdened with an incoherent imagination, from the creative artist whose heightened perceptions of the world are transmuted into disciplined forms. Novels of this type commonly have difficulty with those grey areas in which it is difficult to distinguish the uncreative protagonist from the creative writer (a crucial step that Nabokov could of course make, while Martin, fatally, could not). Throughout the novel Martin's consciousness verges on becoming that of an artist but never quite does so. The train journeys which are such an important motif of these early novels (the source of which is revealed in *Speak, Memory*), anticipated in imaginary trips through picture-space in the nursery, are intrinsically literary, virtual metaphors for a kind of creative displacement:

> At night he saw something wonderful: past the black, mirrory window flew thousands of sparks — arrowlike flourishes of a fire-tipped pen.[30]

Martin is not equipped to resolve in art the poignancy of this restlessness. With uncharacteristic explicitness Nabokov writes in Chapter Thirty-One of 'the strange dim railway platform of reverie', but Martin has to go on experiencing what his creator has formulated and distanced: life is a broken journey, the malaise depicted in *Mary*, with a tug from the future to counterpoise the drag of the past. It is a vision of lights seen from a train that beckons Martin to the pastoral interlude during which he hardens himself in isolation like a guerilla preparing for a fatal mission, after which he is swallowed up by the fiction of Zoorland (a joke name for the Soviet Union). The lights he saw turn out to have no name attached to them. They certainly do not correspond to Molignac, the place he chose in the firm conviction that the mysterious lights had directed him to it.

In other words, his preliminary training for his exploit was carried out under a misapprehension, in a place of no significance; and yet this made no difference, since merely to believe he was in the place of the distant lights was good enough. Sadly, because he is naïvely bent on finding his roots again, he fails to learn the moral: that, in Nabokov's own words, 'fancy is fertile only when it is futile', and Russian literature has grown accustomed to creating in a void. But then he is not, after all, an artist.

More than Nabokov's other novels, this one is written for an emigré audience. *The Gift*, more saturated in Russian literature, is at the same time of more universal interest; the appeal of *Glory* resides in its fairly simple statement of themes which later become much more complex. As a contribution to that late symbolist literature preoccupied with the gulf between the world and the image, the tendency of the word to engulf the deed, it is less impressive than *Despair*, which penetrates further into existential hinterlands.

## Notes to Chapter Two

1. Nabokov confesses in his preface to *The Defense* that he gave Luzhin his (Nabokov's) French governess, his pocket chess set, his sweet temper, and 'the stone of the peach I plucked in my own walled garden' (*The Defense*, London: Panther Books, 1971, p. 10). Yet the author remains distinct from his hero.
2. There is a famous letter of Chekhov's (to his brother Alexander, 1886) in which he notes the impossibility of addressing the natural world directly. 'In descriptions of Nature,' he writes, 'one ought to seize upon the little particulars, grouping them in such a way that, in reading, when you shut your eyes, you get a picture. . . . For instance, you will get the full effect of a moonlight night if you write that on the mill-dam a little glowing star-point flashed from the neck of a broken bottle, and the round, black shadow of a dog, or a wolf, emerged and ran.' This advocacy of metonymy rather than metaphor,

born of naturalist theory, is carried forward into the work of the Formalist critics (see Chapter Seven). By the time he wrote *Bend Sinister* (1948) Nabokov had brought the device to a high pitch of refinement. Only very special conjurors can do such tricks, not the average *fokusnik*. The Chekhov passage can be found in L. S. Friedland, ed., *Letters on the short story, the drama, and other literary topics by Anton Chekhov* (London: Vision Press: 1965), pp. xiv-xv.

3. The reference is to T. S. Eliot's poem, *The Waste Land* (1922). I have noted in subsequent chapters the ambivalent use of Eliot's poetry in Nabokov's work.
4. T. S. Eliot, 'Burnt Norton' in *Four Quartets* (London: Faber & Faber, 1969). I am not trying to suggest that Nabokov's novel has the stature of Eliot's poem.
5. Vladimir Nabokov, *Mary* (Harmondsworth: Penguin Books, 1973), p. 17.
6. *Ibid.*, p. 30.
7. Quilty (*Lolita*) uses the Duk-Duk ranch for making blue films, and tries to get Lolita to take part. It is suggested more than once that in addition to acting as Nabokov's instrument of destiny (McFate), he is a writer corrupted by Hollywood illusions. It is therefore fitting that his death should combine the cinematic genres of gangster movie, slapstick, and horror film (the last, invoking the unkillable vampire, takes us back to German romance and Humbert's magic bullets). See Page Stegner, *Escape into Aesthetics*.
8. *Mary*, p. 40.
9. *Ibid.*, p. 57. Alfyorov is more categorical: "Russia is finished, done for. She's been rubbed out, just as if someone had rubbed a funny face off a blackboard by smearing a wet sponge across it." (p. 26)
10. *Ibid.*, p. 91.
11. *Ibid.*, p. 98.
12. *Ibid.*, p. 101.
13. *Ibid.*, p. 104. The novel, as I have said, explores the sheer walls of a small cell of horological time.
14. *Ibid.*, pp. 105-6.
15. Vladimir Nabokov, *King, Queen, Knave* (London: Weidenfeld and Nicolson, 1968) p. v. This introduction dates from 1967; it is more objective than some of them, but the obligatory reference to 'the Viennese delegation' looks even more evasive than usual.

16. The reference is to Robert Musil, *Der Mann ohne Eigenschaften* (written during the 'twenties and early 'thirties, published in English in three volumes as *The Man Without Qualities*, London: Panther Books, 1968). Set in a decaying Vienna, it blends violent expressionism with the charm of the traditional ruling class, throwing into relief the tensions of an utterly paradoxical society. Nabokov has constantly denied any knowledge, at this stage, of German literature, even of Kafka (cf. the interview with Appel, *op. cit.*).
17. *King, Queen, Knave*, p. 11.
18. *Ibid.*, p. 179.
19. *Ibid.*, p. 247. Musil's Moosbrugger is reduced to similar speechlessness.
20. The sound of the cinema being built comes in through the window of Franz's room, where he and Martha make love, so her moulding of his 'healthy young wax' is associated with the construction of an illusion (*illyuzia*, as we learn from *Dr. Zhivago*, was an early Russian name for 'cinema', later replaced by '*kino*'). Both motifs are of course controlled by that of the magician-inventor who can 'create life', and the whole lot subsumed by the fantasies of Franz's landlord.
21. Not, be it noted, the work of Big Business in the guise of the devil; that would be realism.
22. This device is laid bare (to adopt Shklovsky's terminology, *op. cit.*) in *Invitation to a Beheading*. It is at least as old as Romanticism, and maybe as old as literature itself, but nineteenth century theories of the relation of literature to society tended to obscure it.
23. *King, Queen, Knave*, p. 48.
24. The reference is to an autobiographical incident used in *Glory* but better narrated in *Speak, Memory*, where the sheet of *The Times* stretched before Nabokov's Cambridge fireplace to get the fire blazing itself catches alight — world news turns incandescent — and disappears up the chimney. He calls it a 'firebird' and a 'phoenix', a bright emissary of art.
25. cf. Ch. I. Küchelbecker (see my chapter on *Pale Fire*) is described by his recent editor as combining a contempt for actuality with 'a thirst for *podvigi* in the name of freedom'. In literary-historical tradition, a *podvig* is an assault on eternity with the forces of history. Nabokov, with Pushkin, takes a cooler view of it.
26. Soviet rhetoric habitually uses the term *podvig* with a kind of

upward thrust (which its etymology permits). Mountains are an officially approved (if somewhat over-used) backdrop to *podvigi*.

27. I have something to say, in Ch. Seven, on folk narrative elements in Nabokov; but it would also be rewarding to consider his use of fairy tales.
28. Vladimir Nabokov, *Glory* (London: Weidenfeld and Nicolson, 1972), p. 97.
29. *Ibid.*, p. 97.
30. *Ibid.*, p. 24.

# III

## Laughter in the Dark:
## or, who killed Lev Tolstoy?

Nabokov's admiration for Gogol and Pushkin is as evident as his hostility to Dostoevsky, and the reasons for these loves and hates are suggested elsewhere in this study. But it may be that the pastiches of Tolstoy in *Ada*, the way it makes sidelong allusions to *Anna Karenina* in its efforts to assimilate and annihilate the concept of the family chronicle, were for many readers the earliest evidence that Nabokov has been at all concerned with Tolstoy, positively or negatively. The outrageous jokes that open *Ada*, directed against Nabokov's *bête noire*, the charlatan translator, take *Anna Karenina* as their starting point because it is a novel which is felt to belong, in some special way, to world literature. It is as much an indisputable classic for us as it is for Russians.[1] It thus constitutes a focus of what Steiner has called 'extraterritorial' writing with special aptness.[2] But in addition to this, we sense from the tone of Nabokov's allusions — that typical easy familiarity founded upon thorough knowledge — that Nabokov feels Tolstoy to be *his* Tolstoy as surely as he feels that Gogol and Pushkin are his own. Tolstoy, like Pushkin and Gogol, is another author evaluated, and re-created, by Nabokov in the course of his lifelong devotion to what he seems to feel to be a great lost literature; and his closest engagement with Tolstoy is in *Laughter in the Dark.*

It isn't hard, of course, simply to spot the references to Tolstoy throughout the novel. The seasoned professional actress, husky-voiced and superior, who acts poor Margot off the screen, has the unbelievable stage-name of 'Dorianna Karenina', suggested to her, she tells Albinus, by a 'boy who committed suicide'.[3] She doesn't reveal the story behind the name, inviting Albinus to come to tea if he wants to hear more; and when he asks her whether she has read Tolstoy she answers with classic dumbness 'Doll's Toy? No, I'm afraid not. Why?' Adultery has become the toy of doll-like Margot, her film sequence a vulgar travesty of Tolstoy's concern with the family as the basis of morality. Another overt allusion to Tolstoy occurs in the first few pages of the novel, where Albinus awaits the birth of his daughter Irma. The birth is accompanied by a death, prefiguring Irma's own death, for which Albinus is morally responsible; but the death here is specifically that of Tolstoy. The assistant surgeon announces the birth 'gloomily':

> 'Well, it's all over.' Before Albinus's eyes there appeared a fine dark rain like the flickering of some very old film (1910, a brisk jerky funeral procession with legs moving too fast). He rushed into the sickroom. Elisabeth had been happily delivered of a daughter.[4]

The familiar filmed sequence of Tolstoy's funeral comes to Albinus now as a reminder of an artist who, unlike himself, renounced expediency and ease, and for whom marriage was an agony of the flesh and the spirit experienced at the frontiers of heaven and hell; and of a man for whom to do wrong to a child, as Albinus does, is to be damned (the parallel between Irma and Tolstoy's Seryozha, in *Anna Karenina*, is evident). Tolstoy is long dead; the print of the film of his funeral is worn and the procession goes ridiculously at the double in the way of old films. One might have supposed that the great realist's strenuous effort to disentangle a few threads of meaning in the ravel of human life had been discredited along with the *weltanschauung* that engendered it; yet we cannot feel sure that this is the case. The inexorable moral working-out of

*Anna Karenina* — 'Vengeance is mine and I will repay'[5] — is so sensitively substantiated in the concrete details of Tolstoy's novel that we feel that the outcome could not have been otherwise. Nabokov sets out to make Albinus's fate no less inevitable; and if many readers have felt it to be cruel and arbitrary, this is perhaps because Nabokov, who lacks the framework of Christian ethics which Tolstoy can deploy, has sought to create at the level of metaphor and symbol a logic which dispenses with all points of reference beyond language itself. *Laughter in the Dark* is, of course, schematic and abstract by comparison with *Anna Karenina*, though its tangential allusions to that novel constitute a rich layer of meaning. In manner it resembles more closely one of Tolstoy's late parables translated from an ethical to an aesthetic frame. In the favourite analogy of the chess game, the first move determines the outcome; more exactly, the theme of the narrative must find its formally coherent expression.

If *Laughter in the Dark* might be compared with several of Tolstoy's late parables formally and even thematically, in content it is closest to the story called 'The Devil', which Tolstoy wrote in 1889, and which is furnished with two alternative endings and thus introduces an apparently random element — and an element of reader participation — of a kind that Nabokov characteristically exploits in his fiction. Published only posthumously, in 1911, the story is a condensed moral fable about a married man's obsessive attraction to a serf girl working on his estates: a tale of temptation as commonplace in its essentials as is *Laughter in the Dark*. Nabokov opens by warning us in advance that we have heard his story before; and yet, he says, there was 'profit and pleasure in the telling'. The end of his tale is known from the first paragraph, Nabokov typically disclosing the authorial device ('there is plenty of space on a gravestone to contain, bound in moss, the abridged version of a man's life'[6]). The outcome of Tolstoy's tale is similarly anticipated — not because the author tells us that his hero's life is a book, a fiction over which the author exercises absolute control, but (and herein lies an essential difference) because the epigraph from St. Matthew establishes a frame of reference in which the lust of the eye (Nabokov's theme too) already constitutes adultery and demands either self-laceration or hell fire (the two being nearly identical in terms of Tolstoy's morality) by way of expiation: 'And if thy right eye causeth thee to stumble, pluck it out, and cast it from thee'.[7] Tolstoy does not encapsulate his entire tale in his opening paragraph as Nabokov does; yet it is clearly from such a source as this that Nabokov has learnt the limpid manner suggestive of profundities, the craft of creating a surface which implies murky depths, a quasi-naïve innocence and reticence, which he exploits in *his* opening as Tolstoy does here:

> A brilliant career awaited Evgeny Irtenev. He had everything necessary for it — a fine education at home, a brilliant record as a law student at St. Petersburg University, connections with the highest circles of society through his recently deceased father, and even the Minister's protection in the ministry where he had begun his government service.[8]

This climax of worldly blessings is accompanied by a sinking sense of doom.

Irtenev, in Tolstoy's tale, has taken a lower-class mistress before marrying, for the sake of his health (as he tells himself) and (ironically) for his peace of mind. They meet in the dark. At their first meeting 'he had not even had a good look at her', and later, after he is married and his sense of guilt has grown into an agony,

> . . . He knew that were he to chance upon her somewhere, in the shadows, and, perhaps, touch her, he would surrender to his passion. He knew that only shame before others, before her and before himself held him back. He knew that he was searching for conditions in which this shame might not be noticed — darkness or the physical contact through which shame is smothered in animal lust.[9]

Lisa, Irtenev's wife, is a trusting victim; he forces her into this dull role and then finds her boring, with an egoism very like Albinus's (the scenes of family boredom in Nabokov compare well with those in Tolstoy, the master of domestic neurasthenia). She is also a bright-eyed Argus:

> . . . and she had wonderful bright, tender, trustful eyes. Evgeny was particularly struck by these eyes, and when he thought of Lisa, he would always see before him those bright, tender, trustful eyes . . . He knew nothing of her character, except for what her eyes told him. The meaning of these eyes was as follows . . .[10]

This insistence on clear sight in the married relationship, coupled with unseeingness in the adulterous one, forms part of a pattern of imagery derived in a fairly simple way from the Christian associations of light and dark, the symbolic expression of good and evil. The symbolism is not all so simple: when Stepanida, the serf-girl, smashes and tears at the cherry and hazelnut trees in the grove where they meet when on one occasion Irtenev fails to keep an appointment, the complexity of Tolstoy's understanding of nature and passion becomes apparent; but, in general, Christian terminology and symbolism (Tolstoy can use such a phrase as 'her sense of sin was completely destroyed'), however deformed by pressures of individual psychology — and, indeed, by obsessive naturalistic data — remain valid. In Nabokov's moral fable the recurrent images of black and white are deprived of a moral validation, and become primarily metaphors whose frame of reference is entirely contained by the structure of the novel. For this reason critics have seen here another chess-game, a human puppet-play choreographed on the black and white squares of the chess-board. But it should always be kept in mind that Nabokov's literary chess-games, like the great original from which they derive, the 'Garden of Live Flowers' chapter of *Through the Looking Glass*,[11] are ways of exorcizing by parody a familiar kind of moral utilitarianism — just as Lewis Carroll's Alice, at the Fourth Square of the World Chessboard, discovers the Looking-Glass Insects which play games with Darwin's theories of natural selection:

> 'Crawling at your feet,' said the Gnat (Alice drew her feet back in some alarm), 'you may observe a Bread-and-Butterfly. Its wings are thin slices of Bread-and-butter, its body is a crust, and its head is a lump of sugar.'
>
> "And what does *it* live on?'
>
> 'Weak tea with cream in it.'
>
> A new difficulty came into Alice's head. 'Supposing it couldn't find any?' she suggested.
>
> 'Then it would die, of course.'
>
> 'But that must happen very often,' Alice remarked thoughtfully.
>
> 'It always happens,' said the Gnat.[12]

Like Carroll, and like Adam Krug, the Nabokovesque philosopher-hero of *Bend Sinister*, Nabokov seems to feel

> The faint ridicule of a finite mind peering at the iridescence of the invisible through the prison bars of integers.[13]

— the chess problems being one form of those integers which do, at least, permit us to peer.

The blacks and whites of *Laughter in the Dark*, despite the chess allusions (Rex is a king, Albinus a white pawn and so on), in fact refer primarily not to chess but to photography, and above all to the reversal of blacks and whites on the photographic negative. The Russian title of the original version of the novel, *Kamera Obskura* (1933, Paris) makes this clear, alluding as it does more directly to the organizing motif of the novel, that the eye is a lens which throws inverted and 'negative' images on the inside of the Platonic cave-skull, above all idealized images of desire (mortal beauty, perceived through the eye, is dangerous) — yet the eye is our only means of perceiving that 'iridescence' of which Krug talks, via Joyce's 'ineluctable modality of the visible'.[14] The 'camera obscura' of the original title, as well as being quite literally a camera, is the dark room in which the print is developed, in which the negative is made positive. Thus in *Laughter in the Dark* the final 'development' is Albinus's recognition of the truth in the darkroom of his blindness. Tolstoy's two alternative endings are fused by Nabokov into one. In Tolstoy's tale, Irtenev, persuaded that Stepanida is a 'devil' who has conquered him against his will, argues thus:

> . . . there are only two possibilities: kill my wife or kill her. But, still . . . Yes, yes, there's still a third way: myself, kill myself.[15]

In the first ending, he kills himself; in the alternative, he kills his mistress, and, being judged temporarily insane, is sentenced to nine months in prison and one in a monastery:

> He began to drink while still in prison, continued drinking in the monastery, and returned home a debilitated, irresponsible drunkard.[16]

— a chilling sentence in which 'returned home' is as fearful as 'debilitated' or 'irresponsible'. The moral order of Tolstoy's tale, while leaning on a fulcrum placed outside itself ('God help me!' Irtenev screams, and then 'My God! But there isn't any God. There's only a devil.'), nevertheless substantiates its moral judgements in naturalistic particularities. The alternative endings in fact allow little freedom of choice, and that perhaps is the point: either way Irtenev comes to a sticky end, the return to the family, with all that implies, being perhaps the less desirable of the two alternatives. Nabokov, on the other hand, creates a parodistic schema in which the blacks and the whites (on which bright colours are suddenly and startlingly imposed) are delimited in their meaning by their precise functions within the total structure of the tale — hence the 'coldness' for which he has been censured. The hospital in which Irma is born is all white (Albinus hates its 'hopeless' whiteness). Hospitals commonly are, but the reader is directed towards a further significance by the immediate juxtaposition of this whiteness (associated with home and family: his wife's love 'was of the lily variety', and while pregnant she had the habit of eating snow) with the darkness of the cinema (while Elisabeth was in hospital Albinus was tortured by 'dark' thoughts of infidelity, even of the desirability of her death). Nor is the cinematic darkness neutral: it is 'velvety' and 'rich', and the gangway is 'dark and gently sloping', inviting Albinus to the pleasing fall that awaits him in the shape of Margot, the usherette, whom he follows with his eye until she is 'lost in the darkness'.[17] At this and other crucial points in the novel Nabokov disturbs the narrative sequence by means of a kind of cinematic 'flash-forward' technique, which produces the illusion of the procedures of the spatial art of painting rather than the temporal art of literature — and this is all-important to the theme of the novel. Reinforcing the strange sense of inevitability already created by the one-paragraph summary with which the novel opens, these narrative shifts destroy the time continuum in which free will might operate and Albinus achieve his redemption; but they are peculiarly his destiny, since he is an aesthete and connoisseur whose brainchild is a scheme for bringing paintings 'to life' (by means of animated cartoon film). Thus as he enters the cinema (called the *Argus*, which he notes as a good name for a cinema, though he misses the point that at least one pair of eyes, the author's, is fixed on him rather than the screen) he sees a poster 'which portrayed a man looking up at a window framing a child in a nightshirt'. This is a kink in time of a strangely admonitory kind, since it anticipates the episode in which Irma goes to the window to look for her father, who is with Margot and does not come (therefore does *not* stand looking up at the child), and catches her fatal pneumonia: the peripeteia of the tale, perhaps, after which Albinus, having destroyed his family, sinks into a ghastly parody of it with Margot and Rex. The film itself additionally anticipates the dénouement of the novel:

> He had come in at the end of a film: a girl was receding among tumbled furniture before a masked man with a gun. There was no interest in watching happenings which he could not understand since he had not yet seen their beginning.[18]

In this way the moral pattern of the story is established with an authorial irrevocability worthy of Tolstoy — these ten or so pages being a second, larger, complete statement of the novel, wherein Albinus is given the opportunity to catch a fleeting glimpse of his destiny, but is too blind (can he help it?) to do so. The third intrusion from the future is gross: it comes not in the disguise of a detail of the immediate present, but as a loose and gratuitous sentence which a readier man might have caught by the tail. Albinus, troubled by his Levinesque unreadiness, thinks only of how he might approach Margot:

> 'Any normal man would know what to do,' thought Albinus. A car was spinning down a smooth road with hairpin turns between cliffs and abyss.[19]

The car is his own, as he makes his hopeless attempt to get Margot away from Rex and crashes — and the reference has been inserted at this point by courtesy of the author (or God) who, in an appropriately magical disguise, had watched the whole thing while gathering samphire from the vantage point of Chapter Thirty-One:

> A sharp bend was approaching and Albinus proposed to take it with special dexterity. High above the road an old woman who was gathering herbs saw to the right of the cliff this little blue car speed towards the bend, behind the corner of which, dashing from the opposite side, towards an unknown meeting, two cyclists crouched over their handlebars.[20]

— or maybe he was in the passing plane which could see all the loops in the road just as the author sees all the kinks in time and space. One unreal fold of it conceals Elisabeth, back in Berlin, dressed in black, looking down from her balcony at a white-clad ice-cream vendor: 'it seemed strange to her that he should be dressed all in white and she all in black',[21] strange because in the scheme of the novel white was her colour and their flat, with its cream cretonne wall-covering and white telephone had served to highlight the intrusive splash of red that was Margot's short dress; moreover Albinus, though his name has prepared the way for it, has not yet assumed the white suit of the blind man, or taken up the white stick — his ice-cream cone: Elisabeth has a premonition of the negative image in the camera obscura, the inversion of colours.

Nabokov customarily draws attention to his devices. But if in other novels critics have discovered him displaying them for our admiration, in this one at least — and it is consonant with the homage to Tolstoy — he seems to be making them over-intrusive in order that they shall underline the difficulty of handling a moral theme of this kind in a relativized world. The truthfulness of art is a major part of his subject, and he approaches this subject with a sense of the temerity of the artist who offers to duplicate God's creation. The camera and the cinema both, in a sense, 'ape God's creatures', and Albinus's rash and vulgar appropriation of a random idea of Udo Conrad's — to take great paintings and animate them, 'even religious subjects perhaps, but only those with small figures', and taking care 'to avoid any clash between the movements produced and those fixed by the Old Master'[22] — constitutes a fatal blurring of the confines between life and art symptomatic of Albinus's egotistic aestheticism, and bordering on sacrilege.[23] It is also fatally sentimental, like Albinus's blind passion for Margot. Much is narrated from Albinus's 'point of view', but little is seen by him. His artistic dabbling, exploited by the clever forger Rex, is set against the serious work of the novelist Conrad (as Vronsky's painting is set against Mikhailov's in *Anna Karenina*) who is in exile from political tyranny pondering the possibility of writing in his adopted language — Nabokov making another Hitchcock-like guest appearance. Moreover it is Conrad, the true artist, who sees the truth about the relationship between Margot and the feigned homosexual Rex: the true artist prohibits conventional ways of seeing. Near the beginning of the novel we are told that he has written a story about a conjurer who spirits himself away at his farewell performance. Rex is explicitly compared to a conjurer and Conrad would have him spirit himself away by giving away his secrets, enlightening the unfortunate Albinus, but the latter fumbles his chance, as usual, by missing the clues. Rex is the mountebank always lying in wait for the dilettante, and for this reason Nabokov expatiates in what may seem a disproportionately long passage of undiluted omniscient-authorial narration upon his character and manner (Chapter Twenty-Two):

> Perhaps the only real thing about him was his innate conviction that everything that had ever been created in the domain of art, science, or sentiment, was only a more or less clever trick . . . He watched with interest the sufferings of Albinus . . . the first item in the programme of a roaring comedy at which he, Rex, had been reserved a place in the stage manager's private box. The stage manager of this performance was neither God nor the devil . . . the ghost of a juggler on a shimmering curtain.[24]

Tolstoy's rage against art, in his later years, as just a clever way of telling lies and a pastime for a degenerate ruling class, is foreign to Nabokov, who has been labelled an aesthete often enough for at least a corner of the label to have stuck, and who at all events belongs to the post-symbolist world of relativized values and opaque language. Nevertheless it may not be insignificant that the chapter which contains this unconscionably sincere denunciation of Rex ends in a thoroughly Tolstoyan manner with a brief exchange between the hall-porter and the postman designed to reveal the corruption and still more stupidity of their masters, who endlessly fool themselves with amorous piffle. Tolstoy's short story 'The Cossacks', for example, opens with an all-night banquet in which the hero, Olenin, takes part before leaving for the Caucasus, meanwhile keeping his coachman endlessly waiting, and puzzling the irritated waiter beyond endurance by his inane interest in the complexities of amatory entanglements. From all this urban degeneracy Olenin escapes to the wild Caucasus in search of the simple life and spiritual regeneration. In Nabokov's novel, the porter and the postman sum up Albinus only too accurately (as Margot has summed him up, and as Rex sums him up); and in addition their simplicity seems to add authenticity in the context of a narrative mode shaped by the parable or folk tale:

'It's hardly believable,' said he when they were out of hearing, 'that that Herr's little daughter died a couple of weeks ago.'

'And who's the other Herr?' asked the postman.

'Don't ask *me*. An additional lover, I suppose. To tell the truth, I'm ashamed the other tenants should see it all. And yet he's a rich, generous gentleman. What I always say is: if he's got to have a mistress, he might have chosen a larger and plumper one.'

'Love is blind,' remarked the postman thoughtfully.[25]

It is of course representative of the crucial distance between Tolstoy and Nabokov that whereas in Tolstoy the simple character (often a peasant) has an insight into the real thoughts and feelings of the 'educated' man, which the latter does not want to admit to himself or simply is unable to 'see' — perhaps because of his education, or because of the social role he has to play — in Nabokov, here and elsewhere, the simple character is given an insight not into psychological or metaphysical truth but into the shape of the fiction. If one had to sum up the theme of *Laughter in the Dark* in a single banal phrase, one could do worse than 'Love is blind'. As a statement it belongs to the right register (proverbial wisdom, acknowledged truth, the oft-told tale) and it is the theme, in itself uninteresting, upon which Nabokov builds his baroque divagations; or, to substitute a metaphor closer to the terms in which the novel works (since Nabokov is more a painter than a musician), it is the prepared canvas on which he paints his fanciful interlocking patterns. It reminds us of the fact that all the virtuosity is put at the service of the exploration of a moral problem: how shall we judge, or even describe, a weak but not wicked man who breaks up his marriage in order to pursue a very attractive but very vulgar little girl? What might validate our judgement?

To state the issue in these terms is perhaps to make too simple a thesis of it. Yet Nabokov himself enjoys defining problems and working out, in front of his readers, ways to solve them — a process which is very apparent in *Laughter in the Dark*. The novel explores Albinus's blindness, and in doing so creates a metaphorical system which has its own rules — which are then the rules of the game, which cannot be broken without perpetrating an aesthetic solecism which would at the same time be a bit of moral trickery. This circuitous return to 'reality' is typical of Nabokov's earlier work. Albinus's moral blindness finds its physical equivalent as inexorably as Gloucester's in *King Lear*, because the logic of the tale demands it. From the beginning he is blind to Rex's viciousness (but that might be just lovable naïvety, Rex being so vile). He is also, however, blind to the actuality of others: his wife, his daughter, who are no more than his idea of them (and of Margot he says, when he intends to break with her:

> Like to crush her beautiful throat. Well, she is dead anyway, since I shan't go there any more.[26]

She is always for him an image on his retina). The meetings with Margot, as we have seen, are associated with images of darkness (and his flat, when he rushes back to intercept the fatal tell-tale letter, is a blaze of light). Albinus is shown *choosing* the darkness he is subsequently forced to inhabit. Gradually the motif of blindness emerges distinctly from the pattern of light and dark which Nabokov has drawn: white telephone, black umbrella, black taxi, ivory paper knife and all the rest. In Chapter Seventeen, Rex, meeting Margot again, says he couldn't believe his eyes 'as the blind man said'; and in the next chapter, we are told that

> If, in real life, Rex looked on without stirring a finger while a blind beggar, his stick tapping happily, was about to sit down on a freshly painted bench, he was only deriving inspiration for his next little picture.[27]

His art being that of the caricaturist, he needs material like Albinus. It is only when Udo Conrad, the omniscient author, has overheard Margot and Axel talking together like lovers that Albinus can both recognize that he has been blind and admit it. In Chapter Thirty he accuses Margot:

> Conrad saw you. That French colonel saw you. Only I was blind.[28]

— all such metaphors culminating in the apparition before the accident, of the man with black spectacles 'sitting on the edge of the road breaking stones'.[29]

Above all, what Albinus is too blind to see with those bulging blue eyes of his which have delighted so much in illusion, is that his adulterous liaison has taken on the form of a ghastly parody of family life. Just as Anna and Vronsky are bound, in the end, to set up house, and by doing so to invite judgement in terms of the very code they have flouted, so Albinus, wilfully and totally entering the dark world of his liaison, finds himself caught up in distorting mirrors reflecting misshapen semblances of his marriage. Margot turns out to have a family herself: as vulgar and commonplace as they had to be. The negative image takes on shape in the camera, yet still no-one grasps its human meaning. At the start of Chapter Twenty-Four, where Margot is throwing a fit at the sheer badness of her performance in the film which Albinus has set up for her,

> Albinus, as he tried to console her, unconsciously used the very words with which he had once comforted Irma, when he kissed a bruise — words which now, after Irma's death, were vacant.[30]

— a fine and thoroughly characteristic instance of the 'grammaticality' of Nabokov's moral order, and a new gloss on Albinus's commonplace urge to treat Margot like a child: the words were 'vacant'. The marital fight for the bathroom features in Albinus's relationship with Margot along with other domestic trivia, only now the scene is a hotel. Rex — becoming more and more, as his name suggests, the king pin (*Axel* Rex) about whom Albinus's life turns — is in the next room, the two rooms interconnect via the bathroom, and Axel and Margot use the opportunity to make love while the bathwater runs: 'I went to sleep in the bath,' she called out plaintively through the door. Enlightened by Conrad as to the nature of Margot's relationship with Rex, Albinus threatens to kill her.

'Please, shoot me, do,' she said.

> 'It will be just like that play we saw, with the nigger and the pillow, and I'm just as innocent as she was.'[31]

The most audacious black/white contrast in the novel, invoking Desdemona and Othello, brands Margot as morally obtuse and artistically insensitive (again the relating of moral to aesthetic judgements substantiates the larger theme of the tale) and more importantly forces Albinus into the role of a jealous husband wrongly suspicious of his innocent wife. This, however, is not to be the culmination of the process by which he is made to act out the black farce of a 'negative' marriage. Since it becomes impossible for him to cast Margot in the role of the child, he must play the part himself. When he wakes in hospital after his accident, and lifts his bandage, Margot is waiting to scold him: 'You are a bad boy,' she says; and as he stumbles to a taxi. 'Can't you be a little less timid? Really, you might be a two-year-old.'[32] In the house amid the black fir trees that Rex likes so much, and where Albinus's self-deception acquires a touching quality of helpless innocence, he has to be taught to walk without bumping into things in this new 'home', the dark rooms that have taken the place of his bright apartment. He touches furniture as if glad to feel its solid existence, and (horrible irony) 'patted the different objects as if they were the heads of strange children'.[33] As for Margot, it seemed to Albinus (the wheel having come full circle)

> as though she had returned to the darkness of the little cinema from which he had once withdrawn her.[34]

The darkness is actually his, as indeed it always was — his whole environment, even the whistling of birds outside the window, being an artifice created by the ingenuity of Rex, the *fokusnik* (Russian for a conjurer) who is indeed now the lens admitting only as much of the real world as Albinus is allowed to see. Rescued by Paul and taken back to his wife, he is a pitiful figure, entirely the dependant child:

> Paul talked to him as though he were a child, and cut up the ham on his plate into little pieces.[35]

and he is accommodated — where else? — in the nursery. In any world in which expiation and redemption were possible — in Dostoevsky, for instance, or in Dickens — he might here have purged himself symbolically of his guilt and died wiser. Such things cannot occur in the intricate logic of this novel. We are told only that

> It surprised Elisabeth that she found it so easy to disturb the sacred slumber of that little room for the sake of this strange, silent occupant; to shift and change all its contents so as to adapt it to the blind man's needs.[36]

To her he is now just 'the blind man' and she to him is 'an almost soundless memory drifting about listlessly with a hint of eau-de-Cologne'.[37] His will is fixed on revenge: he goes to what was once his flat, to her, stumbling over 'something which wobbled and jingled — probably a child's bicycle on the pavement',[38] and makes his last gesture of self-destruction, firing into the dark room and destroying its tenant — himself. The neutral stage directions of the last paragraph tactfully make the point that with the extinction of his point of view there is no novel. With Albinus dead, the point-of-view extinguished and the passion that shaped the whole horrible fable spent, the world is a Robbe-Grillet collection of neutral objects. The difference between Nabokov and Robbe-Grillet, in the largest terms, is that although both are builders of labyrinths and obsessed with the fictionality of fictions, Nabokov glimpses, through the transparency of things, through his metaphors, the human reality which gives them meaning. This may be far from consolatory, but in the words of his 1965 preface to his translation of the short 1930 novel *The Eye*, he notes that 'The forces of imagination in the long run are the forces of good', a phrase which Robbe-Grillet would no doubt find meaningless.

It is perhaps worth briefly mentioning *The Eye* by way of concluding this study of *Laughter in the Dark*. Close in date of composition, the two books share certain images and even illuminate each other. The shorter work is much more of a formal game than the longer, an example of Nabokov's creative use of the detective story for its high degree of formal coherence. The use of mirrors in *Laughter in the Dark* — related as always to Lewis Carroll's *Through the Looking Glass* and both writers' impulse to pass through the mirror in the roadway that the novel was once said to be — is less striking than in *The Eye*, where it is perhaps the dominant motif. The entire tale is a point-of-view game: there is no absolute reality, nor even (as in some of Nabokov's fictions) one relatively more firm than the others; but the character of the mysterious Smurov, different from different angles and in the different 'images' other characters have of him seen to depend entirely upon the identity of the narrator. The eye is as deceptive an organ as in *Laughter in the Dark*, but the tale, built on a quite different model from the Tolstoyan parable which underpins *Laughter in the Dark*, has no such fixed metaphoric/moral order. Smurov is a late variant of a character from a Russian literary tradition different from the Tolstoyan. He derives from Lermontov's Pechorin, Turgenev's Rudin, and Dostoevsky's Underground Man, and is properly discussed along with Nabokov's other 'superfluous men'. For the moment it will be enough to say that it is not the swiftness of the hand that deceives the eye, but the fatally unverifiable eye (or I) that deceives hero, narrator, and reader. The making of these mazes is not an idle pastime, nor is it heartless.

## Notes to Chapter 3

1. Nabokov has some acid things to say about those whose knowledge of Russian literature is confined to Tolstoyevsky. But in practice he distinguishes sharply between the moral Tolstoy, whom he respects, and the mystical Dostoevsky, who at his best cribbed from Gogol, and at his worst was 'a much overrated, sentimental, and Gothic novelist'. (*Eugene Onegin*, v. 3, p. 191). Cf. my fifth chapter. It may be interesting in this context to note that in *The Listener* interview (cf. above) Nabokov, talking of *Laughter in the Dark*, said with uncharacteristic directness that in it he 'tried to express the world in terms as candid, as near to my vision of the world, as I could'

2. George Steiner, *Extraterritorial* (London: Faber, 1972) passim. Steiner's theories undoubtedly illuminate Nabokov's work, but he minimizes the damaging effects of a loss of cultural roots. It is clear that Nabokov's attempt to rationalize his loss has been neither altogether persuasive nor altogether sincere. Against *Ada* one ought to set perhaps the best of his few good poems, 'An evening of Russian poetry' (1945). If it is objected that this is an incidental response to writing in an adopted language, being 'extraterritorial', there is still *Pale Fire*, which keeps echoing this poem.
3. Vladimir Nabokov, *Laughter in the Dark* (Harmondsworth: Penguin Books, 1969) p. 123.
4. *Ibid.*, p. 12. The charged lucidity of the writing everywhere in this novel is very striking.
5. 'Mne otmshchenie, i az vozdam.' This is the epigraph to Tolstoy's novel. It is not clear who is speaking.
6. *Laughter in the Dark*, p. 5.
7. *Matthew* v, 29. All references to this tale are to the edition and translation by Arthur Mendel and Barbara Makanowitzky, *The Short Stories of Leo Tolstoy* (New York: Bantam Books, 1960).
8. *Ibid.*, p. 386. cf. the opening of *The Death of Ivan Ilych.*
9. *Ibid.*, p. 417.
10. *Ibid.*, p. 397.
11. Darwin was of course a great artist (cf. Nabokov's *Listener* interview and his lepidopteral asides in *Speak, Memory*). He was not responsible for the crude application of a general theory of natural selection to society, still less for the agonies of writers like Hardy who could not reconcile evolutionary determinism ('science') with a conviction of unique individual value ('art').
12. Lewis Carroll, *Alice's Adventures in Wonderland and Through the Looking Glass* (Harmondsworth: Penguin Books, 1970).
13. Vladimir Nabokov, *Bend Sinister* (London: Weidenfeld and Nicolson, 1960).
14. James Joyce, *Ulysses* (London: The Bodley Head, 1955) p. 33.
15. *The Devil*, p. 426.
16. *Ibid.*, p. 429.
17. *Laughter in the Dark*, p. 13.
18. *Ibid.*
19. *Ibid.*, p. 14.
20. *Ibid.*, p. 152.

21. *Ibid.*, p. 153.
22. *Ibid.*, p. 6. Nabokov himself is the Old Master who has fixed the movements of this novel. He leaves open the question of the 'real' existence of a still older Master.
23. It is at least arguable that the greatest achievements in modern non-representational art have been Russian. Abstraction in Russian art (e.g. Kandinsky, Malevich) has commonly been associated with a specifically religious Weltanschauung. I am not, of course, suggesting that Nabokov is a religious writer.
24. *Laughter in the Dark*, p. 117.
25. *Ibid.*, p. 119.
26. *Ibid.*, p. 15. Ideas of killing her and himself recur (e.g. pp. 40 and 64), but always with the suggestion that he is watching himself in a mirror and trying out his unfamiliar role of wronged and vengeful lover. I find here a faint echo of Tolstoy (*The Devil*) too, but may be imagining it. For both writers murder is a solipsistic act akin to suicide.
27. *Ibid.*, p. 92.
28. *Ibid.*, p. 147.
29. *Ibid.*, p. 151.
30. *Ibid.*, p. 124.
31. *Ibid.*, p. 145. Evidently Albinus has been educating Margot.
32. *Ibid.*, p. 160. The scene in which Margot leads him round the new house, naming things for him, is a triumph. Suddenly the novel is full of colour (formerly black and white had dominated everywhere except in 'the picture-gallery of Albinus's mind').
33. *Ibid.*, p. 163. The negative image of the family is being developed.
34. In fact the house has yellow blinds and blue walls: a microcosm, in fact, presided over by a naked hairy devil, Rex, the king of darkness.
35. *Ibid.*, p. 180. Anna's son plays a crucial moral part in the unfolding of *Anna Karenina*, but no more so than Nabokov's own son Dmitri does in *Speak, Memory*. The treatment of David in *Bend Sinister* reinforces our sense of the scriptural intensity of Nabokov's feeling for the vulnerability of the child.
36. *Ibid.*, p. 181. Evidently Albinus is now being run backwards towards death, like a film that has been shown.
37. *Ibid.*, p. 181.
38. *Ibid.*, p. 184.

# IV

## Two games at chess: **The Defence** (1930 and 1964) and **The Real Life of Sebastian Knight** (1941)

Nabokov's interest in chess, and particularly in the setting and solving of chess problems in the abstract, is well known, and the motif of the chess game can be traced in many of his works. But in two of his novels, *The Defence* and *Sebastian Knight,* chess strategies take on the role of central organizing devices. The hero of the earlier novel is a chess genius and fanatic, and the novel is devoted to his quest for the perfect defence (the Russian title,[1] more than the English, makes it clear that what is being discussed is not only a kind of defensive play known as Luzhin's Defence, but ways of defending Luzhin against himself and the outside world). In the later novel, Nabokov's first in English, the elusive writer is himself a chess piece, the erratic knight, and the chess game, while still a metaphor as it is in *The Defence,* is at the same time a microcosmic structure within which the entire universe of this short novel is contained (as in Lewis Carrol's *Through the Looking Glass,* to which it is indebted).

Nabokov himself obligingly points out in his introduction to *The Defence* (1963) that the novel is shot through with chess motifs. He refers to Luzhin's suicide as a 'suimate' (he has become the solus rex of *Pale Fire,* the exiled king who is

Nabokov's type of the artist[2]) and Luzhin leaves a world which has turned into a monstrous chess board. As Nabokov says:

> . . . my morose grandmaster remembers his professional journeys not in terms of sunburst luggage labels and magic-lantern shots but in terms of the tiles in different hotel bathrooms and corridor toilets . . .

— these tiles forming the pattern of a chessboard onto which he can transfer the abstract game in which he is perpetually engaged. The 'moves' of chapters four to six, says Nabokov,

> . . . should remind one of a certain type of chess problem where the point is not merely the finding of a mate in so many moves, but what is termed 'retrograde analysis', the solver being required to prove from a back-cast study of the diagram position that Black's last move *could* not have been castling or *must* have been the capture of a white Pawn en passant.

All this is interesting, but actually even more involuted and technical than the novel itself; moreover it fails to take into account the extent to which Luzhin's imagination of the world as a chess board is a metaphoric statement of a sickness which has much wider implications. In the end it is quite true that (as Nabokov admits in his last couple of paragraphs of introduction) of all the Russian books '*The Defence* contains and diffuses the greatest "warmth".'[3]

The centre of interest in the novel is its hero,[4] who is presented as young and unhappy, then older and happier, then older still and sick, with relatively little of that preoccupation with the nature of the fiction itself and the reliability or otherwise of the narrator which makes up the subject matter of *Sebastian Knight*. Its peripetaeia is Luzhin's nervous breakdown in Chapter Eight, in which the game of chess, which has hitherto been his defence against the 'real' world in the same way that art is for Sebastian Knight, becomes the trap from which there is no escape. Its elaborate chess metaphors are moulded always by Luzhin's consciousness and thus never make themselves felt as unmotivated formal devices — thus the innocent eccentricity of his superimposing chess patterns on the world:

> He sat leaning on his cane and thinking that with a Knight's move of this lime tree standing on a sunlit slope one could take that telegraph pole over there, and simultaneously he tried to remember what exactly he had just been talking about.[5]

— a passage revealing the closeness of grandmaster and artist — leads inevitably to the complication of:

> With one shoulder pressed against his chest she tried with a cautious finger to raise his eyelids a little higher and the slight pressure on his eyeball caused a strange black light to leap there, to leap like his black Knight which simply took the Pawn if Turati moved it out on the seventh move, as he had done at their last meeting. The Knight, of course, perished, but this loss was recompensed with a subtle attack by black and here the chances were on his side. There was, true, a certain weakness on the Queen's flank . . .[6]

His growing involvement with his shadowy sweetheart thus evokes fear of exposure, by association with the 'queen' who first taught him chess, the red-haired aunt with whom his father was conducting a clandestine affair.

> But the moon emerged from behind the angular black twigs a round, full-bodied moon — a vivid confirmation of victory — and when finally Luzhin left the balcony and stepped back into his room, there on the floor lay an enormous square of moonlight, and in that light — his own shadow.[7]

The surrender of himself to another marks, despite that 'confirmation of victory' (over whom or what?) the inception of Luzhin's dark night of the soul in which he seems to have relinquished the artist's control over the world which chess signified to him and became instead a huge solipsism — a pawn in his own game which is simultaneously a game being played by someone else (concretely embodied as the unscrupulous Valentinov[8]). The boy grandmaster whose most showy trick was to play several opponents simultaneously (chess composing for him a synthesis of the world) is now fatally split between subject and object in a game which he knows he will lose (a split which is strikingly foreshadowed — quite literally — as his image is thrown on to the huge chessboard of his hotel room by the explicitly female moon[9]). This blurring of the confines of Luzhin's art is an incipient disintegration of personality. Unlike Sebastian Knight who, with the devious sidestepping gait of his patron piece seems to survive by virtue of a transgression of the spatial rules which govern the behaviour of the other 'pieces' in the novel, Luzhin has bloomed in the formally coherent world of the chess board like some exotic growth under a bell jar (or like the 'paperweight bearing emerald-blue views touched up with mother-of-pearl beneath convex glass' of Chapter Four which does further symbolic service in *Pnin* and *Pale Fire*[10]). The brief remainder of his life is a struggle to find again the 'combination' which will restore the precarious synthetic stability which chess once gave, a quest in which images of home, jeopardized by boyhood memories of his flight from the railway journey leading him to the 'reality' of Petersburg and school, play an important part in their illusory connotations of the end of his wearying game. The fatal match with Turati is broken off when Luzhin flees in 'a desperate attempt to free himself, to break out somewhere — even if into nonexistence',[11] and hears voices telling him to 'go home'.

> 'What did you say?' he asked again, suddenly ceasing to sob. 'Home, home,' repeated the voice, and the glass radiance, taking hold of Luzhin, threw him out of the cool dusk. Luzhin smiled. 'Home,' he said softly. 'So that's the key to the combination.'[12]

'He would hide there and live on the contents of large and small glass jars' he thinks as he wanders hopelessly, recalling that childhood episode from Chapter One where he had first become aware of his defencelessness.

But the yearning for home (repeated in Chapter Fourteen, when he is intercepted by Valentinov just as he reaches his house muttering 'Home, home . . . there I'll combine everything properly'[13]) leads Luzhin into a squence of games the rules of which he does not know: the social games played by his wife's mother and father and their friends against a backdrop of false Russianism, the gimcrack odds and ends of emigré ménages which both recall and parody the lost homeland which Luzhin yearns for, a social milieu where he plays with a great handicap in an unfamiliar match (as his wife drops off to sleep 'for some reason the word "match" kept floating through her brain — "a good match", "find yourself a good match" '[14]). The sequence following his breakdown at the chess match employs some stereotyped chess motifs (he is picked up by a couple of pawns who escort him to the queen, his fiancée — and her mother, since for Luzhin all women merge into one another). The taxi in which they travel has 'large chess squares' on its door; the generally lurid quality of the colouring prepares for the concerted attempt to consider Luzhin's condition as no more than a disease and to cure him of it by eradicating his obsession with chess completely. The emigré circles into which Luzhin's marriage draws him more and more completely have more than their share of cranks and bores (the last gathering is beautifully 'placed' in the two sentences which close the description of it:

> The guests departed. Luzhin was sitting sideways at the table on which, frozen in various poses like the characters in the concluding scene of Gogol's *The Inspector General,* were the remains of the refreshments, empty and unfinished glasses[15]).

Moreover, the odd visitor from the U.S.S.R. serves to confirm that if emigré life is shallow and sterile, there can be no question of returning to a country inhabited by such boors and vulgarians. There is, in other words, nowhere to go, no geographical correlative for Luzhin's longing for home. There is in fact a good deal of truth in the elegiac observation of the sympathetic old general (in Chapter Eight) that 'it was not Russia we expatriates regretted but youth, youth'.[16] Luzhin *does* regret his youth, if not quite in this simple nostalgic way, and the seeds of his adult misadventures are contained in his childish sufferings.

Luzhin begins life with an oppressive sense of subordination to his father, who is the 'real' Luzhin: the famous author of moralistic children's books, prig and martinet, whom we discover reading a spelling exercise to his son ('Being born in this world is hardly to be borne'[17]), the truth of which he does not suspect (Luzhin characteristically evades the threat by leaving blanks). Against his father's ambitions for him Luzhin tries to evolve a defence: he makes a private world from a handful of objects and impressions (including books by Jules Verne and Conan Doyle, where he thrills to the 'exact and relentlessly unfolding pattern', and Sherlock Holmes' faculty of 'endowing logic with the glamour of a daydream'[18]). A few of these objects, treasured for their talismanic mystery, reappear as mnemogenic props in other Nabokov novels: the stuffed squirrel 'bought once on Palm Sunday at the Catkin Fair' in *Pnin*, the pedometer in *Pale Fire*, and so forth. Puzzles and jigsaws engender an urge towards an 'amazing harmonious simplicity' which can reside only in art. Luzhin stumbles upon the form his art will take when in his father's study a violinist playing at a domestic concert (but taking time off to phone his mistress) shows him a chess set, and remarks to the elder Luzhin, as he 'tenderly' closes the box

> 'What a game, what a game . . . Combinations like melodies . . . The game of the gods. Infinite possibilities.'[19]

The association of chess with stealth and secret, even forbidden, power (as well as with harmony and order) is reinforced when his aunt initiates him into the mysteries of the game: 'The Queen is the most mobile' she says, and as he kisses her hand ('I never expected such tenderness . . . You are a nice little boy after all') his father bursts in furiously and the pieces are scattered (one pawn refuses to fit back into the box). Thus the innocent Luzhin is caught up in a Jamesian web of adult misconduct (his father is his aunt's lover) in which chess itself acquires a guilty sensuous charm (reading old journals for chess problems, he is suspected by his father of looking for pictures of naked women). Hints of his own ambivalent relationship to the game appear early: in childhood sicknesses he recalls especially 'the time when he was quite small

> playing all alone, and wrapping himself up in a tiger rug, to represent, rather forlornly, a king — it was nicest of all to represent a king since the imaginary mantle protected him against the chills of fever'.[20]

— a game which foreshadows Kinbote's sad charade in *Pale Fire*. A pattern is established which Luzhin must play out like Anderssen his sacrifice in the classic game (Anderssen versus Kieseritzky, London 1851) mentioned by Nabokov in his preface (this player is chosen presumably because, as Golombek tells us in *The Game of Chess*, his games are 'famous as masterpieces of combination'[21]). The fact that the radiant realm sought by Luzhin is unknown to geography but resides in a combination of childhood images, adumbrated by the nice old emigré soldier, is developed through a series of allusions to the geography master shared by Luzhin and his wife (since he taught at her school as well as his) and loved especially for his absence (imaginary schoolroom worlds supplanting his platitudinous actualities). Luzhin is pathologically lacking in a sense of place, remembers nothing of the towns he has visited, cannot conceive of a Coriolanian 'world elsewhere' even in the guise of a fabulous dissembling Zembla, and so responds with saddening blankness to his wife's travel projects:

> 'In general, all this could have been arranged more piquantly,' he said, pointing to a map of the world.[22]

Geography offers no refuge comparable to his beloved chess which penetrates a fourth dimension not marked in atlases. His chance encounter with Petrishchev, a boyhood enemy who brings to mind the unhappiest memories of his schooldays, seems only to confirm Luzhin's sense of the unreality of space when his tale of magical adventures in exotic parts is shown to be all fiction. Significantly he evokes their geography master:

> 'Do you remember our geographer, Luzhin? How he used to fly like a hurricane into the classroom, holding a map of the world?'[23]

The real villains of the novel are the psychiatrist with the black Assyrian beard who tries inexcusably (and unsuccessfully) to exorcise the childhood he attributes to Luzhin —

> 'Let me imagine your house — ancient trees all round . . . the house large and bright. Your father returns from the hunt' . . . Luzhin recalled that his father had once found a fat, nasty little fledgling in a ditch . . .[24]

— and inaugurates the sad and misguided therapy apparently calculated to turn Luzhin from a great artist of one kind into a giftless artist of another; and Valentinov, the diabolical fixer who haunts Nabokov's world and is the nearest thing in it to a real embodiment of evil (he appears in *Laughter in the Dark* as Axel Rex, who is presented, like Valentinov, as a conjuror with a whiff of brimstone, a *fokusnik* or charlatan whose black magic evokes a world superficially resembling the totality of meaning that art freely offers but in actuality is one in which the damned act out the costume drama of their own bondage). Typically Nabokov gives the role of antichrist to a film impresario (*Mary* tells us how Russian emigrés habitually sold their shadows into the bondage of celluloid) and even his name (and his black fur collar and white silk scarf) evoke movieland and the glamour of Rudolph Valentino. Valentinov precipitates Luzhin's tragedy by enticing him back into chess through the lure of the silver screen (and it may well be that Kinokonzern 'Veritas', located in Rabenstrasse, slave street,[25] does not exist).

Yet Valentinov, Luzhin's 'chess father',[26] is in the end as insubstantial as the phantoms he conjures up. Luzhin's distraught soul is the central reality of the novel, and the development of the theme that is sounded in his childhood moves to its climax with great pathos and psychological depth, the 'warmth' of which the author speaks. The little chessboard he finds in his old jacket pocket, a much reduced but guiltily treasured model of the universe, serves perfectly as the correlative of Luzhin's tragically frustrated search for protective order, the 'perfect defence'. *The Real Life of Sebastian Knight* (1941) is conceived quite differently, despite the apparent similarity of chess motifs: its hero, far from dominating the novel, endlessly evades the narrator, and its formal devices, based on chess moves, are foregrounded in a way that they are not in *The Defence*. Yet there are deep similarities: the concern with the frontiers of art and its relationship to life, the Proustian obsession with the secret places of childhood and the sources of creativity, combined with the Chekhovian need to make art from the aching void of an endless sense of loss are Nabokovian constants which are given special prominence in both novels.

The name of the hero of this real life story is evidently a significant motif, and it is elaborated upon in the course of the development of the plot. Knight's mixed Anglo-Russian parentage is the starting point for the investigation of a character unbounded by geographical space (queer fragments of classic Russian literature float around in his remembered childhood in St. Petersburg without ever being labelled for what they are). The standard book on Knight, contemptuously referred to by the narrator on many occasions,[27] talks of a Russian education 'forced upon a small boy always conscious of the rich English strain in his blood',[28] whereas the truth is evidently that the possession of two languages and two cultures (if not two countries) was peculiarly and disturbingly liberating.[29] Sebastian wrote poems in English as a child, signing them with 'a little black chess knight drawn in ink', adopting for his own at an early age the knight's gambit which will typify his moves in later life. The knight in chess is characterized by Golombek as a strong defensive piece, and he notes in his introduction to the game that

> The knight has a composite move. It moves two squares, horizontally or vertically, and then another square, vertically or horizontally . . . It has the property peculiar to

> itself of being able to jump over any other piece.[30]

It therefore, as it were, leaves the board intermittently, in order to attack or (more often) defend, and in doing so enters momentarily some obscure dimension outside the planometric conventions of the game. In the same way Sebastian is 'strongly defensive' (and more successful in defensive play than Luzhin); and he disappears at critical moments, evading discovery so bafflingly that it almost seems he has entered another dimension. His relationship with Clare Bishop was bound to be difficult: they are close enough to disagree, and as Golombek says

> One is often met with the question: which is the better piece for the ending, the Kt or the B? The answer is that it all depends on the Pawn structure. If the position is an open one, i.e., if there are plenty of open lines along which the Bishop may travel and especially if the Pawns are not fixed or blocked but are free to advance, then the Bishop is much the better piece . . . How impotent a Kt can be against a Bishop appears in Diagram 175 . . . When, however, the position is blocked, the Kt comes into its own.[31]

The unalterable reason for this appears in Golombek's introduction:

> It (the Bishop) can never change from the colour of the square on which it is initially placed.[32]

Clare is a fixed character, Sebastian a shifting one, and the moves they make correspond to these basic formal realities.

Whereas the game of chess was for Luzhin his alternative world, we are given in *The Real Life* one character, Sebastian, who is, like the knight, within the game yet not confined by it (the game being the whole pattern of conflicts and confrontations that makes up the plot of the novel). When Sebastian is pursued (as he is throughout the novel by his half-brother) he isn't there: the Roquebrune visited by Sebastian, and filled by him with the appropriate respectful sentiments, turns out not to be the one where Sebastian's mother had died. His involvement with Alexis Pan's Futurist activities (a brilliant pastiche of the Russian avant-garde just before and after the revolution in which half a dozen leading figures are discernible) is of short duration, and after Pan's lecture tour (modelled on Mayakovsky's)

> Sebastian talked of the trip as of some quaint incident of which he had been a dispassionate observer.[33]

He isn't wholly involved in the game (and thus avoids Pan's fate — a parody of Esenin's:

> Two or three years later Pan enjoyed a short artificial vogue in Bolshevik surroundings which was due I think to the queer notion (mainly based on a muddle of terms) that there is a natural connection between extreme politics and extremist art. Then, in 1922 or 1923 Alexis Pan committed suicide with the aid of a pair of braces[34]).

His mother said that she 'never really knew Sebastian'; the narrator tells us that 'the manner of his prose was the manner of his thinking and that was a dazzling succession of gaps'; we are told that despite his love of Cambridge 'the most precious part of himself would remain as hopelessly alone as it had always been', and we see him strong in defence like his chess prototype, leaping over the pieces around him rather than running against them as the Bishop must, or indeed as the narrator — perhaps the White Knight — does when he confronts the appalling Mr. Goodman in Chapter Seven and casts him in the part of the black king. Goodman has written of Sebastian in the modernist-apocalyptic vein (e.g. 'The War had changed the face of the universe . . . futility . . . gross liberty . . . the foxtrot . . . glories of standardization') as some kind of spokesman of his age, whereas, as the narrator tells us

> Time for Sebastian was never 1914 or 1920 or 1936 — it was always year 1 . . . Time and space were to him measures of the same eternity, so that the very idea of

> his reacting in any specially 'modern' way to what Mr. Goodman calls 'the atmosphere of post-war Europe' is utterly preposterous.[35]

This is an extreme statement of the writer's autonomy (accompanied as elsewhere in Nabokov by an insistence on his infinite inventiveness: Nabokov opposes the cultural pessimism and conservatism of, for instance, Eliot, by just such claims, not wholly convincing, for the inevitable rootlessness and convenient portability of the artist's world). In his reminiscences, *Lost Property*, Knight (who had no tangible property and in fact has lost about as much as Proust's Marcel has) walks again the 'endless vague wanderings' of his youth towards

> a certain warm hollow where something very like the selfest of my own self sits huddled in the darkness.[36]

The note of naïve nostalgia and romance in this recalls at once an important source for this novel: Lewis Carroll's *Through the Looking Glass*, where the White Knight has some of Sebastian's characteristics.

*Through the Looking Glass* is of course set out as a chess game, and a proper plausibility of moves is carefully observed. Chess is a looking-glass world — not a mirror held up to nature, but a model of ideal reality, a kind of ballet of Platonic forms. Carroll's work thus becomes an important model of anti-realistic fiction, and one of his most amiable and plangent 'characters' serves as the type of the artist. Chapter Eight of *Through the Looking Glass* is headed 'It's my own Invention', and this is the sad but oddly inspiring cry of the White Knight (who appears, appropriately enough, at that chilling moment when Alice is just about to waken the Red King, despite a well-grounded fear that she and all the others may be no more than a part of his dream; his shout of 'Ahoy! Ahoy! Check!' and the identical cry of the Red Knight prevent her). The Knights fight according to the Rules of Battle, which are geared to confining the combatants to a few awkward gestures, ensuring that neither really gets hurt. When the White Knight emerges victorious, he shows Alice all his inventions. These are without any practical use but admirably ingenious, and they are all basically defensive devices designed to help the Knight cope with an importunate and remorseless reality. Even the laws of gravity are a threat to him, since he keeps falling off his horse. But the interesting thing is that in overcoming difficulties by the most roundabout way the Knight becomes an artist. Nabokov writes of Sebastian's 'curves and gaps and zigzags . . . groping along a certain ideal line of expression' and remarks that

> He usually chose the easiest ethical path (just as he chose the thorniest aesthetic one) merely because it happened to be the shortest cut to his chosen object; he was far too lazy in everyday life (just as he was far too hardworking in his artistic life) to be bothered by problems set and solved by others.[37]

— all of which recalls the White Knight's invention of a new way of getting over a gate:

> 'I'll tell you how I came to think of it,' said the Knight. 'You see, I said to myself, "The only difficulty is with the feet: the *head* is high enough already." Now, first I put my head on the top of the gate — then the head's high enough — then I stand on my head — then the feet are high enough, you see — then I'm over, you see.'
>
> 'Yes, I suppose you'd be over when that was done,' said Alice thoughtfully: 'but don't you think it would be rather hard?'
>
> "I haven't tried it yet,' the Knight said gravely: 'so I can't tell for certain — but I'm afraid it *would* be a little hard.'[38]

And as he talks calmly to Alice while head downwards in a ditch there is another pre-echo of Sebastian Knight:

> 'What does it matter where my body happens to be? . . . My mind goes on working all the same. In fact, the more head downwards I am, the more I keep inventing new things.'[39]

It is easy to see why Alice, as Carroll tells us, remembers her encounter with the White Knight more vividly than any other looking-glass experience, especially since he takes his leave with a witty and telling parody of Wordsworth, the great innovator who had connived at his own metamorphosis into the spokesman of Victorian orthodoxy. The little victims of fifty years of cautionary tales and old saws would have relished Carroll's version of one of Wordsworth's finest moral fables, 'Resolution and Independence', for Carroll's White Knight, like Nabokov's Sebastian,

> . . . used parody as a kind of springboard for leaping into the highest region of serious emotion . . . With something akin to fanatical hate Sebastian Knight was ever hunting out the things which had once been fresh and bright (like haddocks' eyes?)* but which were now worn to a thread, dead things among living ones; dead things shamming life, painted and repainted, continuing to be accepted by lazy minds serenely unaware of the fraud.[40]

The knight's gambit, in other words, is the move proper to the artist. By means of it he sidesteps or leaps over material obstacles and evades the traps set for him. It is also the creative gesture by means of which he enters a dimension beyond time and space in which he forges the world anew or (as the Russian Formalist critics said) 'defamiliarizes' and 'complicates' it. And, of course, another precursor of *The Real Life* which Nabokov could not help being aware of is Viktor Shklovsky's book *Khod Konya* (*Knight's Gambit*) published in Berlin in 1923. This collection of essays by the most brilliant and eccentric of the Formalists has a chess-board on its title page on which the knight's erratic moves are indicated. Shklovsky, though writing in the Soviet Union, says that he is directing his book at Russian emigrés, and he provides in it a great deal of frank information about the terrible conditions Petrograd has experienced. But his intention is neither to castigate the

---

*My parenthetical remark—G.H.

emigration nor attack (or defend) the Soviet government: it is to assert the creative individualism of the artist, the Knight whose moves are dictated not by any political directive but by 'the conventionality of art'[41] and the compulsions of literary form. Interestingly, Shklovsky (in the context of some comments on Futurism) remarks that one of the gravest errors of contemporary writers is the hasty analogy they have drawn 'between social revolution and revolution in artistic forms':[42] art is not one of the functions of life, there is no necessary relationship between art and 'byt' (the Russian word implies commonplace material reality), but in actuality

> Art was always free of life, its colours were never those of the flag on the city ramparts.[43]

— ideas very close to those given to Sebastian and to Nabokov's narrator. Moreover, much of Shklovsky's book is a brilliant and choleric assault on charlatans (*fokusniki*), pseudo-artists, and political gentlemen of uncertain intentions who, understanding nothing of art, are grimly and doggedly engaged in formulating the norms and canons of a socialist aesthetic (their opposite number in the West is Nabokov's Mr. Goodman who has his own representative kind of blankness). Nabokov's art demands the reader's total immersion if not acquiescence. Although there is much in the work of the Formalists uncongenial to Nabokov he too, like them, insists that art is a mode of cognition (not a mirror held up to nature) and contains its own proper strategies (hence the chess analogy). Just as the new positivist philosophy finds its proper function to be a discussion of language itself, so Nabokov's novels create, describe, and renew their own devices. But it is just here, in this apparently technical concern, that his greatest creative excitement is generated, and in this Nabokov is much closer to Shklovsky than (say) to I. A. Richards from a theoretical standpoint.

So we come by way of conclusion to the question of the relationship in *The Real Life* between the narrator and Knight. A 'celebrated old critic' cited by the narrator once said of Sebastian:

> 'Poor Knight — he really had two periods, the first — a dull man writing broken English, the second — a broken man writing dull English.'[44]

The closeness of the narrator to his half-brother and of both to Nabokov is evident from the earliest pages of the book, but the full extent of the closeness is revealed only on the last page. As the narrator tries to piece together the 'real' life he not only comes to rely more and more on Sebastian's writings, in which (including the autobiography, *Lost Property*) he fictionalizes his own life, but he is also of course obliged to impose a shape on his material in such a way as to 'invent' Sebastian. Sebastian dies, the 'real life' ends; but he was dead before the quest began, and we begin to see that the novel in front of us, Nabokov's *Real Life*, is exactly what it claims to be. The transition from a dogged piecing together of the evidence to a full creative participation in the fiction (whereby the narrator and Sebastian fuse together and the split selves of the literary emigré are made one through art) is prepared gradually. In Chapter Six the narrator warns us:

> Remember that what you are told is really threefold: shaped by the teller, reshaped by the listener, concealed from both by the dead man of the tale.[45]

Goodman's book, *The Tragedy of Sebastian Knight*, is full of anecdotes purporting to be drawn from Sebastian's life, but actually lifted from Russian and English literature (Goodman, in other words, has not recognized them as fictions). The account of the plot of Sebastian's novel *The Prismatic Bezel*,[46] one of his characteristic attempts to use parody to serious ends, shows it to be a 'real life' adventure, a detective story hinging on an ingenious mirrored doublet of the name of the murdered man (G. Abeson and Nosebag turn out to be the same person; i.e., the fiction reveals the real life of the victim/hero). This novel, like all Sebastian's work, has liberated itself from the time conventions of realist fiction to such an extent that it can (indeed must) be read backwards as well as forwards: it is immersed in what Van Veen will later call, in *Ada*, 'the texture of time'. And it is the train journey of Chapter Thirteen (echoing again *Through the Looking Glass*[47]) in which space-time appears to be decisively overcome, the real Sebastian being on the verge of disclosing himself. The narrator meets a Hoffmannesque commercial traveller called Silbermann who doubles as a private detective and finds a number of possible names for the girl for whom Sebastian left his unswerving Clare Bishop (signing his farewell letter with an 'L', the knight's gambit). Reading backwards to Chapter Eleven, we find that Silbermann is the Mr. Siller of Sebastian's story 'The Back of the Moon' (another looking-glass allusion), 'the meek little man waiting for a train who helped three miserable travellers in three different ways . . . the most alive of Sebastian's creatures'.[48] Fact and fiction dissolve and combine in a blurred past and present. That farewell letter was actually found in the wreckage of an aeroplane which crashed not in 'reality' but in Sebastian's *Lost Property*. By Chapter Fourteen the narrator recognizes that his quest 'had developed its own magic and logic', and that 'in striving to render Sebastian's life I must now follow the same rhythmical interlacements'.[49] In Chapter Fifteen, trying the addresses given him by Silbermann, he stumbles into a chess game. The little boy standing watching it is described by his father as

> '. . . an all-round genius. He can play the violin standing upon his head, and he can multiply one telephone number by another in three seconds, and he can write his name upside down in his ordinary hand.'[50]

The chess clue is a good omen: it shows that the narrator is on the right track now, a fact confirmed at the moment when Mme. Lecerf reveals that it was she, not her friend, who was Sebastian's mistress with the whispered remark that she once upon a time

> '. . . kissed a man just because he could write his name upside down.'[51]

Moreover, Chapter Fifteen ends with the mystery man known as Uncle Black (since black is his chess colour) telling the boy (who likes to draw racing cars) a story which runs

> 'Once upon a time there was a racing motorist who had a little squirrel; and one day . . .'[52]

— a tale which charmingly muddles fact and fancy and leads us to the most unreliable of all the narrators, Mme. Lecerf herself (who would rather flirt with the narrator than talk about Sebastian). Her large country house of course echoes the setting of *The Prismatic Bezel.* In Chapter Eighteen, the account of Sebastian's *The Doubtful Asphodel* tells us that as a commentary to the main subject (the gradual death of the hero) other motifs enter:

> We follow the gentle old chess player, Schwarz, who sits down on a chair in a room in a house, to teach an orphan boy the moves of the knight . . .[53]

— an unsolicited echo of that chess game. Other characters and events (Lydia Bohemsky, the pale wretch, etc.) exist similarly within two fictions: Knight's and the narrator's — not to mention Nabokov's. It is not surprising that Mme. Lecerf found Sebastian obsessed by his dreams, and

> the dreams in his dreams, and the dreams in the dreams of his dreams.

The narrator arrived too late to be with Sebastian as he died (worse: he kept vigil at the bedside of someone else whom he 'only' imagined was Sebastian) but has nevertheless picked up a useful hint: that 'any soul may be yours, if you find and follow its undulations'.[54] His closing words reveal that he has gone some way towards solving the problem of his identity (the emigré bilingual writer whose adopted tongue has no personal past is not unrelated to his inventor): 'I am Sebastian, or Sebastian is I, or perhaps we are both someone whom neither of us knows'. As Alice remarks (*Through the Looking Glass*, Chapter Eight)

> 'So I wasn't dreaming after all . . . unless — unless we're all part of the same dream. Only I do hope it's *my* dream, and not the Red King's! I don't like belonging to another person's dream,' she went on in a rather complaining tone: 'I've a great mind to go and wake him, and see what happens.'[55]

— whereupon the Red and the White Knight appear, and prevent her, which takes us back several moves in what is more of a chess problem than a chess game. The novel is an elaborate synthesis in which, writing in a foreign language which he knew well but evidently not perfectly, Nabokov explores his new identity. It occupies a pivotal place in his conception of the literary sensibility, since it enacts an acceptance of homelessness which implies a reconciliation of the split halves of the protagonist of *Despair* (1936) in combination with a determination to reduce his cultural belongings, so richly displayed in *The Gift* (written between 1935 and 1937), to an absolute minimum. It prepares the way for the joyous and humane *Pnin*, in which Russia, though the memory of it tugs at Pnin's heartstrings, is kept well under control. When the theme of estrangement and loss recurs, in *Lolita* and *Pale Fire*, it does so in forms no longer so immediately related to a specifically Russian experience.

## Notes to Chapter 4

1. *Zashchita Luzhina*. Nabokov does not explain this in his preface to the English version of the novel.
2. This is perhaps too much of a generalization: after all, the knight is the artist in the other chess novel discussed here. I think the distinction is that the artist protects himself by means of the knight's gambit, but presides Timon-like over his private kingdom, in which language, his only subject, has to perform every kind of royal service. cf. *An Evening of Russian Poetry*:

   Beyond the seas where I have lost a sceptre
   I hear the neighing of my dappled nouns,
   soft participles coming down the steps,
   treading on leaves, trailing their rustling gowns,
   and liquid verbs in *ahla* and in *ili*,
   Aonian grottoes, nights in the Altai,
   black pools of sound with 'l's for water lilies.
   The empty glass I touched is tinkling still,
   but now 'tis covered by a hand and dies.
3. This does not mean that Nabokov generally lacks warmth, but he seldom allows his hero such unequivocal sympathy and pathos as here: especially in the case of those heroes who, like Luzhin, are 'neurotic'.
4. Although he may be taken as the type of the artist, he is first and foremost a confused and unhappy *man*.
5. Vladimir Nabokov, *The Defence* (London: Panther Books, 1971). For obvious reasons the first edition spells the title differently. The reference here is to *ibid*., p. 79.
6. *Ibid*., p. 92. To lose a Knight is to lose the strongest defensive piece, which protects itself by its strange ability to leave the board and pass into another dimension. The weakness on the Queen's flank is Luzhin's way of talking about being tied down by marriage. The reified artifice of his language is neurotic but not, like Hermann's (*Despair*) vicious.
7. *Ibid*. This is the conclusion of the same passage, in which Luzhin's fear of women is sensitively explored.
8. Another *fokusnik* or conjuror. With the Russian word in mind, Nabokov here and in other novels seems to see the conjuror-figure as a 'false' artist whose function is to provide a 'focal' point thematically: he 'focuses' the issues at stake, engineering the peripeteia. But such characters are no more than mechanics, and it is wrong to identify them with the author.

9. Nabokov dislikes mythic archetypes — but this one keeps within the confines of the text.
10. Props like this are handed round from book to book, mostly on loan from *Speak, Memory*. In *Transparent Things* the author tries to get some of them back, with a desperate sense that they have passed beyond the reach of his art.
11. *The Defence*, p. 110.
12. *Ibid.*, p. 111.
13. *Ibid.*, p. 192. The need for a stable home turns it into a kind of positive absence which obsesses Luzhin.
14. *Ibid.*, p. 144. In most of Nabokov's novels the role of women is determined by men. This one is unusual in that Luzhin's wife is, as the author himself notes in his introduction, a character 'in her own right'.
15. *Ibid.*, p. 183. The allusion to Gogol suggests that Luzhin, like him, has a holy dread of what is called in Russian *byt*, which is perhaps best paraphrased as 'unredeemed time'. Both artists and neurotics are driven to transcend *byt*. Luzhin gets sympathy (unlike Hermann or Smurov) because he is more the former than the latter.
16. *Ibid.*, p. 101.
17. *Ibid.*, p. 12. Truth lurks unheeded in the most utilitarian phrases. Cf. the epigraph to *The Gift*: 'An oak is a tree. A rose is a flower. A deer is an animal. A sparrow is a bird. Russia is our fatherland. Death is inevitable.' (An extract from Smirnovsky's *Textbook of Russian Grammar*.)
18. *Ibid.*, p. 26. Cf. my earlier note on detective stories and structuralist critics.
19. *Ibid.*, p. 33.
20. *Ibid.*, p. 55.
21. H. Golombek, *The Game of Chess* (Harmondsworth: Penguin Books, 1963) p. 200. It will be the hopeless endeavour of Luzhin's life to 'combine' his talent with his everyday self, to fit together the pieces of that jigsaw 'poozel' of the natural world started in the nursery (p. 28).
22. *Ibid.*, p. 146. From chess master Luzhin turns into chess piece.
23. *Ibid.*, p. 156.
24. *Ibid.*, p. 127. It would be wrong to assume that Nabokov has *in fact* repudiated Freud just because of his frequent anti-Freudian quips. Page Stegner (op. cit.) remarks that 'the clear connections Freud makes between the artist and the neurotic are totally alien to Nabokov', which is only half

true (the word 'totally' is otiose, and there seems to be some suggestion that Freud's association of artist and neurotic is more unequivocal than is in fact the case). Later in his book, Stegner says that Nabokov's objections to Freud 'strike one quite often as themselves obsessive', which I agree with.

25. 'Raben' is a raven in German, a bird of ill omen, but *rab* is the Russian for 'slave'. Nabokov's infrequent allusions to German (a language he claims not to speak) often contain such inter-lingual Russianisms.
26. To Valentinov, Luzhin is always 'my boy'. Paternity matters in some of Nabokov's novels (*The Gift, Laughter in the Dark, Pnin, Pale Fire* — even *Lolita*) almost as much as it does in *Ulysses* or *Les Faux Monnayeurs*.
27. Mr. Goodman's book is called *The Tragedy of Sebastian Knight*, and it is a work in the apocalyptic-modern vein. With the analogy of *The Gift* in mind (where Fyodor invents the critic Strannolyubski as an index of his 'strange love' for his subject) it is tempting to see Goodman merely as a negative projection of the narrator's: they certainly indulge in oddly suggestive mask-play. I feel, however, that in dealing with this novel more than with any of the others, it would be wrong to throw the emphasis on to specific characters. All of them, evidently, have functions rather than identities, which is why — in the absence of a 'finished' text to secure their relationship to one another — they are so elusive.
28. *The Real Life of Sebastian Knight* (Harmondsworth: Penguin Books, 1971) p. 13.
29. The bearing of this on Nabokov's case hardly needs underlining. This is his first novel in English and he is evidently flexing his muscles. There are some odd turns of phrase here and there. In the fate of St. Sebastian — shot to death with arrows — Nabokov maybe alludes to his own case: this was the most insecure period of his life, and it is only after the desperate farce of *Bend Sinister* that we find the assurance of *Pnin*.
30. *The Game of Chess*, p. 11.
31. *Ibid.*, pp. 144-5.
32. *Ibid.*, p. 11.
33. *The Real Life of Sebastian Knight*, p. 26.
34. *Ibid.*
35. *Ibid.*, p. 55. Again Nabokov protests too much (or is it only his narrator, who has lent Goodman a black mask?) *Bend*

*Sinister* does not take history so lightly: here Nabokov makes it clear that his anti-historicism is an effort to wake up from a nightmare. Between the two novels came the death of his brother in a Nazi camp.

36. *Ibid.*, p. 58.
37. *Ibid.*, p. 69.
38. Lewis Carroll, *Through the Looking Glass*, p. 308.
39. *Ibid.*, p. 310.
40. *The Real Life of Sebastian Knight*, p. 76.
41. Viktor Shklovsky, *Khod Konya* (Moscow-Berlin, 1923). This is the book absurdly represented in the standard English translation of Trotsky's *Literature and Revolution* as *The March of the Horse.*
42. *Ibid.*, p. 37.
43. *Ibid.*, p. 39.
44. *The Real Life of Sebastian Knight*, p. 6.
45. *Ibid.*, p. 44.
46. *Ibid.*, p. 76 et. seq. Sebastian's titles are pointers to his 'real life'. The word 'bezel' denotes the faceting of a gem.
47. cf. Lewis Carroll, op. cit., p. 220. The chapter is entitled *Looking-glass Insects.*
48. *The Real Life of Sebastian Knight*, p. 86.
49. *Ibid.*, p. 113.
50. *Ibid.*, p. 119.
51. *Ibid.*, p. 143.
52. *Ibid.*, p. 123. Time shifts in Nabokov's work are often accompanied by the appearance of squirrels. This delightful creature, which haunts the lawns of childhood, leaps airily from book to book to reach its apogee in *Pnin* (see Julia Bader, *Crystal Land*).
53. *The Real Life of Sebastian Knight*, p. 147.
54. *Ibid.*, p. 172. Sebastian dies at St. Damier ('Holy Chessboard') and to reach what he thinks is his deathbed the narrator passes through a chess puzzle (p. 167) very like that in *Through the Looking Glass*, 'normal' sensations of 'progress' being in abeyance in both. The telegram informing the narrator of Sebastian's fatal illness spells his name the Russian way, 'Sevastian' (p. 160). The holy chessgame of art mediates between subject and object, between the self and the world and, in doing so, enlarges the possibilities of life. The narrator has discovered not Sebastian but himself, the tell-tale Russian 'character'.
55. Lewis Carroll. op. cit., pp. 299, 346.

# V

## Divided selves: **The Eye** (1930, 1965) **Despair** (1936, 1966) and **Lolita** (1955)

The most distinctive tradition in nineteenth century Russian fiction is perhaps that of the so-called 'superfluous man'. This term, an ungainly translation of a commonplace category in Russian literary criticism (*lishni chelovek*), is used to signify a novelistic hero (originating actually in Pushkin's poetry, especially *Eugene Onegin* and *The Bronze Horseman*, and owing much to Byron) whose distinguishing feature is the lack of what might be termed a centre of self.[1] The forms he takes (or rather 'generates', since he is all process) in fiction from Lermontov to Dostoevsky and beyond are extremely various, and the formal instability of the Russian novel, a relatively unestablished genre which had itself not yet defined its identity, permits a fluid experimentalism (denied in other areas of Russian life and thought) which constitutes an odd 'modernity'. There is a continuous creative and exploratory relationship between author, protagonist, and fictional techniques in such works as *A Hero of Our Time*, *Oblomov*, *Rudin*, *The Diary of a Superfluous Man*, or *Notes from Underground* which seems to anticipate the influence of existentialist thought on the modern novel.[2] Unlike in other respects, these works have in common this intense preoccupation with the problematics of the relationship between the writer and his material, especially his 'hero' (Lermontov's title has a representative ambivalence) who is a tentative *alter ego* projected into the world. He shares with his creator positive traits of intelligence, sensitivity, and conscience, as well as negative traits of pathological frigidity (Pechorin), 'Asiatic' willessness (Oblomov) phoney nobility of soul (Rudin) which have been interpreted by materialist critics as the inevitable scars left by the struggle of a radical vision against autocracy.[3] For the Russian writer of the nineteenth century the pressure to be the consciousness of the age conflicted with the demand that he be keeper of its conscience. There was a kind of schizoid condition, induced by a contradiction, explored in detail in modern fiction, between the social pressures from without and the psychological pressures from within, both being made manifest in the forms of the genre itself.

The instability of nineteenth century Russian fiction, then, reflects the absence of a substantial stratum of bourgeois liberal culture such as the English or French novelist could either rest upon or react against. Writing is a single-handed and desperate activity, for the writer, as well as writing in fear of the censorship, must create from the void. It is also striking that this 'void' is cherished as freedom, and thus potentiality: this is true of works otherwise as different as *A Hero of Our Time* and *Oblomov*. Lermontov's novel is not a finished work but a kind of do-it-yourself kit which must be assembled each time anew by the reader,[4] and Gogol's fantastic world exists only as long as his words are kept spinning in the air by the narrator, who is thus a kind of conjuror (like Humbert Humbert, he 'has only words to play with'[5]). If this condition makes impossible the achievement of a George Eliot in Russian fiction, it fosters, on the other hand, a kind of creative uncertainty (even in the comparatively stable universe of Tolstoy) which has perhaps come to seem closer to us now than ever before.

There are, of course, many other factors which contribute to the inventiveness of Russian literature during what is undoubtedly one of the most miraculous cultural efflorescences known to man. The fresh delight of discovering the potential of Russian as a literary language, the impact of European rationalism (which Russia caught like influenza, having a very low natural resistance), the triumph of 1812 and the fervour and frustration of the failed uprising in 1825, the constant expansion of the Empire and the discovery of contiguous 'alternative societies' on the very borders of European Russia — all this impinges on an immature society caught in painful internal contradictions. Writers belonged inevitably to a kind of schismatic and embattled caste, denoted by the Russian word *intelligentsia* (taken over into English where it becomes only a ghost of itself). Even after the Revolution, which soon demanded a realist literature reflecting a coherent society founded upon shared objectives, Russian literature continues to evolve from its schismatic origins: the rift, indeed, has become wider since Stalinism. Anyone who has seen Russian 'unofficial' painting, for instance, will have been struck by its obsession with 'schizoid' themes, the counterpart of the bland classicism of most of the 'official' art.[6] Writers of the emigration, who have felt an urgent (no doubt exaggerated) responsibility for safeguarding the Russian literary tradition have generally, insofar as they have succeeded in outwitting nostalgia, felt the need to define their relationship to the old intelligentsia. The question of 'superfluity' has been given a new and bitter significance. Nabokov is no exception to this. Questions of identity have been crucial for him as for earlier Russian writers, and so has the problem of continuity, both personal and cultural.[7] To treat Russia as an inert object of nostalgia, to lament one's loss and to carry around with one a 'portable Petersburg' (*Glory*) is not only to confirm Russia's remoteness — to turn it into a far-off Zembla — but also to reject a part of oneself: that Russian part which is hermetically sealed off in a container labelled 'the past'. In the resonant metaphors of *Speak, Memory* Nabokov directs all his art to the transcendence of this fatal nostalgia and the divided self engendered by it: whence the assertiveness, even arrogance, with which he stakes his claim to the Russian language and Russian literature, as if both were constantly threatened by fools and charlatans, and only he had been entrusted with the keys of the kingdom.[8] In Nabokov's case the fact that the liberal dissidence which was his birthright (and for which his father was imprisoned by the Tsar, and murdered by right-wing extremists) seemed doomed even in those countries to which he fled in the hope of preserving it must have intensified the temptation of nostalgia. England's exclusiveness, which he seems never to have penetrated,[9] gave way to Germany's chauvinism and totalitarianism[10] and France's fall.[11] Even America, perhaps, which he seems to have loved as a free country,[12] in the end proved exhaustible, and he has settled in the traditional home of the homeless dissident, Switzerland, where his Russian forbears sought shelter from autocracy. His hostility to the Soviet regime has always been countered by his hatred of right-wing revanchistes,[13] and his strenuous defence of his liberty of conscience (together with the more mundane frustrations of being always a foreigner, amply illustrated in his novels) must have influenced his conception of his art as a looking-glass land of truth and freedom. But if, like Humbert, he 'has only words to play with', he is all the more alert to the possibilities of deception and evasion inherent in language. No writer sees more clearly than Nabokov that literature and a kind of compensatory fantasy are closely akin but that they are by no means the same thing: that the true writer sheds his sicknesses in his books, while the charlatan passes off his delusions as art and his wonderfully sick soul as creative sensibility. This is the theme of at least three novels: *The Eye*, *Despair*, and *Lolita*.[14]

Of these three, *The Eye* is the simplest, though its extreme compression should not blind us to its scope. It is a more clinical record of a nervous breakdown than *Despair*, and at the same time closer to those antecedents in Russian literature which I have briefly described. Its plot is simple, and for once Nabokov's introduction is more helpful than mystifying:

> A serious psychologist . . . may distinguish through my rain-sparkling crystograms a world of soul dissolution where poor Smurov only exists in so far as he is reflected in other brains, which in their turn are placed in the same strange, specular predicament as his.[15]

The reader is forced into the role of analyst, since all he has to go on is a first-person narrator, who demonstrates his unreliability — and his acute sickness — from the first words of the novel. An emigré, intelligent enough to diagnose the sadness and falsity with which his fellow emigrés cling to the 'phantasmata' of old Russia, he nevertheless needs this emigré society to confirm, mirror-like, his own existence. He is afraid that, without it, he may cease to exist. At the same time he fears the gaze of others, *le regard des autres*,[16] even the 'clear gaze' of the children he teaches, because it seems to exert a power over his uncertain sense of identity. This already seems 'abnormal' (if that word may be permitted for the time being). As R. D. Laing puts it, in *The Divided Self*, in 'normal' circumstances:

> Each has his own autonomous sense of identity and his own definition of who and what he is. You are expected to be able to recognize me. That is, I am accustomed to expect that the person you take me to be, and the identity that I reckon myself to have, will coincide by and large.[17]

Smurov lacks this sense. From the early passages describing his affair with Matilda, for instance, we see an exaggerated craving for love and warmth combined with a tendency to dissociate himself from the sexual act, so that it becomes depersonalized and unsatisfying.[18] Yet he dreads equally the surrender of self in a close relationship, which he conceives as a threat to his already insecure identity.[19] Turgenev charts this, his own case, with great art, in tale after tale, the classic instance being *Rudin*, a novel which throws much light on *The Eye*. Smurov suffers from what Laing rather portentously calls 'ontological insecurity':[20] his fears 'engulfment' (being dominated by another), 'implosion' (being swamped by reality), and 'petrification' (being treated by others as an object, an 'it'), all of these fears being part and parcel of the exaggerated need to have one's identity confirmed by others. One of Smurov's characteristic defences against these threats is admirably described by Laing: he 'engulfs' himself, since

> Thoroughly to understand oneself (engulf oneself) is a defence against the risk involved in being sucked into the whirlpool of another person's way of comprehending one-

> self. To consume oneself by one's own love prevents the possibility of being consumed by another.[21]

It is in this sense that he is an 'eye' (actually the meaning of the Russian title is rather 'one sent out by an army to reconnoitre'). But turning himself into the object of his own scrutiny merely confirms his dissociation:

> I was always exposed, always wide-eyed; even in sleep I did not cease to watch over myself, understanding nothing of my existence, growing crazy at the thought of not being able to stop being aware of myself, and envying all those simple people — clerks, revolutionaries, shopkeepers — who, with confidence and concentration, go about their little jobs.[22]

The intrusion of 'revolutionaries' into the list economically evokes the political background of Smurov's disease, elsewhere enlarged upon. The belief that there *are* 'ordinary' people, and that they are happy (because stupid), is a neurotic trait given also to Hermann in *Despair.*[23]

Smurov thinks of people as parts of their bodies, gestures, never as selves. This is a defensive ploy on his part, which Laing relates to the myth of Perseus and the Medusa's head: the schizophrenic carries a kind of device for turning others to stone, thus avoiding 'petrification' himself. But Smurov, and Hermann, go further: like Laing's schizophrenic patients, each has a tendency 'to identify himself . . . with that part of him which feels *unembodied*', thus treating their bodies as dissociated objects, 'felt as the core of a false self' (Laing), observed with detachment or, more often, disgust. This is the crux of the split between what Laing calls 'the false-self system', or persona, and the 'self' (felt to be the 'true' self). The attack on Smurov by Matilda's husband is observed with detachment by Smurov himself, and one might almost take it for fantasy — especially since Smurov has already had just this kind of fantasy about this man, and is evidently ready to accept him as an objective correlative of his confused sexual guilt (and fear of impotence, in the cane motif). The chronic dissociation recalls Kafka:

> The contemplative immobility of my two pupils, the different poses in which they froze like frescoes at the end of this room or that, the obliging way they turned on the lights the moment I backed into the dark dining room — all this must be a perceptional illusion — disjointed impressions to which I have imparted significance and permanence, and, for that matter, just as arbitrary as the raised knee of a politician stopped by the camera not in the act of dancing a jig but merely in that of crossing a puddle.[24]

The kinship between Smurov's habitual dissociation and the device of 'estrangement' ('making strange', *ostranenie*) regarded by the Russian Formalist critics as the key technique of modern art is worth noting, as well as the closeness of both to Brecht's so-called 'alienation effect'. The relationship between art and neurosis already referred to is best explored in relation to *Lolita*, but for the moment Nabokov's characteristic use of the motif of photography — like the cinema, a treacherous usurper of art's function — will serve to illustrate the chaotic fragmentariness of a world seen from no stable centre of self.

The fear of 'engulfment' or of 'petrifaction' which prompts the involuted ducking and weaving of 'superfluous men' as they keep moving on in order to be able to dissociate themselves from their former selves (which they leave behind them like pillars of salt or stone totems surveying a surreal landscape) drives Smurov to a still more drastic recourse: he kills himself (as does Hermann). This is startling, since he is telling the story — yet at no point does he say that it was merely 'as if' he had killed himself, but gives a circumstantial account of the suicide. He conceives suicide as a kind of trip to the country, a sudden opening up of clear vistas of unspoiled natural beauty, but admits in retrospect this was a delusion (thus Hermann, walking out into the countryside near Prague, finds he has taken his subjective debris with him, and envies Felix his untrammelled, 'natural' freedom of movement). The puzzling aspects of the matter (given that writing can be seen as a kind of suicide, which is an exegetical abyss neatly bridged by Nabokov himself in *Despair*) can be resolved once again with Laing's assistance. For the neurotic, 'What is "existentially" true is lived as "really" true':

> Undoubtedly, most people take to be 'really' true only what has to do with grammar and the natural world. A man says he is dead but he *is* alive. But his 'truth' is that he is dead. He expresses it perhaps in the only way common (i.e. the communal) sense allows him. He means that he is 'really' and quite 'literally' dead, not merely symbolically or 'in a sense' or 'as it were', and is seriously bent on communicating his truth. The price, however, to be paid for transvaluating the communal truth in this manner is to 'be' mad, for the only *real* death *we* recognize is biological death.[25]

I do not think Nabokov would agree with some of the assumptions here (and Laing's own later work, based in part on Blake, places rather different emphases on such words as 'real' and 'communal'); nevertheless, the fact that a schizoid subject can consider himself literally dead should make it perfectly possible to understand Smurov's case. Revisiting his room, he finds the bullet hole in the wall, confirming the death of his 'false self' (which his 'real self' has survived). His unembodied self has been set free to assume whatever form it pleases: he can enter the pure fiction of insanity, where he is the master of his world (instead of its victim), the author of the dazzling novel which is his own life; but, as Laing remarks,

> The withdrawal from reality results in the 'self's' own impoverishment. Its omnipotence is based on impotence. Its freedom operates in a vacuum. Its activity is without life. The self becomes desiccated and dead.[26]

— while the false self mounts its improbable charades: a new, infinitely malleable false self.

I have referred to the narrator as 'Smurov'. In fact they are not at first identical, and it is some time before we realize that 'Smurov' is the fictional projection of the narrator's false self. His meeting with the two sisters, Evgenia and Vanya, seems at first unremarkable; then gradually it dawns that these two (and especially Vanya, with her masculine name) are drawn with improbable obviousness from classic Russian fiction (Turgenev and Chekhov come at once to mind, though Pushkin's Tatyana and Olga are the great originals). One recalls those crucial episodes in which the ineffectual hero (Oblomov, Rudin, even Pechorin in his way) fails to rise to the challenge of the offered relationship with the lively and, in Turgenev and Chekhov, 'progressive' (and so slightly boyish) girl whose love is an unending threat and provocation to the talented but hopeless protagonist (*Oblomov* charts this relationship and confrontation most graphically, and with the fullest mythic power: Oblomov retreats to a mother-figure, the great provider Mrs. Pshenitsyn — her name, deriving from *pshenitsa*, wheat, reveals her as the earth-mother — to return to whom means death). The narrator registers his favourable reaction to Smurov, met in the company of the sisters: like Rudin in Turgenev's novel, he is a fascinating outsider, full of charm, intelligent, witty, an excellent conversationalist; in addition, Smurov is given the 'interesting pallor' of the more Byronic 'superfluous men'. Early on there are clues that he is a kind of composite literary fabrication, that the narrator, after his 'suicide', has synthesized a new literary personality in this great tradition, thus creating for himself a screen to shelter behind as well as a reassuring image to fill his existential void:

> He was obviously a person who, behind his unpretentiousness and quietness, concealed a fiery spirit. He was doubtless capable, in a moment of wrath, of slashing a chap into bits, and, in a moment of passion, of carrying a frightened and perfumed girl beneath his cloak on a windy night to a waiting boat with muffled oarlocks.[27]

It all falls too patly into the convention to be plausible. Lermontov's descriptions of Pechorin have a similarly stereotyped quality (imposed upon the Byronic demonism), but this is because Lermontov, too, is already, a hundred years earlier, *using* the literary type in a manner much like Smurov's; while its resemblance to early passages describing Rudin —

> Images followed upon images; comparisons started up one after another — now startlingly bold, now strikingly true . . . each word seemed to flow straight from his soul, and was burning with all the fire of conviction . . .[28]

— suggests that the persona is in part sustained, as in Turgenev's novel, by the insecurity and emotional needs of the 'intelligentsia' which acclaims it: a fragile basis for an admiration which can quickly give way to disgust. The book dealer, Weinstock, appropriately enough, embodies the rootlessness and paranoia of this community, with his pathetic seances. Only one character, Mukhin (like Pigasov in *Rudin*, but much more sympathetic) seems even to *want* to call the delightful imposter's bluff. Smurov's narrative, just like his persona, borrows heavily from Russian literature (including a nice allusion to *The Station Master* of Pushkin, broken off with 'but that's another story'.[29]) Challenged by Mukhin, he breaks down into Dostoyevskian snivellings. The narrator justly remarks that Smurov's 'image was influenced by the climatic condition prevailing in various souls', but excludes, of course, his own. His involvement with Vanya is all a matter of guessing and eavesdropping (Nabokov himself has drawn attention to Lermontov's compulsive use of this device in *A Hero of Our Time*, where it both solves problems of first-person narrative and reinforces the reader's sense of the hero's estrangement). He doesn't even get to the point of decisive failure, like Rudin, since Vanya loves Mukhin, Smurov's unmasker. The conclusion of the story belongs to the world of Gogol rather than Turgenev (though the latter's rather uncharacteristic *Diary of a Superfluous Man*,[30] which helped to define the phenomenon, is never very far away). Smurov, declaring his happiness, enters a world of sheer madness: the split is permanently accepted, he is happy to be just a huge bloodshot Eye (or 'I') enjoying fetishistic fantasies of Vanya. But Gogolian, too, is that sharp note of pain in the last sentence:

> Oh, to shout it so that all of you believe me at last, you cruel, smug people.

It is striking how often Laing uses the word 'despair' in *The Divided Self*. In confronting the schizophrenic, he says,

> We have to recognize all the time his distinctiveness and differentness, his separateness and loneliness and despair.[31]

adding in a footnote that 'Schizophrenia cannot be understood without understanding despair'. The solipsism characteristic of one kind of schizoid behaviour is described as offering 'a false hope' (i.e. of integration): it 'leads on to despair'. It is the Kierkegaardian experience of fear and trembling, the Kafkaesque knowledge that the hoped-for deliverance will be infinitely delayed, or Hermann's admission that the best title for the novel he has been writing (the novel of his life which is the substance of this novel of Nabokov's) is *Despair* — a title made the more desperate by the fact that Hermann has obsessively believed that his novel is his salvation (his fantasies, like Smurov's, take literary forms, but much more elaborate ones). The murder itself was to be a work of art which would (like Smurov's suicide) allow the murdered man to enter a fiction of his own making: only one thing went wrong, he tells us, but by the time he tells us, we know we are dealing with a psychopath. In his introduction to the novel, Nabokov draws a comparison between Hermann and Humbert (of *Lolita*), at the same time discriminating between them:

> Both are neurotic scoundrels, yet there is a green lane in Paradise where Humbert is permitted to wander at dusk once a year; but Hell shall never parole Hermann.[32]

This is, of course, unfair to Humbert (in the way Nabokov has oddly been in other comments on him), but sums up Hermann well, and Nabokov's attitude to him. He is damned, his life is a journey through Hell, his 'novel' a schizoid projection of shameless borrowings from Dostoyevsky (with a dash of Turgenev here and there) and an unforgivable misappropriation of one of Pushkin's greatest lyrics (helpfully quoted by Nabokov in his introduction[33]). It is the novel in which Nabokov's infallible humour, controlling the most unpleasant material, comes closest to abdicating.

Hermann is a sad emigré (though with German blood) living in Berlin (some of the action, however, takes place in Czechoslovakia, a country where Slav roots generate alien linguistic growths[34]). His business is failing (he is a chocolate manufacturer: the word 'chocolate' is made into the kernel of Hermann's banal detective story, or riddle, since by a neat word-game it is interpreted as 'chock' — the sound, in context, of a stick, 'oh' — exclamation of surprise or shock — or despair — and 'late' in the meaning of deceased).[35] 'Chocolate' generates Hermann's sick fancies and starts them on their mad career, since the trademark of his firm, shown on the wrappers, is a lady in lilac with a fan, and Hermann appropriates this image and presents it as that of his mother (telling us at the same time that he is lying: his mother was working class, and Hermann is ashamed of his origins[36]). The tissue of fantasy, drawing upon an imaginary Russia of ancestral houses, is initially only partial — Hermann knows what he is doing, and, like Dostoyevsky's Underground Man, likes to tell us what a rogue he is (in human relations, to borrow Laing's terms, he can experience only 'impotence' or 'omnipotence', and would rather name himself a villain than be thought one). From the fantasy of his mother, rocking on a hot summer day with 'all the blinds down, and the wind from some new-mown field making them billow like purple sails',[37] springs the precise imagery in which Hermann's schizophrenia is formulated; his neurosis is sexual, of course, in origin, schizoid in form, and involving a desperate act of transcendence which, going beyond Smurov's, is conceived as a suicide in the form of a murder. Nostalgic for the childhood, pastoral calm, and happiness he has in fact never known, Hermann tries to shed his mature self (both by suicide and by writing: as in *The Eye* the neurotic pseudo-artist sees the embodiment of himself in words as a fatal exposure and reification, rather than as the shedding of a sickness) and enter the being of a crude, simple, bucolic soul, Felix — the eternally happy man who exists only in the mind of such insecure souls as Hermann. To do this, of course, he has to get rid of the actual Felix: so he murders him.

There is little documentation of the origins of Hermann's despair, of course. One has to read between the lines and pick up such clues as the couple of references to the Nansen Passport, that temporary pseudo-identity offered to refugees (Hermann notes that people had said he looked like Amundsen, or maybe 'there had been some mix-up with Nansen'[38]). There can be no mistaking, however, the wasteland rootlessness that follows Hermann everywhere, into the countryside around Prague, for instance, where he meets Felix, and into his fantasies of natural renewal, roads stretching serenely into the distance with surreal Fermanns and Helixes striding down them.[39] The murder itself has an aura of ritual atonement and takes place in a sacred grove, as if to redeem the dreary hotel existence of the commercial traveller with only his mirror to contemplate — the source of Hermann's despair. And Hermann's malady is accompanied, as I have said, by profound sexual disturbance. He is not, he decides, a narcissist: he considers that Felix has helped him to cheat Nemesis by 'helping his image out of the brook'.[39] Rather he is a sort of voyeur: like Smurov he is an Eye. The condition is intimately connected with schizophrenic symptoms, as well as with the act of writing. Laing describes it well:

> A patient, for instance, who conducted his life along relatively 'normal' lines outwardly but operated this inner split, presented as his original complaint the fact that he could never have intercourse with his wife but only with his own image of her. That is, his body had physical relations with her body, but his mental self, while this was going on, could only look on at what his body was doing and/or *imagine* himself having intercourse with his wife as an object of his imagination. He gave the guilt he was subject to for doing this as his reason for seeking psychiatric advice.[40]

With this in mind, there should be no difficulty in understanding Nabokov's chilling account of Hermann's relations with his wife in Chapter Two, his contempt for her 'mediocrity' (i.e. normality), his blindness or indifference to the fact that she is sexually involved with Ardalion, his general disgust with the flesh and contemptuous treatment of her body and others' (the episode where he demands that she strip so that Ardalion may draw her focuses all these themes). As Laing says, 'the unembodied self of the schizoid individual cannot really be married to anyone'.[41]

Resurrected as Felix, Hermann hopes that he will re-integrate himself, find the ground of his being. Felix is natural man, in Hermann's fantasies of him. Naked (as he is twice), he is ambivalently a shaggy specimen of animal maleness (with notable genitals) and a corpse waiting to be dressed willy-nilly in Hermann's city clothes (thus magically effecting the transfer to Hermann of the animal happiness which he supposedly possesses). And one does not have to join the Viennese delegation[42] (Nabokov's disclaimers are anyway scarcely to be taken at face value) to note that it is Felix's stick, with his name on it, that, as Hermann deludedly supposes, gives the game away. That stick attracts attention early on: Hermann notes near the beginning of Chapter Two that his wife believed that the word 'mystic'

> was somehow dimly connected with 'mist' and 'mistake' and 'stick', but that she had not the least idea what a mystic really was.[43]

In Chapter Eight, Hermann, giving her a character-sketch of the non-existent brother who is to commit suicide, tells her he is 'a murderer and a mystic'. I have already referred to the 'chocolate' pun: a benighted passerby knocks the lampposts with his stick, and the sound is a kind of 'chock'; and Felix (Chapter Eleven) leaves in Hermann's car his stick, his 'S-T-I-C-K, gentle reader'.[44] Associated with the post which marks the place of the rendezvous (Ardalion's sacred wood), it is a queer kind of libidinous talisman engendered by Hermann's neurosis. Hermann himself is the 'murderer and mystic'; his wife's understanding of the word 'mystic' was not far off the mark, since his 'mysticism' is actually the mist of delusion and leads him into the 'mistake' of leaving the 'stick' behind. The novel is full of baroque clues of this kind (in this respect *Laughter in the Dark* resembles it) which suggest the moral pattern inevitably enacted by true art (Nabokov has no false modesty about making this claim for his work) in total disregard of the immoral pretentions of the bogus artist-hero. Hermann is set against Ardalion as Albinus is against Udo Conrad (*Laughter in the Dark*).[45] The real artist does not confuse art and neurotic fantasy but with a conjuror's ease and a serene omniscience constructs his intricate models of the truth — to the despair of his feverish untalented emulator.[46]

The confusion of neurosis with mysticism suggests Dostoyevsky; and indeed this is the most 'Dostoyevskian' of Nabokov's novels, in the sense that although the disembodied noses Hermann draws come from Gogol, and he makes interesting play with Turgenevian lyric modes, he recognizes himself that the literary persona, or 'double', he is constructing in the false novel which lies embedded and comfortably subsumed in Nabokov's true fiction, derives from Dostoyevsky, even as, with the bad faith of derogatory asides, he tries to distance himself from this persona as he has from the others.[47] Deprived of a continuous sense of self — and there are, as I have said, concrete reasons for this — and of memory (he is shut off from his past self, with which his present self is totally discontinuous), Hermann builds one of those 'portable Petersburgs'[48] beloved of emigré Russian writers. The 'superfluous man' belongs naturally (though not, of course, exclusively) to Petersburg, that artificial and premeditated city which, modelled on the great geometrical schemes of Western enlightenment, autocratically enforce a split in the Russian psyche between the medieval benightedness of the mass of the people and the modern administrative efficiency of the West. A condition akin to mass schizophrenia produced by Peter the Great's new capital — conceived symbolically as a wilful defiance of nature — is explored first by Pushkin in *The Bronze Horseman*,[49] where glowing tributes to the beauty and harmony of this lovely city — the window on western civilization — are juxtaposed with evocations of nature's vengeful wrath (Petersburg was built on marshes by slave labour, and subject to disastrous floods) and the miserable fate of the innumerable petty civil servants pressed into the service of the monstrous bureaucracy needed to run an over-centralized Empire from an inappropriate site. The centre of the Russian intelligentsia and Russian cultural life in its heyday, it was inherently unstable, and the fact that all this excellence was swept away by the upsurge of what Nabokov elsewhere calls 'Tartary' (Mother Russia), after the Revolution, left emigrés (and I am stating now an emigré view of events) nostalgic for what was, even before the event, a kind of hallucination. The hallucinatory quality of Petersburg may be felt not only in *The Bronze Horseman* but also in Gogol's short stories and even more frighteningly in Dostoyevsky's work (Bely's novel *St. Petersburg,*[50] the Russian *Ulysses,* is the modern statement of the theme from which much contemporary Russian fiction, including Nabokov's, directly derives). Hermann embraces this hallucination, with all its Dostoyevskian associations, and makes it the setting of his mad schemes.

His dependence on second-hand literature is, of course, symptomatic. Along with his superficial Marxism, it stands for an inauthenticity of being (associated with his suicidal tendencies) which is contrasted with the scrupulous individualism and originality (his life is a Bohemian cliché of drink and apparent indolence, but his art contains nothing spurious) of Ardalion. A hypertrophied language is an over-literary language, one that is fed by literature rather than by life (cf. *Lolita*). In the little town with its equestrian statue (Chapter Four) Hermann sees first the village near Astrakhan where he lived during the war, and then the portable Petersburg already mentioned (the statue is described as having a 'snake writhing under that hind hoof', but this is, as Hermann admits, a fiction derived from Falconet's statue of Peter). This at once, in turn, generates reminiscences of Turgenev and Dostoyevsky — and Nabokov, who is, of course, the 'Russian author to whom my manuscript will be forwarded when the time comes' — in itself an allusion to the literary device of the 'edited manuscript' used by Lermontov in *A Hero of Our Time,* and Turgenev in his *Diary of a Superfluous Man.*[15] As the discussion with Felix proceeds, Hermann realizes that it 'smacks of thumbscrew conversations in those stage taverns in which Dostoyevsky is at home',[52] recognizing that he is constructing a pastiche of 'our national expert in soul ague';[53] but despite the irony, and the fact that Dostoyevsky is eventually degraded to 'dusty' and 'dusky', *Crime and Punishment* becomes *Crime and Slime,* and Raskolnikov is metamorphosed into Rascalnikov, Hermann is unable to see that his own 'mysticism' is, like Dostoyevsky's, a mixture of mists and mistakes (Nabokov, while demonstrably accepting Dostoyevsky's achievement as an abnormal psychologist — in both senses — resists 'metaphysical' approaches to him). Such things, as his wife pathetically remarks, only happen in books; it is all not just mad but second-hand, stereotyped. When Hermann takes refuge in France after the murder, the style of his 'novel' changes in accordance with the development of his plot. He stimulates now a kind of serenity with the help of Turgenev, and closes his last page in Chapter Ten with a false resolution reminiscent of the evasive let-out of the end of *Fathers and Sons*, remarking as he does so:

> Do you feel the tang of this epilogue? I have concocted it according to a classic recipe. Something is told about every character in the book to wind up the tale; and in doing so, the dribble of their existence is made to remain correctly, though summarily, in keeping with what has been previously shown of their respective ways . . .[54]
>
> — before making a gesture of despairing abdication:
>
> Finis. Farewell, Turgy! Farewell, Dusty!
> Dreams, dreams . . . and rather trite ones at that. Who cares, anyway?[55]

The 'real' plot of the novel goes on, ending with Hermann now desperately trying to enter the fantasy world of the cinema (he had passed himself off to Felix as an actor) even as he says to the waiting police (winding up his aborted novel): 'Thank you. I'm coming out now'.

Hermann comes 'out' of his fantasy world to meet death: the end of his fiction is the end of his life. Humbert tells us on the last page of *Lolita* that 'neither of us (i.e. himself or Lolita) is alive when the reader opens this book'[56] — Humbert because he expects the death sentence for his murder of Quilty (the novel is cast in the form of his plea to a tribunal consisting of God and the reader) and Lolita because she existed only in the lurid light of Humbert's imagination (outside of this she is merely Dolly Schiller, a provincial housewife). Like Hermann,

Humbert takes refuge in a hypertrophied world of words; like Hermann he is alienated, literally an alien, whose famous first words reveal at once that he speaks English with a foreign accent ('Lo-lee-ta: the tip of the tongue taking a trip of three steps down the palate to tap, at three, on the teeth. Lo. Lee. Ta.'[57]). Like Hermann, he has a double: the man who is *really* guilty (or Quilty). Like Hermann, he lives a literary fabrication: it has been often observed that the novel seems to have been generated from Edgar Allan Poe's *'Annabel Lee'* and (less often noted) Belloc's *Do you remember an inn, Miranda?* But although Humbert too is a 'superfluous man', it would be wrong to press the analogy too far. Not only, as I have said, is he paroled from hell (Nabokov himself tells us) once a year[58] (this seems ungenerous given that Humbert's tragedy turns upon his exaggerated sense of sin and redemption in a morally neutral world); but what is more we cannot see past him to any 'objective' reality beyond his own consciousness. This universe of the fiction, teetering on the brink of solipsism, is, like Beckett's, both tragic and comic.

*Lolita* expands infinitely into considerations of the interaction of Europe and America (history versus geography, 'culture' versus 'community') but is at bottom a moral tale in which a fantastic pilgrim's progress (or regress) is enacted in a world in which material objects, instead of congealing into allegorical patterns as they do in Bunyan's chronicle, lie scattered like bones in a spiritual desert awaiting the life-giving word which will cloth them in imaginative flesh. Entering an alien language, Nabokov (while still profoundly concerned with cultural displacement) has drawn closer to his lost hero than he ever was to Hermann: he, too, 'has only words to play with'. This does not mean that the novel is not concerned to organize the word-games of which it is composed into moral sense. Humbert, indeed, is represented as burdened by the desire to break out of his prison-house of language (a prison strikingly represented by Gaston and his attic portraits of great cultural inverts who lean ominously down on you).[59] His cultural baggage, which he drags with him across an uncomprehending continent and back, is at one and the same time the only world in which he feels at home (domestic America being to him as grotesque as his own sick fantasies, and inevitably hostile) and the spiritual Axel's Castle which holds him in its magnetic magic. Here the erotic spell is woven which turns a hoydenish American teenager into Helen of Troy: and more, since to Faust's lust and insatiable curiosity Humbert adds love.[60] The narrative is shaped by the time of memory and desire.

This quest is evidently one which penetrates and deforms its object. But if this makes it neurotic, it is from this, too, that it derives its mythic power. D. H. Lawrence, in his *Studies in Classic American Literature*,[61] has written of Poe (whose 'Annabel Lee' with its 'kingdom by the sea' — Humbert's riviera — its knowing boy/girl love, its envious winged seraphs — gentlemen of the jury — its necrophilia and dread of death pulses through Humbert's mind) that, concerned with the disintegration processes of his own psyche, Poe is 'more a scientist than an artist'.[62] His 'ecstasy of spiritual, nervous love' divorced from a 'real central or impulsive being in himself' drove him to murderous dissection:

> What he wants to do with Ligeia is to analyse her, till he knows all her component parts, till he has got her all in his consciousness. She is some strange chemical salt which he must analyse out in the test-tubes of his brain, and then — when he's finished the analysis — *E finita la commedia!* But she won't be quite analysed out. There is something, something he can't get.[63]

And Lawrence sees that this 'mechanical consciousness' is what

> gives Poe his extraordinary facility in versification. The absence of real central or impulsive being in himself leaves him inordinately mechanically sensitive to sounds and effects, associations of sounds, associations of rhyme, for example — mechanical, facile, having no root in any passion.[64]

Behind the synthetic brilliance of Humbert's prose lies a similar dissociation as, enacting a tragic parody of the early pioneers, he rides on his enchanted hunt through the Valley of

Many-Coloured Grass (the setting of Poe's story 'Eleanora'), which Lawrence appropriately glosses as 'the valley of prismatic sensation'.[65] Poe's sensibility is that of the analytic Puritan conscience searching for an ultimate meaning in the exercise of a monstrous will, consuming itself in the face of a blank and hostile land. Humbert's experience, while containing elements of a Europe/America antithesis, is fundamentally at least as typically American as Poe's. Like Poe, he suffers from the American disease of hypertrophied consciousness; and, again like Poe, is haunted by the ghostly conflict of Good and Evil, God and the Devil battling for supremacy in his conscience. For Humbert has a conscience and he has a mind, and he is driven to madness by the mindlessness and blank functionalism he finds all about him. In the end his case is representative, which is why it seems so tragic. It refuses to be subsumed by generalizations about the materialism of the American way of life or the brilliance of Nabokov's prose style. 'Look at this tangle of thorns,' he tells us at the end of his first paragraph, and indeed it does almost look like a crown.

Humbert is haunted by images of primal rose gardens as poignant as those in 'Burnt Norton', but Nabokov, with a cultural apparatus strictly extra-territorial (his ancestral houses having all been nationalized) cannot exorcise them by referring them to a given religious and literary tradition, inexorably working back through the recreation of metaphysical concepts to the place we started from as Eliot does.[66] Humbert's mind is heterodox, his life severed at the root. The key to *his* kingdom is what he euphemistically calls (in Chapter Five, evoking his frustrated childish sexuality) the 'sceptre of his passion' With this deadly love he will unlock the gates of space and time and enter again his 'first world', where Annabel Lee, who never grows up, is playing still on her 'intangible island of entranced time'. The undertaking demands great art; but Humbert, like Hermann, feels that art is to madness close allied. The comprehension and evaluation of Humbert's sickness demands an even greater art: Nabokov's, which has assimilated Humbert's fantasies. We should not be misled by Humbert's virtuosity into equating the two, for behind the scenes Clare Quilty, the agent and former collaborator of one Vivian Dark-bloom (an androgynous anagram of V. V. Nabokov lurking in the pages of *Who's Who in the Limelight*[67]), plots the abduction of Lolita with the inside information of a demon born of Humbert's ineluctable conscience. One may easily, of course, accuse the author of complicity in the tipping of the moral balance against Humbert, but then one could bring the same accusation against Tolstoy for setting at the head of *Anna Karenina* the words 'Vengeance is mine and I will repay' and suppressing the explanatory phrase, 'saith the Lord'.[68]

Humbert ransacks his literary culture to provide examples of Great Nympholepts of History, and exhausts a world of sexual experience in his quest for the archetypal nymphet; so that when, at last, McFate (Humbert's understudy for the role of Destiny) leads him to Lolita, he welcomes his damnation as a blessed release, embracing the dolorous haze of Swinburne's Lady of Pain (Dolores),[69] and reaping the whirlwind: for she is as destructive as Carmen,[70] and her 'theme tune' a song called 'Little Carmen', to the mechanical jingle of which (modelled on Belloc's nostalgically masochistic poem about Miranda and an inn, echoed at *The Enchanted Hunters*) Humbert fantasises intercourse (technically masturbation, the only 'real' sexual act in this novel). The key which will unlock Humbert's rose-garden, releasing him from the chic suburban horrors with which Charlotte has cluttered his life and giving him back the past which Charlotte has sought to destroy, is in his pocket. The parodies of Eliot (specifically 'Ash Wednesday' and 'The Waste Land', in Chapters Five and Thirty-Five) by no means lay his ghost. In the crucial Chapter Twenty-Eight (set in *The Enchanted Hunters*, a Disneyland reconstruction of the House of Usher where Humbert's quest gets snarled up with the cheapest kind of bogus frontier mythology, while Quilty writes and waits in the wings) Humbert talks of God and the Devil, of evil and sensuality, and of himself as 'Jean-Jacques Humbert' (cf. Leopold Bloom's metamorphoses, the sad collage of his consciousness strung on a thread of basic decency). He tells us of his innocence (and his guilt) and above all of his naïvety and sorrow, and all the while he holds the key to 'the hermetic vision which I had locked in':[71] a drugged nymphet. If we think of the last section of 'The Waste Land' (*What the thunder said* . . . and a thunderstorm is gathering around the inn) we discover the germ of this episode, and perhaps the main theme of the novel:

> I have heard the key
> Turn in the door once and turn once only
> We think of the key, each in his prison
> Thinking of the key, each confirms a prison
> Only at nightfall, aethereal rumours
> Revive for a moment a broken Coriolanus.[72]

Humbert is the broken Coriolanus, the shattered hero, both shattered *and* a hero, whose key, whose phallus (its tag he calls a 'dangler'), is to serve to release him from the prison of his loneliness and frustration — a release accompanied by a rush of water (the thunderstorm echoes that of Eliot's poem, and the motif is taken up parodistically in the noise of waterfalls — lavatories flushing recall the waterfall of Belloc's poem, and the sound of the sea in Poe's, and the play on 'Poe' is too childishly obvious to mention). There can be no such release; Humbert's seduction by Lolita, for whom sex is a summer camp game, forbidden by dull adults (but otherwise quite devoid of the associations of sin and guilt which make it meaningful for puritanical, cultured Humbert), opens the door not to freedom but to the padded cell of gloomy lust in which the enchanted hunter becomes a hunted enchanter, a mad artist-magician trapped for ever in the web spun from his entrails. As Smurov turned himself into a literary stereotype and Hermann became a character in his own novel, so Humbert lives now in the fictional microcosm of his car, perpetual timeless motion passing through a hallucinatory Valley of Many-Coloured Grass. And even in this hermetic tomb the eye of God sees the future Cain, killer of brother Quilty: the key becomes a gun in Humbert's last desperate bid for freedom.[73] His trek across a chromium desert (with cokes, chewing-gum, and ice-creams falling from heaven like plastic manna) takes place under the all-seeing eye of a strange dehumanized conscience which conceals itself in word-games. Another great American novel comes to mind (one to which *Lolita* is evidently indebted): Fitzgerald's *The Great Gatsby*:

> But above the grey land and the spasms of bleak dust which drift endlessly over it, you perceive, after a moment, the eyes of Doctor T. J. Eckleburg. The eyes of Doctor T. J. Eckleburg are blue and gigantic — their retinas are one yard high. They look out of no face, but, instead, from a pair of enormous yellow spectacles which pass over a non-existent nose. Evidently some wild wag of an oculist set them there to fatten his practice in the borough of Queens, and then sank down himself into eternal blindness, or forgot them and moved away. But his eyes, dimmed a little by many paintless days, under sun and rain, brood on over the solemn dumping ground.[74]

But if for Fitzgerald the dead god is totemic, for Humbert (as for Poe) he is cabbalistic, a secret lurking wisdom. Humbert speaks at one point of 'the revenge that the Gods of Semantics take against tight-zippered Philistines',[75] but Quilty embodies the revenge that the Gods of Hermeneutics take against those who only have words to play with (cf. *Pale Fire*). Crossing what he calls the 'crazy quilt' of America (Book Two, Chapter One) towards Beardsley (how much old European corruption lurks in these innocent American names), through 'scenic drives' parodying Dante's divine landscape, and piled with the debris of European culture, slotting in here and there a 'quick connection' with Lolita (the terse vulgarity underlines Humbert's lack of all other 'connections'), he becomes the 'hunted enchanter', the Poe-figure (Poe the Poet), dissecting living tissue in a necrophiliac search for the quick of life.

> My only grudge against nature was that I could not turn my Lolita inside out and apply voracious lips to her young matrix, her unknown heart, her nacreous liver, the sea-grapes of her lungs, her comely twin kidneys.[76]

After his abduction of Lolita, Quilty scatters the trail with clues (false names and addresses left by him and Lolita to preserve their incognito), as sure of hitting their mark — Humbert's superstitious fascination with language — as Weber's magic bullets.[77]

Humbert can only enter Beardsley society by a schizophrenic splitting: 'I used to review the concluded day by checking my own image as it prowled rather than passed before the mind's red eye'.[78] He obscurely recognizes that (quite apart from the 'Annabel Lee' jingle) he is acting out Poe's neurosis (in Chapter Sixteen he remarks that he felt instinctively that 'toilets — as also telephones — happened to be for reasons unfathomable, the points where [his] destiny was liable to catch' — the po and the P.O.); but if I have chosen not to refer to Laing's book in dealing with *Lolita* it is because art and neurosis are related in this novel differently from the way they are related in *Despair*. If Humbert's penchant for metaphor is seen as a noose into which he runs, there is at the same time a feeling (both comic and tragic) that he could not have acted otherwise, and that (in however dim and muddled a fashion) his possession of a mind and an (albeit deadly) capacity for love stands as a small guttering candle amid the neon and car headlights: a poor thing but his own. His self, like Hermann's, is divided (and the gentlemen of the jury, the envious angels, will not be); but his overburdened conscience, laid bare in the poem he presents to Quilty before he shoots him[79] (not for nothing a pastiche of 'Ash Wednesday'), prompts the novel itself, an extraordinary act of truth-telling. *Lolita* passes in recapitulation through madness and death and emerges with an uncanny visionary clarity. Nabokov's art would never again be so perfectly integrated.

# Notes to Chapter 5

1. This is a broad generalization, but so is the term itself. Pechorin (*A Hero of Our Time*) is a disgruntled officer with more intelligence than is good for him: he might have taken part in the unsuccessful Decembrist uprising of 1825. Oblomov is a landowner whose past and present dissolve together in a haze of sloth. Gogol's and Dostoyevsky's superfluous men are victims of the Petersburg malaise, cogwheels spinning in a geometric void.
2. Cf. Geoffrey Clive, *The Broken Icon: Intuitive Existentialism in Classical Russian Fiction* (London: Collier-Macmillan, 1972).
3. Evidently, this will not do: but the radical-reforming tradition in Russian criticism simplifies in this sort of way. See Matlaw, *Belinsky, Chernyshevsky and Dobrolyubov.*
4. The excellent translation Nabokov and his son made of this novel (Doubleday, 1958) seems little read. This is all the more unfortunate in that Nabokov's preface to it is a model of criticism.
5. Vladimir Nabokov, *Lolita* (London: Weidenfeld and Nicolson, 1959) p. 33.
6. Abram Tertz (Sinyavsky) interestingly contends that Socialist Realism should be called Socialist Classicism.
7. Cf. my study of *The Gift*.
8. The startling pronouncements come, of course, from a lifetime of study: and even where academic scholarship prevails, as in the Pushkin commentary, lively insights stud the footnotes. On the other hand, Nabokov has covered his tracks so carefully that the casual reader is led into the erroneous belief that his confident 'placings' are more original than is in fact the case.
9. Cf. the handling of Cambridge in the novels and *Speak, Memory*.
10. Nabokov is unedifying on Germany as only a Russian knows how to be; there seems to be no aspect of German life or culture that does not fill him with contempt. The pages on German *poshlust* (affected vulgarity) in the Gogol study (Vladimir Nabokov, *Gogol*, New Directions 1961, pp. 65-6) are splendid: he does not, of course, suggest that Germany has a monopoly of the vice. In *Speak, Memory* (London: Weidenfeld and Nicolson, 1967, p. 305) he refers to a bed of pansies in a German park, 'each of their upturned faces show-

ing a dark, moustache-like smudge' like 'a crowd of bobbing little Hitlers'. This image alone does all that is necessary.

11. In Paris (on the same page of *Speak, Memory*) he sees a shabby little girl, apparently from an orphanage, 'who had deftly tied a live butterfly to a thread and was promenading the pretty, weakly fluttering, slightly crippled insect on that elfish leash (the by-product, perhaps, of a good deal of work in that orphanage)'. He tries to divert his son's eyes.
12. In the essay entitled 'On a Book Entitled *Lolita*' he warmly dissociates himself from anti-Americanism, adding (somewhat misleadingly) that he is 'trying to be an American writer'. (*Lolita*, p. 305).
13. Nabokov's father was killed by one such, in Berlin.
14. I say 'at least', because this evidently could be said of *Pale Fire*, too. But in that novel the perspective is somewhat different.
15. Vladimir Nabokov, *The Eye* (London: Panther Books, 1968) p. 9.
16. In the foreword to *Despair* (London: Panther Books, 1969) Nabokov wonders whether anyone will call Hermann 'the father of existentialism'. Sartre's *L'être et le néant* is evidently apposite, even though he is taken to task in this same preface for his 'remarkably silly' review of *Despair*.
17. R. D. Laing, *The Divided Self* (Harmondsworth: Penguin Books, 1965) p. 36.
18. *The Eye*, p. 15. The umbrella and the moleskin coat are Freudianisms as gross as Smurov's appropriations of literary stereotypes.
19. *Ibid.*, p. 17. 'The summit of love-making was for me but a bleak knoll with a relentless view.'
20. *The Divided Self*, p. 39.
21. *Ibid.*, p. 51.
22. *The Eye*, p. 17.
23. Cf. Racine, *Phèdre*, Act Four, Scene Six: Phèdre imagines the innocent revels of Hippolyte and Aricie, who actually have their own problems:

    Helas! ils se voyoient avec pleine licence;
    Le ciel de leurs soupirs approuvoit l'innocence;
    Ils suivoient sans remords leur penchant amoureux;
    Tous les jours se levoient clairs et sereins pour eux!

    In *Bend Sinister* Nabokov is specially contemptuous of pseudo-democratic efforts to determine what 'everyman' is and wants, as if anyone were 'ordinary'.

24. *The Eye*, p. 24. The 'pupils' here are tutees not eyeballs.
25. *The Divided Self*, p. 37.
26. *Ibid.*, p. 141. The play on 'omnipotence' and 'impotence' is worthy of Nabokov himself.
27. *The Eye*, p. 44. Cf. also p. 41. The ambivalence of the narrative point-of-view is very piquant, and extraordinarily like that of Turgenev's *Rudin*, where there is a comparable merging of subject and object.
28. Ivan Turgenev, tr. Constance Garnett, *Rudin* (London: Heinemann, 1911) p. 63.
29. *The Eye*, p. 53. One might as well say it is a reference to *A Hero of Our Time*, of course: though it may have been Byron who instituted this interestingly ambiguous relationship between flagging males and pert teenage girls.
30. The last page of this work, ostensibly found after the diarist's death (chance is a major factor in the superfluous tradition), peters out in idiotic scribblings. Cf. the fragmentary pages that open Sartre's *La Nausée*.
31. *The Divided Self*, p. 38.
32. *Despair*, p. 9.
33. The device recalls Fyodor's encapsulation of biography within a sonnet in *The Gift*. But Hermann is despairingly trying to write his own life story. In this he resembles not Fyodor but Kinbote in *Pale Fire*.
34. *Despair*, p. 15.
35. *Despair*, p. 58. I make this sound very clumsy: but of course it is a public utterance of a private derangement, so naturally gauche.
36. *Despair*, p. 14. The 'social' theme is not important, of course.
37. *Ibid.*
38. There are a number of references in Nabokov's work to the Nansen passport (wryly referred to sometimes as the 'nonsense' passport). This temporary document issued to stateless persons seems to have made them automatically second class citizens wherever they were.
39. *Despair*, p. 23.
40. *The Divided Self*, p. 86.
41. *Ibid.*, p. 87.
42. One of Nabokov's favourite denigratory phrases to describe Freudian therapists. His dislike of them, based on a hostility to Freudian determinism as well as a suspicion of 'progres-

sivism' generally, is also, of course, a dislike of rivals. Nabokov surely believes that art — especially his own — contains and transcends neurosis and is itself therapeutic. This belief has been fairly widespread among artists. In the preface to *The Eye* (p. 9) Nabokov distinguishes between Freudians and 'serious psychologists' — i.e. those of whom he approves, presumably.

43. *Despair*, p. 32.
44. *Ibid.*, p. 196.
45. There is a touch of Axel Rex about Hermann, too. The Kierkegaardian distinction between the aesthetic, ethical, and religious visions of life seems applicable to Nabokov's work. Art, for him, must achieve an intensity of vision which seems scarcely secular and which outstrips moral categories; but he comes down heavily against 'aesthetic' tampering with life's delicate natural pattern.
46. This is why I think some criticism of Nabokov has been wide of the mark in over-elucidating his work. Modernism (and of course he is a modernist, despite all the diatribes against abstract art etc.) soon left behind the jejune aestheticism of its origins.
47. This does not simply derive from Dostoyevsky: it is also what Dostoyevsky does himself. But he is more conscious of this than Nabokov ever admits, and this is what makes him great — not a minor Gothic novelist, as Nabokov tries to tell us.
48. See Chapter 1. The finest portable Petersburg (after Bely's) in Russian literature may be that of Mandelshtam ('V Peterburge my soidyomsya snova'). He was not an emigré. The first two lines of his poem serve as epigraph to a poem by the emigré Georgy Ivanov, beginning 'A quarter of a century has passed abroad', one of the best-loved 'portable Petersburgs' of the emigration. Both poems are in the Penguin Book of Russian Verse, ed. Obolensky (Harmondsworth: Penguin Books, 1962).
49. This great poem may be stalked but not bagged in Edmund Wilson's prose translation (*The Triple Thinkers*, Penguin Books, 1962, pp. 57-71).
50. The last prose statement of the Petersburg malaise (1913) this is at the same time a modernist classic, comparable to (though not as fine as) Joyce's *Ulysses*.
51. See note 30, above.
52. *Despair*, p 92.

53. *Ibid.*
54. This is not just a clever pastiche, as I hope I have shown. The point is that Turgenev shamelessly switches to the timeless-idyllic mode in order to diminish the impression left by his 'superfluous' nihilist hero Bazarov, who apparently died of typhus but *in fact* was murdered by Turgenev because his gross and ungainly person had become a shade too persuasive: either he or Turgenev had to go. This vexed relationship between author and fiction is very typical of the 'tradition' I have been sketching here.
55. *Despair*, p. 175.
56. *Lolita*, p. 300.
57. *Lolita*, p. 11. The point is that the English 't' is not dental but alveolar: moreover there is a suspicion of a Russian palatalized 'l' in the second syllable. Those who have heard Nabokov reading on record (Spoken Arts 902) will recognize the accent.
58. Preface to *Despair*, p. 9.
59. *Lolita*, p. 178. Nijinsky was not an invert, but the creature of one (Diaghilev).
60. Lionel Trilling perhaps put this too emphatically, but he was essentially right.
61. D. H. Lawrence, *Studies in Classic American Literature* (New York: Doubleday Anchor 1955). If Nabokov is an American novelist, he is one in the sense in which Poe was an American poet: both invented new terrains and peopled them with old monsters.
62. *Ibid.*, p. 74. Nabokov is himself a scientist in something like this sense, though not, like Poe and Humbert, a vivisectionist.
63. *Ibid.*, p. 78.
64. *Ibid.*, p. 87.
65. *Ibid.*, p. 85.
66. The allusion is to T. S. Eliot, *Little Gidding*.
67. *Lolita*, pp. 32-3.
68. Cf. Chapter 3 above.
69. One of many allusions to the literature of the decadence, which knew Poe not only by direct acquaintance but also transmitted via Baudelaire and Mallarmé.
70. Bizet's opera, with its *femme fatale* heroine and yearning for an ultimate love (which is death, merging, loss of self) is an evident motif in *Lolita*. A rare musical allusion: Nabokov does not care for music.
71. *Lolita*, p. 122.

72. T. S. Eliot, *The Waste Land,* lines 411-416. It is odd how often Eliot crops up in Nabokov's work: he is wantonly disparaging about him, but in this novel — despite the facile parody of Eliot attributed to Humbert on p. 18 — seems closer than usual to Eliot's pessimism.
73. Here, too, it is a phallus, 'aching to be discharged' (p. 284).
74. Scott Fitzgerald, *The Great Gatsby* (Harmondsworth: Penguin Books, 1971, p. 29).
75. *Lolita,* p. 148.
76. *Ibid.*, pp. 161-2.
77. Humbert's pills are magic bullets, but also nothing more than a mild sedative. The facts constantly fall short of Humbert's fantasies.
78. On p. 192 he sees himself as 'a shabby emigré'.
79. *Lolita,* p. 292.

# VI

## History as Nightmare: **Invitation to a Beheading** (1935, 1960) and **Bend Sinister** (1947)

*Invitation to a Beheading* and *Bend Sinister*, while perhaps not remarkably alike in method — the earlier novel is one of Nabokov's most 'mannerist' and ornamental, while the later organizes its chilling theatrical effects by flatly juxtaposing the real and the surreal — are nevertheless comparable in theme. *Invitation to a Beheading* has often been compared to Kafka in its combination of political and metaphysical allegory. It takes for its hero a man imprisoned by some weird political tyranny for the obscurest of crimes: he is guilty of being opaque in a world which demands glassy translucency. His prison cell (which is archetypal: it even has a spider which the warder scrupulously looks after) allows him the merest glimpse of sky, plus an inscription in the stone: 'You cannot see anything. I tried it too.'[1] Born anonymous and unwanted, the consequence of a chance coupling in the park, he doesn't doubt (any more than Joseph K. does) his 'basic illegality': his crime is known as 'gnostical turpitude', which means more or less that, like Joseph K., he is 'accused of guilt'. Far from maintaining his innocence, Cincinnatus C. devotes his time in prison to trying to find out when his execution is to be and to contemplating the visionary world he builds in his imagination to supplant the real world to which he is denied access by his imprisonment (but which he sometimes catches radiant glimpses of). The journal he keeps is murkily metaphoric in its quest for the elusive truth which he feels is hidden at the heart of his experience; waking life, he says, is semi-sleep, and from this waking sleep one will eventually awake — 'but how I fear awakening'![2] Giving expression to the reality he intuits behind the forms of the 'real' world subjects language to impossible stresses: as for the Symbolists — Mallarmé, for example — so for Cincinnatus too the articulation of reality demands the deformation, even the destruction, of language:

> Brought up into the air, the word bursts, as burst those spherical fishes that breathe and blaze only in the compressed murk of the depths when brought up in the net.[3]

A recurrent motif in the novel is the absurdity of literary realism, which merely duplicates the shadows on the cave wall.

The political theme of *Bend Sinister* is given much more circumstantial documentation: the novel is pretty clearly, on one reading, a bitter response to Stalinism (though it is also, characteristically, a satire on political satires). Krug, the philosopher hero, is subjected to very literal harassment and shut away in a very material prison for a crime much less rarified than Cincinnatus's — non-cooperation with a boring and brutal dictatorship. Insidious ideological pressure turns into sheer terrorism, and denouncers and sycophantic *apparatchiki* are themselves denounced and liquidated at an accelerating nightmarish tempo which is hardly more grotesque (or more theatrical) than the historical facts of Stalin's purges and 'show' trials;[4] so that whereas in *Invitation* the political theme, as in Kafka, is part of a larger metaphor, and Cincinnatus's drama is metaphysical, in *Bend Sinister* history is the literal nightmare from which Krug, like Joyce's Stephen Dedalus in *Ulysses*,[5] longs to awaken (the fact that he can do so only by going mad is an index of the book's pessimism). Yet the coruscating black humour of the political satire does not obscure a deeper theme analogous to that of the earlier novel. Krug's crime is in essence, like Cincinnatus's, a kind of 'opacity' or 'gnostical turpitude', a complexity of consciousness and an extreme self-awareness (or consciousness of his own identity) which he stubbornly asserts against the historical process.[6] Whereas in the optimistic *Invitation* Cincinnatus painfully wins through to selfhood, in the bitter *Bend Sinister*, Krug, a philosopher, attributing from the very beginning the highest value to mind, is destroyed mentally. His equivalent of opacity is circularity; in Russian, the word *krug* means 'circle', and the novel sets his circularity against historical linearity in many ways: [7] his stoop is often noted (in combination with his slow and awkward gait) in preparation for the transformation of it in Chapter Seventeen to an apocalyptic gesture;[8] as he is thrust into the government car (history, in the shape of Ekwilist party, travels habitually by fast black cars modelled on the Soviet *Zis*). When the murder of his son has liberated him from this world by destroying his last reason for living, he is 'torpid recurved Krug (still in the larval stage)', and in the 'perfectly round' waiting room, a miniature world in which he notes 'four doors at the cardinal points', where he hopes to find David, his pupation is prepared. He makes his last appearance as the moth that strikes against the author's window as he writes, set free just as he is gunned down by Paduk's soldiers;[9] then off into the night of death:

> I had just time to make out its streamlined brownish-pink body and a twinned spot of colour; and then it let go and swung back into the warm damp darkness.[10]

A moth frightens Rodion, Cincinnatus's jailor, at the end of *Invitation*, and it serves as a symbol of escape: it 'disappeared as if the very air had swallowed it'.[11] Nabokov's butterflies and moths commonly enact the mysterious metamorphosis of which human beings too, if they are very lucky, are capable. *Bend Sinister* ends with the author glimpsing the puddle Krug had noted at the beginning of the novel, a 'nether sky', a 'sample of the brightness beyond'. So Krug comes full circle. There was indeed a 'handle' to the apparently flawless sphere of his mind — David — but Paduk's thugs, devoid of family feeling, discovered this too late and then bungled the affair. So Krug enters the perfect sphere of death unencumbered, helped on by his compassionate creator (Nabokov). A passage in Chapter Fourteen, approaching the theme of death through Krug's philosophizing (Nabokov is clever enough to remark that Krug feels his intellectual powers have declined, thus evading an obvious problem), tells us, through metaphors clearly evoking *Invitation*, that

> Death is either the instantaneous gaining of perfect knowledge (similar say to the instantaneous disintegration of stone and ivy composing the circular dungeon where formerly the prisoner had to content himself with only two apertures optically fusing into one; whilst now, with the disappearance of all walls, he can survey the entire circular landscape), or absolute nothingness, *nichto*.[12]

So *Bend Sinister* too, for all the effectiveness of its satire of totalitarian politics and the laconic brilliance with which it encapsulates the human issues at stake in the grotesque farce of Stalin's show trials,[13] is finally metaphysical in its concerns, as *Invitation* more evidently is.[14] Krug delays too long before arranging to escape (his 'circularity' is in many ways a disability[15]) and in Chapter Fifteen we find him trying to leave the country with the help of a man who is really Paduk's agent. As he finds the meeting-place on the map, he thinks of his dead wife Olga, and her way of 'lifting her left eyebrow when she looked at herself in the mirror', and asks himself.

> Do all people have that? A face, a phrase, a landscape, an air bubble from the past suddenly floating up as if released by the head warden's child from a cell in the brain while the mind is at work on some totally different matter?[16]

Krug's quest is in essence a Proustian search for lost time, like Cincinnatus's. Material reality thereafter intrudes forcibly upon consciousness. For Cincinnatus the terms are reversed: there is a *real* jailor's daughter (at least, if the prison is real, so is little Emmie) who may help him to escape; the two apertures through which he views the world are (he is sure) in the wall of his cell, not in his skull; yet consciousness may dispose of material reality, transcending it by a kind of metaphysical leap. *Invitation* belongs as unmistakably to the period of formalistic modernism as *Bend Sinister* does to the politically pessimistic forties (it is pretty well contemporary with Orwell's *1984*).

The epigraph to *Invitation* provides the essential clue to the understanding of the book, though it is very characteristic of Nabokov to give expression to such an unequivocally Platonic ontology in the disguise of an imaginary philosopher and in French.[17] The novel itself has no such aphoristic certainty and is bound by the Wittgensteinian counsel that one had best be silent about things of which one cannot speak. Nevertheless it too is a *Discours sur les ombres*.[18] Cincinnatus is under sentence of death (like the rest of us, he 'believes himself mortal', having little apparent evidence for any other belief). He accepts the role of condemned man and the conventional phrases and appurtenances appropriate thereto (the pencil and paper to write his memoirs, 'In spite of everything I am comparatively', the spider, 'official friend of the jailed') as well as certain curiosities which he doesn't question (the jailer invites him to dance a waltz[19]). Above all he accepts time, being especially concerned about the future, in the shape of the precise time of his impending execution, which no one has told him. By means of the crude spacial analogues which we use to describe our experience of time he conceives himself as a kind of point along a graph, acknowledging the time which Eliot describes in *Four Quartets* as 'moving in appetency on metalled ways'. He hears a clock striking nearby —

> A clock struck — four or five times — with the vibrations and re-vibrations, and reverberations proper to a prison.[20]

— clock time being prison time. Another symbol of the prison-house of linearity is, cleverly, the novel itself: 'The right-hand, still untasted part of the novel . . . had suddenly, for no reason at all, become quite meagre.'[21] It is evident that Cincinnatus's liberation cannot take the linear and material form in which he conceives it: it can only be a liberation from time into what

Bergson called 'durée' and Nabokov himself elsewhere talks of as 'spacetime' (in order to emphasize its characteristic relativity). Art is the most important instrument of liberation, since its symbolic structure and metaphoric texture obliges language to abandon that one-dimensional linearity with which everyday discourse has endowed it (giving language itself, in the process, the power to shut us into its conventional prison[22]). Moreover, the novel embodies a special conception of time different from the time measured for practical purposes by the clock. The most evident difference is the primacy of subjective time in art. But in addition, and with great complexity, the counterpointing of themes developing at different tempi, the larger musical structure of recapitulation and development, the discrepancies between reading time and narrative time, all such devices (to state them here in no more detail) enable the novel to penetrate 'durée' or space-time, which is intrinsically more 'real' than the impoverished fiction proposed to us by clocks and watches.[23] And (as Nabokov's term implies) the penetration of real time implies the penetration of real (inner) space, spatiality of the world which we habitually accept as real (and which is our prison) being as dully conventional as its temporality.

The conventionality of Cincinnatus's prison has already been alluded to. It is foregrounded by Nabokov as a motif to which he wishes to call special attention. All the characters are actors, and they play their part in a shabby theatrical set — though Cincinnatus does not realize this. The prison director appears looking like a cross between a ringmaster and a banker, and

> His face, selected without love, with its thick sallow cheeks and somewhat obsolete system of wrinkles,[24]

is evidently taken without much discrimination from the properties cupboard. He, like the other prison officials, specializes in a kind of uplifting rhetoric ('Prisoner, in this solemn hour, when all eyes are upon thee . . .') which is as vulgar in its way as his stubbing out his cigarette in the sauce in Cincinnatus's plate. The vulgarity is general throughout this prison 'society', and the censored newspapers (entitled *Good Morning Folks* and *Voice of the Public*) suggest that the same combination of vulgarity and music-hall jocosity governs the world 'outside' (whatever that may be). It is a world of what in Russian is called *poshlost* (or *poshlust*, Nabokov transcribes it both ways), a quite special kind of vulgarity beautifully characterized by Nabokov in his book on Gogol.[25] M. Pierre, the headsman who pretends to be a fellow prisoner, is a masterpiece of vulgarity, with his flabby hands and family snapshots, his conjuring tricks and his funny stories. He is the *fokusnik*, the mountebank or false artist who appears elsewhere in Nabokov's novels,[26] who rhapsodizes with a sickly blend of sentiment and pornography on the delights of love and of Nature, and whose *chef d'oeuvre* is the so-called 'photohoroscope' he makes of Emmie's life:

> Extensively retouched snapshots of Emmie's present face were supplemented by shots of other people — for the sake of costume, furniture and surroundings — so as to create the entire decor and stage properties of her future life . . . By means of retouching and other photographic tricks, what appeared to be progressive changes in Emmie's face had been achieved . . . but one had only to look closer and it became repulsively obvious how trite was this parody of the work of time.[27]

In fact the theatrical manipulations of his 'art' form the quintessential expression of the prisonhouse of space and time in which Cincinnatus is trapped.

Everything conspires to reduce Cincinnatus to the 'opacity' of his isolated self: his attempts to escape or to make contact with other people are endlessly frustrated, and the positive value of this process is not seen until the last pages of the novel. He looks forward to a meeting with his wife, Marthe; the meeting is deferred over and over again, and when, in Chapter Nine, she comes, she is accompanied by her whole monstrously vulgar family, before whom Cincinnatus is made to feel obscurely guilty, and who import their whole everyday world of inertly naturalistic objects (like the props of some human interest drama) into his cell (their furniture includes 'a mirrored wardrobe, bringing with it its own private reflection'[28]). When she appears again she reproaches him for involving her in so much unpleasantness, and manages to be unfaithful to him with his jailor in the middle of their conversation (her infidelities haunt Cincinnatus's memories and imaginings). Rodion, the jailer, is a parody of the devoted serf of Tolstoy's 'The Death of Ivan Ilych'.[29] Emmie, the director's daughter, seems to hold out some promise, but it may be that Cincinnatus misinterprets this. He associates her with the possibility of escape: she is a child, and it is often said that Cincinnatus is child-like, and at the beginning of Chapter Four, in an episode terminated by 'the merciless bong of the clock', he puts to her his burning question:

> 'Emmie . . . I implore you — and I shall not desist — tell me, when shall I die?'

as if she knew the answer. He attaches importance to her drawings in the catalogue of the prison library, which seem to represent a fleeing prisoner being led by a little girl. It may be that his escape can be effected by means of a return to childish innocence (and as he takes his bath he sees his body as the body of a child, with its 'meek', 'dear', 'innocent' toenails which gaze at him with 'childlike' attention as he sits on his 'cot' — the prison bed — whereupon Emmie's little red and blue ball rolls into his cell and out again). But although the discovery of childhood is a major factor in the liberation into 'spacetime' which Cincinnatus eventually experiences, this is not to be achieved by simple regression. Emmie cannot take Cincinnatus very far, as the crucial encounter with her makes clear. In Chapter Six, Cincinnatus had seen Emmie framed in the semblance of a window — representing the Tamara Gardens, object of his dreams and fantasies — and had asked her

> 'Won't you please take me out there?' — both of them were peering into the artificial remoteness beyond the glass.[30]

The approach of Rodion makes it clear that Cincinnatus, who

thought he was far from his cell, had been walking in a circle: he comes from the 'wrong' direction, like 'a reflection in a mirror', and the association of motifs makes of Emmie only a very tenuously hopeful figure. By Chapter Fourteen, when she has become rather disagreeably intimate with Cincinnatus, we find her declaring her willingness to help (though again the context makes it ambivalent):

> 'Tomorrow I'll die?' asked Cincinnatus.
> 'No, I'll rescue you,' Emmie said pensively (she was seated astride him).[31]

And then, finding himself outside of the prison by some curious quirk of the bogus 'escape' tunnel organized by M'sieur Pierre, he also finds Emmie, apparently ready to act out the drama depicted in those childish drawings of hers Cincinnatus had found on the library catalogue. Instead, she leads him into the director's apartment by the back way, and into one of those ghastly domestic gatherings which exemplify what is called in Russian *byt*, the time-bound world of vulgar materialism, the routine and the commonplace succession of meaningless trivia which was Dostoyevsky's way of defining hell and which even the dynamism of Mayakovsky's Futurism was (as he confessed before shooting himself) unable to transcend.[32] *Byt* is an obsessive theme of Russian fiction, and in Nabokov's novels is often associated with what he calls the 'stale Russianisms' of the Emigration:

> The hanging kerosene lamp, whose light did not reach the back of the dining-room (where only the gleam of a pendulum flashed as it hacked off the solid seconds), flooded the cosily spread table with a familiar light, which graded into the chinking sounds of the tea ritual.[33]

Oblomovka is one element in the structure of Cincinnatus's prison.

Cincinnatus's release can come only with a recognition that opacity, the 'crime' for which he has suffered so much, turning 'this way and that, trying to catch the rays, trying with desperate haste to stand in such a way as to seem translucent', is not only no crime but in fact the artist's response to the human condition.[34] As he recognizes this, the materials of his prison themselves become transparent, even the fleshy M'sieur Pierre: 'Through the headsman's still swinging hips the railing showed.'[35] The theatrical set which he has called 'reality' dissolves into its constituent 'chips of painted wood, bits of gilded plaster'; but this is the culmination of a long process by which Cincinnatus learns how to give substance to the inner reality which he describes in Chapter Eight, the *durée* which time and matter obscure.[36] This involves in part a repossession of the wonder of childhood and the interrelatedness of what he is now and what he was then (if it is impossible to divide past from present, the future becomes more than ever an empty hypothesis). The Tamara Gardens, which he entered in Chapter One only to find himself walking back into his cell, must be seen to be not a mocking mirage of freedom[37] but a substantive reality of memory and imagination, along with the hills in the distance 'hazy from the ecstasy of their remoteness' — it is useless getting on a table to try to glimpse the 'real' gardens through the window, since these *are* the real gardens. The childhood images evoked by Emmie help Cincinnatus to repossess the world of memory: in this sense she sets him free, but in no other. And there is *one* other person who helps him, even though she too is part of the whole huge theatrical deception of 'reality', as he knows. This is his mother, who, though very unprepossessing and in any case almost a stranger to Cincinnatus, is the midwife/muse who helps Cincinnatus give birth to the artifice of reality, even though he endlessly calls her bluff:

> 'You're still only a parody,' murmured Cincinnatus.
> She smiled interrogatively.
> 'Just like this spider, just like those bars, just like the striking of that clock,' murmured Cincinnatus.[38]

It is an important episode in the process of Cincinnatus's evolution towards freedom, and this scepticism about the 'reality' of the prison is accompanied by his mother's little anti-realist parable which takes its place as the clinching formulation in the novel's discussion of the nature of fiction.

This is the tale of the *nonnons*, which Cincinnatus's mother recalls from her childhood (they therefore belong among those remembered motifs of which reality is composed[39]). They were popular, she says, not only among children, but among adults too. *Nonnons* were 'absolutely absurd objects, shapeless, mottled, pockmarked, knobby things, like some kinds of fossils' which were held up to a distorting mirror by which 'everything was restored, everything was fine,'

> and the shapeless speckledness became in the mirror a wonderful, sensible image; flowers, a ship, a person, a landscape.[40]

The parable is a complex one, though its essential meaning is clear. The classic theory of mimesis claims that art is a mirror held up to nature, and the novel has been described as a mirror in the roadway (by Stendhal, among others, a writer whom Nabokov dislikes). If this theory is true in any sense at all, it is true only in the terms of this parable: art is a distorting mirror held up to distorted reality; warped by the conventions inherent in our perception of it, it must be deformed into truth in a crooked mirror. This is evidently a variant of Nabokov's through-the-looking-glass theory of art, commented on elsewhere.[41] It implies a high degree of formal self-consciousness in fiction, but not necessarily abstraction;[42] in fact it often comes close to lending itself to social and political satire, as indeed it had done in the work of Jonathan Swift. This childhood memory of the muse/mother/midwife (the creator, not the imitator) strikes a spark which 'proclaimed such a tumult of truth that Cincinnatus's soul could not help leaping for joy'. He does not know why; in fact it is because the novel in which he is the protagonist is the perfect *nonnon* mirror, the tricks and distortions of which produce (to the initiated eye, as Nabokov himself admits) a perfect pattern of sense, won from the distorted forms presented by the 'real' world.

The *nonnon* parable complements Cincinnatus's own reflections on realism. Among the books in the prison library (the librarian being a sympathetic but ineffectual guardian of a sort of reality — more real, at least, than anything else in the prison) is a famous new novel called *Quercus*, 3,000 pages long.[43] Its protagonist is an oak which lives about 600 years, and

> . . . employing the gradual development of the tree . . . the author unfolded all the historic events — or shadows of events — of which the oak could have been a witness . . . It seemed as though the author were sitting with his camera somewhere among the topmost branches of the *Quercus*, spying out and catching his prey.

This is the monstrous apotheosis of Zola's 'roman experimental', the novel which assembles its material and studies it with the disinterestedness of the scientist, adhering to a constant viewpoint and observing strict laws of mechanical causality. Such novels, for all their comprehensiveness and their sternly positivistic attitude to the facts actually do no more than perpetuate the illusion that the material world has an autonomous existence distinct from the sentient centres experiencing it. In other words such fiction is conventional to the point of mendacity, like Cincinnatus's prison, and in the end its lovingly observed spiders turn out to be made of rubber.[44]

*Bend Sinister* contains a discussion of literary realism not unlike those in *Invitation*, though it is (of necessity, in this more political novel) more completely integrated into the text. Paduk's father (printer of the works of 'cranks and frustrated politicians') has invented a kind of typewriter called a 'padograph', a device which could be built to imitate the handwriting of its owner more or less accurately. It was a device, of course, with an 'inane undertow of clumsy forgery', but

> the thing caught the fancy of the honest consumer: devices which in some new way imitate nature are attractive to simple minds . . . Philosophically the padograph subsisted as an Ekwilist symbol, as a proof of the fact that a mechanical device can reproduce personality, and that Quality is the mere distributional aspect of Quantity.[45]

Grotesquely, one of the perks of declaring loyalty to the Ekwilist régime, as Paduk tells Krug, will be 'a motorcar, a bicycle, and a padograph'. This machine for the large-scale-imitation of nature is a fitting symbol of the new order, which Nabokov economically characterizes by means of samples of its prose (such as the preposterous circulars received by Krug in Chapter Thirteen and the documents he refuses to sign, or the cartoon strip of the doings of Mr. and Mrs. Etormon ('Everyman') who are adopted as mascots by Paduk and the Ekwilist party). There are numerous samples of the literary modes of the Ekwilist party (including the poem composed by the assassin Emrald[46] in honour of Skotoma, senile and unwitting instigator of Ekwilism), all of which bear a marked resemblance to actual documents of Nazism and Stalinism; and the debilitating effect of political jargon and rhetoric is nowhere more clear than in the sad efforts of the President of Krug's college to emulate it. More even than the obscene Ruler and his brutal and vulgar henchmen, Nabokov's target is the conventionality and banality of their evil régime, of all evil.[47]

Against this banality, he sets a literary synthesis compounded, for the most part, of Proust and Shakespeare, two improbable companions who share nothing but their faith in the power of language to renew thought and feeling by means of metaphor: the quintessential artistic function of language, as Nabokov sees it. Metaphor and metonymy link disparate phenomena across great gulfs of time and space, creating those new wholes which Eliot claimed it was the special property of the poet's mind to discover.[48] Nabokov's quest for the clinching metaphor, the exact pattern of sound or sense (comparable to his entomological pursuit of lepidoptera) is (like that pursuit) an attempt to capture the strange particularity of experience.[49] He talks in *Speak, Memory* of his interest in lepidoptera being stimulated by entomologists at the turn of the century querying the over-generalized taxonomy (mostly German) which had hitherto been considered adequate.[50] Butterfly-collecting was for him the exact description of metamorphoses and deviations which had prevously been subsumed under some more or less generalized typology. Proust embodies this process when he renders minute sensations and impressions too fine for language to register unless stripped of all the coarse encumbrances that conventionally obscure meaning, whereupon the moment of perception, arrested, detaches itself from the material in which it is embedded and takes its place in a subjective order of similar perceptions, illuminating all the rest. Krug, pausing on the bridge in Chapter Two, notes the natural imperfections in its stone:

> Let us touch this and look at this. In the faint light (of the moon? of his tears? of the few lamps the dying fathers of the city had lit from a mechanical sense of duty?) his hands found a certain pattern of roughness: a furrow in the stone of the parapet and a knob and a hole with some moisture inside . . . I had never touched this particular knob before and shall never find it again. This moment of conscious contact holds a drop of solace. The emergency brake of time.[51]

The passage is strikingly set in the midst of Krug's attempts to get past two sets of sinister Ruritanian guards and cross the bridge (he suggests in despair turning the bridge round: 'give it a full turn' — a nice encapsulation of his heretical circularity of which this Proustian arrest of time is a larger manifestation). The impression of the texture of the bridge is also an impression of the texture of time.[52] It is associated with his wife:

> On this particular night, just after they had tried to turn over to me her purse, her comb, her cigarette holder, I found and touched this — a select combination, details of the bas-relief.[53]

The sensation thus acquires by association a Proustian mnemogenic quiddity, and forms one link in the spiralling time-gyre which carries all such memories of his dead wife,[54] combining them with poignant intuitions of the threat that hangs over his son into a touching demonstration of the primary human reality of family life (cf. *Pale Fire*). In addition a faint hint of Shakespearian yokels in the first set of guards (especially Krug's yarn about the grand apples of Bervok, which is virtually his password) anticipates the novel's Shakespearian theme.[55]

As in *Invitation*, the texture of time, Bergsonian *durée*, must be intuited beyond concrete time, or clock time. We have seen that the novel describes a circle, in more senses than one. Moreover, if it is a kind of *A la recherche*[56] (Krug's quest being primarily for his dead wife, who at the end of Chapter Six, in a ghastly dream very like one that Cincinnatus has, performs a kind of ultimate striptease, taking herself to pieces) it is also a *Temps Retrouvé*. That dream of Olga's complete obliteration concludes a nightmare in which Krug, back in school, fails an examination which Paduk passes with ease. In the last scene of the novel Krug's prison is his old school where, by some Viconian recurrence, he plays a last football game with Schamm's cissy sealskin bonnet and dies in a heroic assault on the Toad. It would have been a kind of victory for Krug, this total immersion in *durée* (which restores his memories of his wife and their happiness together in proportion to his increasing social isolation), if it were not for the little historical handle which marred his perfect circularity: David, murdered in a lurid 'experiment' not much more horrible than those history records in totalitarian régimes (driving to that hopeless meeting with David, Krug significantly has no words to describe his feelings: the future, inaccessible to language, is an illusion).

Clocks tick remorselessly throughout the novel, measuring the nightmare of history and the unredeemed world of *byt* (the vulgarity of which is as vividly evoked as in *Invitation*). Krug, for a joke, once read backwards a lecture on space; but he exercises no such easy control over history. At the momentous university conference, Dr. Alexander (whose fate is instructive) sets going the clock which has stopped, thus facilitating the signing of what Azureus calls 'that really historical document'. Maximov's clock 'rapped out the seconds in pica type' and after his arrest Ember notes that the two clocks in the house

> are probably still going, alone, intact, pathetically sticking to man's notion of time after man has gone.[57]

Time accelerates as Krug plans his escape and the Ekwilists arrange his arrest, culminating in Mariette's attempted seduction ('She had a pillow under her arm and an alarm clock in her hand'[58]), which she doesn't manage to organize before Paduk's gangsters arrive, despite her exhortations ('Let's go on, we have just enough time to do it before they break the door, please'). A detailed timetable charts the stages in Krug's wait for his son; though of course when he finds him it is too late. Against this accelerating tempo (and the state's hymns of praise to the future) is set Krug's rapt re-run of the past, in which events are not constricted by idiotic laws of sequence.

Loose parallels are drawn between Krug and Hamlet, Krug and Lear. In the middle of the novel Ember and Krug discuss *Hamlet* in a way that recalls Stephen's exposition of his theories in the Public Library in *Ulysses;*[59] but the primary objective in setting off Ember's despairing account of Professor Hamm's crudely politicized account of the play against Krug's story of a vulgarized American screen version seems to be to show that the civilized literary consciousness represented by these two men is more than equal to enacting a transcendence (by parody) of vulgar materialistic assaults on Shakespeare, from East or West (the Ekwilist version rewrites him in terms of the victory of the masses, the American inserts simplified visual images of everything that Shakespeare evoked by means of metaphor). The Toad's performance as Poor Tom, designed to underline Krug's nakedness, is sadly mis-timed: this Lear ('Mad Adam',[60] as Paduk so rightly called him) has his own drama to act out in which Paduk has no say. However, it is Shakespeare who has given Paduk his proper identity: a 'paddock' (various spellings) in Shakespeare is a toad, and it is a term Hamlet applies to Claudius.[61]

One can, in short, understand why Nabokov, in his introduction to *Invitation*, rejects comparisons between his work and Orwell's; and yet despite the fact that the political themes in these two novels are in substance metaphoric, their vindication of individual freedom is inevitably political.[62]

## Notes to Chapter 6

1. Vladimir Nabokov, *Invitation to a Beheading* (Harmondsworth: Penguin Books, 1969) p. 26.
2. *Ibid.*, p. 78. Cf. *Through the Looking Glass*, where life is the Red King's dream. The distorting mirrors of Nabokov's novel are very like Carroll's looking-glass, but there is also a Kafka-like element of guilt: Cincinnatus has shut himself in to the cell of himself. Cf. the 'camera obscura' of *Laughter in the Dark* and sundry keys and locks elsewhere (*The Gift*, *Lolita*, etc.).
3. *Ibid.*, p. 80.
4. Those who doubt reality's talent for imitating the maddest theatrical fantasy are referred to Robert Conquest, *The Great Terror* (Harmondsworth: Penguin Books, 1971). The 'show' trials arranged by Stalin were unique combinations of fact and fancy. Pp. 129 and 147 are specially relevant.
5. James Joyce, *Ulysses*, p. 31: 'History, Stephen said, is a nightmare from which I am trying to awake.' Joyce, like Nabokov, found a cyclic theory of time more productive than teleological notions of liberation struggles. But the roundest mug may have its handle: 'What if that nightmare gave you a back kick?' (*Ibid.*).
6. The Gnostics were heretics who claimed access to a 'special' wisdom.
7. The microcosmic nature of Krug's universe (i.e. he projects outwards a small private order) has led some critics to see the whole novel as a dream. This seems needless, given that life *is* a dream. The use of Shakespeare's *Hamlet* to structure plays within plays and microcosms within macrocosms (not to mention the individual and society) is an overt Joyceism. Other modern muses in the wings and flies include Mallarmé and Kafka (actually under the sofa).
8. Recognition scenes involving fathers and sons are also Joycean: they use *Hamlet* and Homer in the Joycean way. The language into which Krug erupts at the end of this chapter is significantly not a spoof but pure (highly demotic) Russian. No doubt this is a response to the nightmare's kick, but one cannot talk of Krug's 'blindness' as one talks of Albinus's (*Laughter in the Dark*).
9. Vladimir Nabokov, *Bend Sinister* (London: Weidenfeld and Nicolson, 1960) p. 210. The novel ends in the author's 'com-

parative paradise', his study.

10. *Ibid.*
11. *Invitation to a Beheading,* p. 173. Rodion is terrified of it: with its 'squirrel face' it comes in from the dark of a private reality.
12. *Bend Sinister,* p. 153.
13. See note 4.
14. The often-made comparison with Kafka is essentially right, if resented by Nabokov (*Invitation to a Beheading,* p. 7).
15. No doubt it is a form of solipsism, but not, like Hermann's, a derangement.
16. *Bend Sinister,* p. 155.
17. Cf. *The Gift,* where this gnomic phenomenologist again appears.
18. If there are shadows, there must be a light and there may be 'real' things behind it all. Nabokov appropriates Plato's cave allegory but is more interested than Plato in the mechanics of the performance. Essences are beyond human language.
19. *Invitation to a Beheading,* p. 12.
20. *Ibid.*
21. *Ibid.*, p. 11.
22. The clearest exposition of this in the novel is on pp. 76-83. It is a classic modernist extension of the differentiation between *Langue* and *Parole* in Saussure's *Cours de Linguistique Generale* (1916) which, assimilated by the Formalist school of critics, greatly influenced Russian modernism.
23. See Chapter 1, above.
24. *Invitation to a Beheading,* p. 14.
25. Vladimir Nabokov, *Nikolai Gogol,* pp. 63-74.
26. In this novel perhaps more than any other Nabokov demonstrates that art's illusions, like life's, reveal their meaning to the trained eye.
27. *Invitation to a Beheading,* pp. 145-6.
28. *Ibid.*, p. 85.
29. For all his admiration of Tolstoy, Nabokov seems not to share his social views.
30. *Ibid.*, p. 65. Cf. the 'feigned remoteness' of the second line of Shade's poem in *Pale Fire.* To pass through this mirror is to right the distorted and partial image provided by the 'real' world. It is 'real' enough, this 'remoteness', though not geographically. At this stage Cincinnatus sees only that the window is actually a glass case.

31. *Ibid.*, p. 127.
32. For the line 'Liubovnaya lodka razbilas' o byt' in Mayakovsky's last fragment *Uzhe vtoroy* (*Past one o'clock*) Herbert Marshall has 'The love-boat of life/has crashed on philistine reefs' while Hayward and Reavey have 'Love's boat has smashed against the daily grind'. *Byt* seems to be a specially Russian word.
33. *Invitation to a Beheading*, p. 145.
34. Like the 'oppressive' forces in Kafka's world, the prison is there because Cincinnatus at bottom *wants* it to be. Of course he changes in the course of the novel.
35. *Ibid.*, p. 191.
36. Cf. Chapter 1, above.
37. Cf. note 30, above.
38. *Ibid.*, pp. 112, 114.
39. I have noted the wanderings of some such from novel to novel.
40. *Ibid.*, p. 115.
41. See, for example, my comments on *The Real Life of Sebastian Knight*.
42. In the work of the Russian Formalists, the preoccupation with form is often an attempt to renew traditional forms with the help of 'low' or extra-literary material. Fundamentally this takes the form of juxtaposing the spoken and the written language. (See my chaper on *Pnin*.)
43. *Invitation to a Beheading*, p. 104. One can think of many querci, especially in the American novel: now Solzhenitsyn seems to be growing a Russian strain.
44. *Ibid.*, p. 180. The disintegration of the cell is connected with the appearance of the moth.
45. *Bend Sinister*, p. 62.
46. One of the instructors at Wordsmith (*Pale Fire*) is called Gerald Emerald, and Kinbote metamorphoses him into the assassin Izumrudov. I would not make too much of the anti-utopian reading, but it would be equally wrong to ignore it.
47. Often, when Nabokov says evil is banal, his critics seem to hear the reverse: banality is evil. Nabokov criticism is distinguished by a holy terror of banality. The reader will note that the present writer does not share this fear.
48. T. S. Eliot, *The Metaphysical Poets*, op. cit.
49. Cf. Chapter 1, above.
50. A Chekhovian love of the particular detail, the part revealing

the whole, has been noted in his work by Simon Karlinsky (Appel and Newman, op. cit.).

51. *Bend Sinister*, p. 14.
52. 'Texture of Time' is, of course, Van Veen's thesis in *Ada*, q.v.
53. *Bend Sinister*, p. 14.
54. As so often in Nabokov's novels, normative value is given to family life.
55. If history is not a nightmare, it is a costume drama: in fact the ability to regard it as the latter may prevent it becoming the former. Cf. *Pale Fire*.
56. Proust's great novel seems to have become more and more important to Nabokov. *Speak, Memory* and *Ada* are thoroughly Proustian, even though they perhaps minimize the hard intellect that there is in Proust: another modern Proustian, Samuel Beckett, has more of this quality.
57. 'Man's notion of time' is the most striking image in Nabokov's early, immature novel *Mary*. It need hardly be pointed out that the phrase does not mean the same as Poulet's 'human time', in his *Studies in Human Time*.
58. *Bend Sinister*, p. 171.
59. James Joyce, *Ulysses*, p. 172.
60. A circular phrase, the same backwards as forwards. Old Adam is in *As You Like It*, which is where Bervok belongs (if not to Falstaffland). A *mirok* (p. 10) is not a kind of potato but a little world of one's own or inner world (from Russian *mir*). Cf. Hamlet bounded in a nutshell, king of infinite space: except for those bad dreams of his, which are certainly *not* ambition (eating too many *mirki*?)
61. *Hamlet*, Act. 3 Scene 4.
62. Cf. Chapter 1, above, and Henri Bergson: *Matter and Memory*.

# VII

## A debt to Gogol: **Pnin** (1957)

Russian literary criticism in the first decades of this century (and especially the group known as the Formalists[1]), in the course of a revaluation of the literary tradition, became much preoccupied with a phenomenon known in Russian as *skaz*. Defined by Harkins[2] as 'a narrative told by a fictitious narrator rather than by the author directly', the term comes to denote all those narrative devices that call attention to the fictionality of the tale told, by means of persistently foregrounding the inventiveness of the teller. Cognate with the word *skazka* (a folk-tale), *skaz* and its techniques originate in popular oral narratives, in which the linear progression of the story is constantly interrupted by elaborate digressions and delaying devices which serve to heighten tension or, like a conjuror's patter, to distract the hearer's attention from a narrative improbability. The commonest devices are a kind of musical *stretto* (the repetition of motifs — sometimes very lengthy — with effects of diminution and augmentation) and sonic 'irrelevancies' of one kind and another: interjections, ejaculations, and of course silences. The folk narrative is habitually accompanied by gestures, the storyteller reinforcing his point with a wave of the hand, or even going so far as to act out a sequence. The language of the tale itself, moreover, is likely to incorporate verbal equivalents of gesture, a sort of sonic gesturing. The narrator's relationship with the audience becomes crucial. Where the Victorian novelist may take his reader for a moment into his confidence in order to point a moral or to pose a rhetorical question, the popular entertainer — and in this respect Dickens is one — has a complex and ever-changing relationship with an audience which may indeed be familiar with the substance of the tale — its outcome and even its precise incidents being known beforehand — but for this reason is all the more attentive to the teller, whose job it is to entertain his hearers not by repeating what is familiar but by 'defamiliarizing' it, by playing upon the conventions which define his relationship to them, so making the tale new.

The Formalists' interest in *skaz* was not primarily anthropological. In fact it was — as we see in such a seminal text as Eikhenbaum's *Illuzia Skaza* (*The 'skaz' illusion*, 1918) — part of a complex set of critical attitudes to literary texts rather than to folk narratives per se.[3] The intense moral concern of nineteenth century Russian literature, its special role as the consciousness of an oppressed people, had helped to shape the revolutions of 1905 and 1917. On the one hand the radical and meliorative strain seemed to have found a valid outlet in action, but on the other — as in western Europe — historical crises seemed to have exhausted or discredited certain normative models of language. Modernism in Russia as elsewhere sought new literary modes, new bearings were taken in the literature of the past in order to discover among the debris of a shattered humanitarianism (an avant-garde poet called nineteenth century literature 'a kind of salvation army'[4]), forms of sensibility and expression which would stand the pressure of confused and contradictory modern experience. As Eliot discovered in the intellectual metaphorism of seventeenth century poetry and the enacted dialectic of Jacobean drama the basis of a 'Prufrock', so the Russian Formalists, closely associated with some of the greatest creative talents of their day, found in Sterne the archetypal novelist,[5] and in Gogol and Leskov the great exemplars of a narrative fusion of high and low literary modes, combining a mastery of ambivalent point-of-view and a baroque ornamentation with an eschewal of rhetoric in an idiom which, on the other hand, never lost touch with popular sources and the rhythms of speech. Here, it seemed, was an inspiration to modern writers, and indeed Eikhenbaum can enlist with complete appropriateness some of the finest modern Russian writers, claiming that all of them are influenced in one way or another by *skaz.*[6]

Some of Eikhenbaum's arguments have lately become familiar. As 'bookmen', he says, we only *see* words:[7] the written language and established genres have forced speech and gesture into a subordinate position. But identifying the *skaz* elements, in the widest sense, in a literary text will, he claims, help us to establish a richer critical approach to it; since although the folk tale is essentially an improvised affair and the realist novel evidently is not, every novelist who matters to us now will be found to be trying to preserve the *illusion* of improvisation at those points at which he needs to keep a hold on the spoken language. This is true even of Tolstoy, while Gogol, with his gestures and grimaces

> doesn't simply narrate, he play-acts and recites. Typically, he began with the folk-tale, placing these tales in the mouth of Rudi Panko. And then he created special 'skaz' forms, with outbursts and word-games of all kinds.[8]

A real artist, says Eikhenbaum, carries within himself the primitive but organic powers of the living teller of tales. A literary heritage is a kind of museum; but 'our own mad but creative age is marked by a return to the living word'.[9] And in the same year he published an essay on Gogol, 'How Gogol's Overcoat was made',[10] in which he developed his ideas of *skaz* with close reference to Gogol's masterpiece, and at the same time succeeded in formulating the essential preoccupations of experimental literature. The essay clearly influenced Nabokov's book on Gogol (though he does not acknowledge it) and is worth considering in some detail because it throws light on the relation between *Pnin* and Gogol's tale. The interest of this relationship is not merely academic: by exploring, in *Pnin*, the resources of Gogol's devices, Nabokov has fabricated his own critical schema and incorporated it in the very texture of his novel.[11] In this way a new currency is minted which is backed up by that weighty 'gold reserve of Russian literature'[12] which Pnin carries about with him.

Eikhenbaum begins by distinguishing between those tales in which the story (*anekdot*) is rich in itself, the narrative devices merely serving as a formal link between events, and those where *skaz* plays a dominant part, in which

> the narrator in one way or another manoeuvres himself into the foreground, as if merely making use of the plot as a means of weaving together various stylistic devices[13]

— thus shifing the centre of gravity towards verbal intricacies as small as the pun or as large as the short anecdote, and producing comic effects from the technique of narration itself. There is a kind of comic tale which relies primarily on mimicry, gesture, plays on words, distortions of syntax and so on, and behind which we feel the presence of an actor.[14] Gogol's plots, he says, are usually extremely thin, and it is a known fact that the need to find a story embarrassed him.[15] On the other hand he was a masterly raconteur, as contemporary sources tell us, excelling in both sentimental declamation and in a gestural kind of comic narration (derived from that of the tale-tellers of his native Ukraine[16]). Even in dictating a story to an amanuensis he would act it out.[17] His narratives are bound together in part by the logic of mime: the sonic properties of words, their rhythms and harmonies, create the illusion of a complementary semiotic system parallel to the sense. He collected names, for example, with Dickensian glee, for the sheer sound of them or for the suggestive properties of their semantics, incorporating them in narratives which had his listeners in fits of laughter, while he remained himself apparently unmoved and intent on his virtuoso performance. The actors in his tales, says Eikhenbaum — evidently drawing on Bergson's 'Le Rire' for support — are automated attitudes, set poses and gestures:

> The author himself, his joyous and playful spirit presiding over them, is the producer of the play and its real hero.[18]

'The Overcoat', of course, combines pathos with its word-play. Traditionally the pathos of the tale had been treated as a discrete element, Akaky being considered an early instance of the 'little man' as hero. Eikhenbaum, however, refuses to separate out the elements in this way, suggesting that the pathos is subsumed by the grotesque. The way Akaky is christened — his name being introduced along with an accretion of 'irrelevant' detail — he takes as typical of one important kind of Gogolian word-play, whereby a strictly logical progression masks absurdity with a show of inevitability:

> The clerk's name was Shoenik. There is no doubt that this name derives from shoe but we know nothing of how, why or when. His father, his grandfather, and even his brother-in-law wore boots, having new soles put on them not more than three times a year.[19]

The string of improbable saints' names run through by the family before 'Akaky Akakievich' is reached creates a kind of uniformly exotic context in which the name and patronymic chosen, with its stuttering repetition, sounds, says Eikhenbaum, like a nickname: this he calls a 'sonic gesture', a device, he says, beloved of Gogol. The best example of the sonic gesture may be in the second paragraph of the tale, where Akaky's appearance is described: a bit pock-marked, a bit red-headed, a bit short-sighted, a bald patch, wrinkled, and with a hemorrhoidal complexion. Here a transcription of the Russian may allow the sound patterns to be perceived, along with the loose articulations of the syntax, even by a reader who does not know Russian:

> Itak, v odnom departamente sluzhil odin chinovnik, chinovnik nelzya skazat' shtoby ochen' zamechatelnyi, nizenkovo rosta, nyeskol'ko ryabovat, nyeskolko ryzhevat, nyeskolko dazhe na vid podslepovat, s nyebolshoy lysinoy na lbu, s morshinami po obeim storonam shyok i tsvetom litsa shto nazyvaetsa gemoroidalnym.[20]

Repetitions of similar sounds ('ryabovat', pock marked;

'ryzhevat', red-haired; 'podslepovat', short-sighted) mark a rhythmic wave that breaks on the ridiculous '*gemoroidalnym*'. This is the process Eikhenbaum calls 'sonic semantics': the meaning of the words as logical units is subsumed by the total sonic effect.

Gogol allows his characters to speak only very seldom, and then in a stylized way (i.e. there is no attempt to create naturalistic dialogue). As Eikhenbaum rightly points out, Akaky Akakievich's idiolect fits seamlessly into the narrative mode. Petrovich's speech, equally stylized, is conceived primarily as a formal contrast to Akaky's, and the process by which he is introduced (a fine example of a rage for accuracy leading to total absurdity) is pure *skaz*: the narrator has a job remembering all the relevant (?) details. Eikhenbaum begins the final section of his article by reiterating and intensifying his central point: the teller of the tale is an actor, almost a comedian, lurking behind the words on the page. The disinterested narrative of the first few lines of 'The Overcoat' is at once interrupted by the narrator's sarcasm, giving an impression of improvization; the narrative as it develops is constantly interrupted by such digressions, as the narrator intervenes. It may seem that Akaky's desperate outburst, when he is taunted beyond endurance, constitutes a different kind of narrative and a different approach to the hero; but Eikhenbaum's attitude to this outburst of sentiment is to attribute its effectiveness precisely to that quality which raises the tale from the anecdotal to the grotesque thus implicitly dismissing the tradition of Gogol criticism which emphasizes the author's humanitarianism and social commitment, and preparing the way for Nabokov's approach. The episode, he claims, is marked by an authorial intrusion comparable to an actor's direct 'aside' to the audience — and it is 'naïve', rather than 'humanitarian'. Nabokov's most memorable description of the tale is more impressionistic but no less opposed to overstating its human pathos:

> The story goes this way: mumble, mumble, lyrical wave, mumble, lyrical wave, mumble, fantastic climax, mumble, mumble, and back into the chaos from which they had all derived.[21]

Moreover, Eikhenbaum points out that immediately after a passage of moral indignation there follows a string of brilliant and thoroughly typical verbal games culminating in the very funny (and thoroughly Pninian):

> Even when Akaky Akakievich's eyes were resting on something, he saw superimposed on it his own well-formed, neat handwriting. Perhaps it was only when, out of nowhere, a horse rested its head on his shoulder and sent a blast of wind down his cheek that he'd realize he was not in the middle of a line but in the middle of a street.[22]

The genre of the grotesque demands that the small world of the tale be shut off from reality, and that didactic and satiric modes be excluded. Naturalistic details certainly *are* admitted, but only by a process of distortion, so that normal perspective is lost. The nineteenth century social critics — the utilitarian school of Belinsky brilliantly travestied by Nabokov in *The Gift*[23] — had stressed that Akaky was primarily the object of our concern and sympathy, but it is evident that, within the tale, his consciousness becomes its own scale of measurement. His death is as grotesque as his birth — 'back into the chaos', as Nabokov says — but after it he lives briefly on as a ghost:

> Who would have imagined that that was not the end of Akaky Akakievich, that he was fated to live on and make his presence felt for a few days after his death as if in compensation for having spent his life unnoticed by anyone? But that's the way it happened and our little story gains an unexpectedly fantastic ending.[24]

— a tone of voice, by the way, often used by Nabokov.[25] Pnin, too, is resurrected, maybe for the same reason, since like Akaky's return from the dead Pnin's rebirth in *Pale Fire* serves to illuminate the vanity and self-deception of the living. Shade, presiding over Wordsmith's senior common room with his bad parody of the Johnsonian manner lends himself unworthily to Pnin-mockery.

> 'I think I heard you, the other day, talking to — what's his name — oh, my goodness.' (laboriously composing his lips)
>
> Shade: 'Sir, we all find it difficult to *attack* that name.' (laughing)
>
> Professor Hurley: 'Think of the French word for tire: *punoo.*'
>
> Shade: 'Why, sir, I am afraid you have only punctured the difficulty.' (laughing uproariously)[26]

When Pnin drove off the edge of the page at the end of the novel, or rather was driven off by the author, he seems to have found precarious sanctuary in the formal arbours of New Wye. Like Bergson's Jack-in-the-Box, he is a puppet turned parable.

Nabokov's book on Gogol is a highly personal affair, but perhaps, in the light of Eikhenbaum's essay, not quite so 'curious' as Mottram and Bradbury find it.[27] In fact it is itself a rather remarkable example of *skaz*, especially in its use of long passages of quotation in his own vivid translation. Gogol himself is the *donné*, which like his plots (and here Nabokov is in complete agreement with Eikhenbaum) is of little interest: indeed in recounting the horrible details of his death Nabokov notes that 'the scene is unpleasant and has a human appeal which I deplore'.[28] His reason for describing it is not to enlist sympathy but to bring out 'the curiously physical side of Gogol's genius',[29] another observation which seems to accord with Eikhenbaum's findings; and there follows a brilliant digression on noses of the kind that Eikhenbaum notes in 'The Overcoat', and which in the changes it rings on proverbs is pure *skaz*. The freedom of the *skaz* narrator to play with the time continuum of his tale (a device much admired by Shklovsky in the work of Sterne[30]) is suggested in the title of Nabokov's first chapter, 'His Death and Youth';[13] and the first part of this introductory chapter (in which Nabokov characteristically feels for the themes rather than the facts of Gogol's life — as he says in *Speak, Memory*, every life has its themes) passes through a sequence of vivid anecdotal glimpses to come to rest by an apparent process of logic on the surreal image of Gogol killing lizards:

> In Switzerland, he had quite a field-day knocking the life out of the lizards all along the sunny mountain paths. The cane he used for this purpose may be seen in a daguerreotype of him taken in Rome in 1845. It is a very elegant affair.[32]

This may be compared with the paragraph in 'The Overcoat', in which the narrator, having introduced the tailor Petrovich and his wife, goes on:

> Now that we've mentioned his wife, we'd better say a word or two about her, too. But unfortunately very little is known about her, except that Petrovich had a wife who wore a bonnet instead of a kerchief, but was apparently no beauty, since, on meeting her, it occurred to no one but an occasional soldier to peek under that bonnet of hers, twitching his mustache and making gurgling sounds.[33]

(In the Russian the syntax is much more gossipy and the final phrase is literally 'and emitting a sort of peculiar voice'.) This trick of throwing into relief a weirdly irrelevant detail and by doing so endowing it with a quality of pure and troubling grotesquerie is a device that Nabokov has learnt from Gogol.

The picture of Gogol built up by Nabokov (though that sober phrase does not do justice to it) confirms Eikhenbaum's in many details, even though there is less show of 'scientific' disinterestedness. The mutterings of passers-by that Gogol noted when he first went to Petersburg, he says, turned into a narrative style: 'The monologue was echoed and multiplied by the shadows of his mind.'[34] Gogol was 'an actor of genius', though evidently his forte was the monodrama. Above all he was no realist, as Eikhenbaum too insists:

> Gogol, of course, never drew portraits — he used looking glasses and as a writer lived in his own looking-glass world.[35]

Consequently (and Nabokov makes the point in his chapter *The Government Inspector* — the chapter is called 'The Government

Specter') he feels no obligation to develop his motifs in accordance with external verisimilitude, only in conformity with inner necessity:

> A famous playwright has said . . . that if in the first act a shot gun hangs on the wall, it must go off in the last act. But Gogol's guns hang in mid-air and do not go off — in fact the charm of his allusions is exactly that nothing whatever comes of them . . . Gogol's genius deals not in the intrinsic qualities of computable chemical matter (the 'real life' of literary critics) but in the mimetic capacities of the physical phenomena produced by almost intangible particles of recreated life.[36]

The term Eikhenbaum uses is *'vosproizvodit'*, roughly 'to mimic', but not in the orthodox sense in which realism is mimesis.

It is (one hopes) already clear that *Pnin*, the most delightful of Nabokov's novels, maybe his most popular, and the one that first attracted substantial public attention in the English-speaking world, is actually the product of a native Russian tradition refracted through the English language and the lenses of modern Russian criticism. In the chapter of the Gogol study in which he discusses *Dead Souls*, Nabokov coins a characteristic aphorism: 'Fancy is fertile only when it is futile', glossing it as signifying

> the remarkable creative faculty of Russians, so beautifully disclosed by Gogol's own inspiration, of working in a void.[37]

In Gogol's work, as in *Pnin*, the narrator holds the stage single-handed, though it must not become apparent that he is alone: you must be persuaded that you see a group of actors. His skill (again as in *Pnin*) distracts your attention from the fact that there is nothing more substantial in the world he creates than his own presence in it. Any message or moral, any note of social hope, you will have to supply yourself: the text does not preclude it, but the narrator is preoccupied with other matters.

This is not cold virtuosity, in Gogol's work or in *Pnin*. Nineteenth century Russian literature, always under pressure to make sweeping statements about the condition of society or the cosmos, preserved its deep spontaneous creativity by incorporating a profound moral and aesthetic relativism.[38] Still less is the grotesquerie of Gogol or of *Pnin* trivial: Nabokov is contributing to a great alternative tradition. The realist novel, with its watertight assumptions about causality, its rigidly sequential conception of time, its feigned unselfconsciousness, has come to seem the most unreal and unworkable of literary modes. Since the experiments of the modernist period we have perhaps come to value most highly those writers who, fully conscious of the conventional nature of fictions, renew them through a process of 'spontaneous generation'.[39] The 'dishevelled grammar' that Nabokov finds in Gogol and recreates in *Pnin* has come to seem more responsive to the way things 'really' are than the literalism of a Turgenev. The highest praise Nabokov can give the famous climax of *Dead Souls*, with its rhetorical invocation to Rus, the nimble troika ('Whither are you speeding so?' etc.) is to say that:

> Beautiful as all this final crescendo sounds, it is from the stylistic point of view merely a conjuror's patter enabling an object to disappear, the particular object being — Chichikov.[40]

This is an exaggeration, like other points in Nabokov's study of Gogol, but it puts the emphasis in the right place, on what really is creative in Gogol's work. Behind it lies Bergson's *Le Rire* (1900), a book which I have already suggested has a special importance for Nabokov's own novels. Underlying its conception of comedy is a theory of gesture, deliberately unemotional ('laughter has no greater foe than emotion'), which puts us in mind of the research into gesture being undertaken by Pnin's colleague Clements. One extract from Bergson may serve to sum up this argument and lead into a consideration of Nabokov's novel; it is evidently the stock onto which Eikhenbaum grafted his folkloristic growths, and (like the art of *Pnin*) shows how a comedy of gesture does not so much negate seriousness as throw it into dumb relief:

> to prevent our taking a serious action seriously, in short, in order to prepare us for laughter, comedy utilizes a method, the formula of which may be given as follows: *instead of concentrating our attention on actions, comedy directs it rather to gestures.* By *gestures* we here mean the attitudes, the movements and even the language by which a mental state expresses itself outwardly without any aim or profit, from no other cause than a kind of inner itching. Gesture, thus defined, is profoundly different from action. Action is intentional, or, at any rate, conscious; gesture slips out unawares, it is automatic . . . Action is in exact proportion to the feeling that inspires it . . . About gesture, however, there is something explosive . . .[41]

Gesture, the *skaz* element to which Eikhenbaum had given such a large significance, plays the most important part in *Pnin*, and Nabokov characteristically directs the reader's attention to it. Pnin is himself a sonic gesture: travestied as 'the French for a tire' in *Pale Fire* he is introduced to his Cremona audience as 'Professor Pun-neen', an ambulating wordplay, and the amiable Joan Clements ('John' to Pnin) hears his name over the phone as 'a preposterous little explosion', and (in her own words) 'a cracked ping-pong ball. Russian'.[42] Although he is 'more of a poltergeist than a lodger'[45] (objects behave as strangely in his vicinity as those melon-rinds that find themselves transported about by Akaky Akakievich's hat[44]), Laurence Clements comes to value him as a fellow 'human surd' — it being only one small syllable from the surd to the absurd[45] — and as material for his current research on

> the philosophical interpretation of pictorial and non-pictorial, national and environmental gestures.[46]

Pnin is 'a veritable encyclopaedia of Russian shrugs and shakes' and expertly demonstrates

> the movements underlying such Russian verbs — used in reference to hands — as *mahnut'*, *vsplesnut'*, *razvesti*: the one-hand downward loose shake of weary relinquishment;

> the two-handed dramatic splash of amazed distress; and the 'disjunctive' motion — hands travelling apart to signify helpless passivity.[47]

These are voluntary gestures, Pnin being conscious of their form and significance. There is also a rich profusion of involuntary gestures, ranging from the poetic description of Pnin's tongue feeling its tentative way across the gaps left by his recently extracted teeth, that tongue, a 'fat seal', which once,

> used to flop and slide so happily among the familiar rocks, checking the contours of a battered but still secure kingdom, plunging from cave to cove, climbing this jag, nuzzling that notch, finding a shred of seaweed in the same old cleft[48]

— characteristically, as in the case of Gogol, this rises to rapturous flights of fancy in the description of something that is not there — to gestures of a simpler and non-verbal kind, like Pnin falling downstairs at the Clements's feet 'like a supplicant in some ancient city full of injustice',[49] or his early struggles with snapped spectacle frames and broken zippers. His dislike of Charlie Chaplin, unnamed but vividly evoked in the account of the film show in Chapter Three, Section Seven,[50] is understandable: Pnin, a nonpareil, has no use for rivals.

Or for mimics: what the narrator refers to as 'the Pninian gesture and the Pninian wild English' lend themselves to unkind imitation. Jack Cockerell 'impersonated Pnin to perfection' — even to the perhaps apocryphal (and thus more Pninian than Pnin himself) declaration that he had been 'shot' (when he meant he had been fired). This of course is at the end of the novel, though Cockerell had done his Pnin impersonation as early as Chapter Two, at the Clements's party, while Pnin himself, at this stage very imperfectly in control of the English language, was informing 'John' that

> This is not a clean glass in the bathroom, and there exist other troubles. It blows from the floor, and it blows from the walls[51]

— the apparent poverty of Pnin's English being an actual comic richness (like Akaky's meandering Russian[52]). Cockerell's imitation is — what else could it be? —a mere shadow of reality; and untrue at that, since by the end of the novel Pnin has actually developed in English as in other things to such an extent that he would not, as the narrator tells us, have made so obvious a mistake as to substitute 'shot' for 'fired' (quite apart from the not quite irrelevant human issues at stake here[53]). But the greatest Pnin imitator is not Cockerell, all crow and no bite, but the narrator, who is a much more substantial threat to our hero — and who shall say how reliable *he* is, or how much he invents and fictionalizes? The ultimate answer is of course 'everything', but infinity is notoriously difficult to measure.

At first the narrator hardly disturbs us: he does what he is paid for, narrate, and since he is not an aged Ukrainian peasant but, it seems, a literate and cultivated American we pay little attention to his faintly charlatanic knowingness (this is not, it would seem, part of the fun, as it might be in a different context). We are told that it was 'none other than' Professor Pnin on the train and that he was 'ideally' bald without being pulled up by what is evidently, on reflection, a queer perspective on one's hero. The string of alliterations and assonances that follow ('His sloppy socks were of scarlet wool with lilac lozenges') may strike us as mannered, or we may even want to call them, after Eikhenbaum, 'verbal gestures', but the narrator plays the realist third-person-past-tense game that is the novelist's bread-and-butter comprehensively enough for the illusion to endure rather more totally than it does in Gogol's world with its constant knavish or foolish asides to the reader. When we learn that Cremona is 200 versts west of Waindell, the alliteration lulls us into acceptance of the quaint Russianism, which may, we assume, in any case be a mirage thrown up by Pnin's hazy consciousness: though if so the blunt 'he taught Russian at Waindell College' is oddly cold. That Pnin was beloved 'not for any essential ability but for those unforgettable digressions of his' puts us in mind of Gogol and his creatures without (I suppose) prompting us to consider *who* might have forgotten Pnin's digressions should anyone have been inclined to do so.

And even the tell-tale 'a letter he had written *with my help*' is ignorable, given the comic impetus the tale has by now built up. We are reproached for our inattentive attitude one third of the way through the novel in connection with a fairly trivial matter of a mistaken date ('O Careless Reader'! says the narrator) without perhaps thinking more of it. But there is much more to be thought about, and it is central to the novel.

For the Gogolian comic devices of *Pnin* — the sonic patterns that create their own pseudo-logic as they lead deeper into absurdity, the intrinsically comic names, the fascinating digressions, the passages of 'spontaneous generation' and the rest — indicate their debt to Gogol by being devised as a part of a structure in which they constitute not so much the method as the matter. It is evident from Nabokov's book on Gogol that his admiration of Gogol's narrative skill is accompanied by a fascination with Gogol's hallucinatory adumbration of a metaphysic; his sense of the proximity of an abyss which by threatening to swallow man and all his devices provides a fictional 'sense of an ending'.[54] The page contains the whole world of the fiction and the whole fiction of the world, and when Cockerell has the last word (he prepares to tell the quite false story of Pnin arriving at Cremona with the wrong lecture — an unopened door we have passed by early in the tale) there is no one to contradict him — except the narrator, who cannot be relied on to do so, since he has ousted Pnin, his creation, and taken over his job. There is here an extension of *skaz* that cuts its Gogolian ties to a folk mode and moves into a different and more sombre realm of fantasy whereby, like Braque painting on to one of his pictures the nail by which it might be supposed to be hanging, complete with shadow, Nabokov not only 'lays bare his devices' (as the Formalists said[55]) but dissolves the boundary between fiction and reality in such a way as to suggest not so much that the fiction may not be real as that reality may be only a fiction. And in the novel itself the Gogolian grotesque (that alternation of pathos and clowning) is developed towards the frontiers of the phenomenal world in such a way as to evoke a doubt about their authority which is more modern than anything in Gogol.

Pnin's pathos is more complex than Akaky's. Akaky's 'Let

me be. Why do you do this to me?'[56] is echoed by Pnin when Dr. Wind — the first of a succession of characters who outplay Pnin at the chess game of life, unless the narrator is the first — tells him that he has claimed, or 'taken', Liza. 'Lasse mich, lasse mich' Pnin wails — in German, the language in which he is most helpless and which he most dislikes — the novel is shot through with that eternal Russian hostility to all things German so marked in Nabokov's book on Gogol. But at the same time there is a quite un-Gogolian element in this pathos: a gift (or is it a disease?) of reverie through which Pnin tries to repossess the world of his youth, the Russia still dimly glimpsed which moves Pnin to tears even by way of the banalities of a Stalinist propaganda film. His ineptitude contains an Oblomovesque yearning to lapse out of life into a small but perfect alternative universe. This is of course seen in the novel in terms of the emigré's tendency to build from his blurry memories and his carefully safeguarded 'private' language (Russian is described as practically dead) a small clearing in the forest, off the beaten track, where a kind of Bergsonian *durée* holds at bay the purposeful linearity of American life, and where Pnin can discuss with scholarly assurance a part of that great inheritance of Russian literature which at Waindell — or Vandal as he pronounces it — had been a string of comic pearls cast before likeable swine or a heavy tome dragged unnecessarily back to the college library. Moreover, the literary discussion at Cook's Castle revolves around a time-trick in *Anna Karenina* whereby — if one compares relevant dates — it will be seen that Levin and Kitty live more slowly than Vronsky and Anna:

> 'You will notice,' he said, 'that there is a significant difference between Lyovin's spiritual time and Vronski's physical one. In mid book, Lyovin and Kitty lag behind Vronski and Anna by a whole year. When, on a Sunday evening in May 1876, Anna throws herself under that freight train, she has existed more than four years since the beginning of the novel, but in the case of the Lyovin's, during the same period, 1872 to 1876, hardly three years have elapsed. It is the best example of relativity in literature that is known to me.'[57]

This discourse is closely followed by one of the mild heart attacks from which Pnin suffers and which accompany his retreat, by means of his own time-trick, into a vision of his childhood in which the material world with which he is habitually on such bad terms takes on a kind of artistic coherence and intensity. It is this shared faculty (or affliction) of transcendence that makes Victor rightfully Pnin's son: Pnin's memories reach out to meet Victor's fantasies (the daring escape of the king his father anticipates the delusions of Kinbote in *Pale Fire*), and Pnin's overtures to Victor start with him symbolically sending his son a picture of a Grey Squirrel (with a text explaining that 'squirrel' is from a Greek word meaning 'shadow-tail'). The squirrel, a childhood memory, has habitually accompanied Pnin's reveries as a shadow-creature like him, a creature for whom he feels sympathy and kindness.[58] Other things intuitively bind them together: Victor's painting, involving the 'naturalization of man-made things', the beautiful reflection and deformation of the world in a shiny black car,[59] for instance, echoes what Pnin does with the objects and automated inhabitants of the 'real' world. Both demand the mirrors of art, though while Pnin's comedy liberates the world from automatism through laughter, Victor's phenomenology liberates it by revealing the endless flux and interpenetration of apparently impenetrable matter, impressionistically. If one were obliged to select one episode in which the essential concern of the novel is revealed, it would be Pnin buying a football as a present for Victor:

> 'No, no,' said Pnin, 'I do not wish an egg or, for example, a torpedo. I want a simple football ball. Round!'
>
> And with wrists and palms he outlined a portable world. It was the same gesture he used in class when speaking of the 'harmonical wholeness' of Pushkin.[60]

In this 'portable world' Pnin hopes to meet Victor and find solace for his friendlessness as well as a sanctuary for his frustrated love, a small eden (*Martin Eden* is the book he fails to buy for Victor). His sad effort to give some small part of his life the 'harmonical wholeness' of great art is frustrated by the illusoriness of art and the equal illusoriness of life. His house is another private world snatched from him *en passant* by the aggressive colleague whom Humbert Humbert styles McFate, the chess opponent whom the clearsighted Middle Ages represented as Death. Victor doesn't like football and is too old for Jack London (he has got to the stage of reading *Crime and Yawn*) but his beautiful present to Pnin (too beautiful to be quite convincing, and that presumably is the point) proves that the 'son' has acknowledged his 'water father'.[61] If the overcoat is Akaky's mistress, as Nabokov suggests, by virtue of the longing and the joy with which he invests it, the aquamarine flint glass bowl in the washing-up water is symbolic of Pnin's lost and thwarted love. The superb timing of the dramatic sequence in which he almost breaks it forces the reader to share his own sense of its ineffable value. Gesture here becomes art: it is worthy of Chaplin.

The fictional world of *Pnin*, magicked into existence by a great shaman,[62] is dismissed by him too: not, as we have seen, with the autumnal glow of a retiring Prospero which critics have discovered in *Transparent Things*, but with the more than Gogolian sense that it is only a chance kink in space-time that releases life momentarily from the void that bounds it. Like Petrushka — whom the showman at the end of Stravinsky's ballet has shown to be just a doll stuffed with sawdust — Pnin proves that in some queer sense he *was* alive by returning to haunt New Wye (in *Pale Fire*), though his proper name has been dissolved once and for all into the 'preposterous little explosion' which is his 'true' identity.

## Notes to Chapter 7

1. I have referred to these critics in earlier chapters: the definitive study of their work remains Victor Erlich, *Russian Formalism* (The Hague: Mouton, 1969).
2. William E. Harkins, *Dictionary of Russian Literature* (Paterson, New Jersey: Littlefield, Adam and Co., 1959).
3. A theory of skaz also underlies Shklovsky's study of *Tristram Shandy* (Petrograd 1921: translated in Lemon and Reis, *Russian Formalist Criticism*).
4. Khlebnikov, the Futurist poet, who (with the other Futurists) was associated with the Formalists. Obviously this represents a very extreme view.
5. Victor Shklovsky, *Tristram Shandy Sterna i teoriya romana*, Petrograd 1921. See note 3, above.
6. Bely, Remizov, Pilnyak, Zoshchenko, Babel, Bulgakov and others are writers who use the 'skaz' techniques introduced by Gogol and Leskov. Cf. Boris Eikhenbaum, *Illuzia Skaza*, reprinted in Jurij Striedter, *Texte der Russischen Formalisten* (Munich: Fink, 1969) Vol. 1, p. 160 (the text is in Russian and German).
7. *Illuzia Skaza*, p. 160.
8. *Ibid.*, p. 164.
9. *Ibid.*, p. 166.
10. A French version of this essay is available in Todorov's anthology, *Théorie de la Littérature*. My own references are to the Russian text in Jurij Striedter, op. cit., p. 122.
11. I think this discussion of *Pnin* also throws light on Nabokov's study of Gogol, which is an essay in what Russian critics called 'ostranenie', 'making strange'.
12. Vladimir Nabokov, *Pnin* (Harmondsworth: Penguin Books, 1971) p. 55. The volume is actually called, in Nabokov's transcription, *Sovietskiy Zolotoy Fond Literatury*, or Soviet Gold Reserve of Literature.
13. Striedter, p. 122. The translations from this volume are my own.
14. *Ibid.*, p. 124.
15. *Ibid.*
16. *Ibid.* Reading such passages in Eikhenbaum's essay one thinks at once of Dickens.
17. *Ibid.*, p. 126.
18. *Ibid.*, p. 130. Eikhenbaum has a good phrase for 'automatism':

'okamenevshie pozy'.

19. Nikolai Gogol, *The Overcoat*, in *The Diary of a Madman and Other Stories* (New York and London: Signet Classics, 1960) transcription, *Sovietskiy Zolotoy Fond Literatury*, or Soviet Gold Reserve of Literature.
20. Quoted by Eikhenbaum, op. cit., p. 136. No translation does it justice.
21. Vladimir Nabokov, *Nikolai Gogol*, p. 149.
22. Gogol, *The Overcoat*, p. 72.
23. Cf. Matlaw, *Belinsky, Chernyshevsky, Dobrolyubov*.
24. Gogol, *The Overcoat*, p. 94.
25. A tone which lays bare (as the Formalists would say) the devices of realism by suggesting that not reality but the story is prior to the narrator, and has enlisted his talents in order to get itself told. The placing of the word 'unexpectedly' is a Gogolian thumbprint.
26. Vladimir Nabokov, *Pale Fire* (New York: Lancer Books, 1963) p. 189.
27. The Penguin Companion to Literature, Vol. 3 (Harmondsworth: Penguin Books, 1971), ed. M. Bradbury, E. Mottram and J. Franco.
28. Nabokov, *Gogol*, p. 2. In the Pushkin edition Nabokov seems to be saying that his study of Gogol was not quite serious. This is untrue, but there *is* a degree of strain in Nabokov's antihumanitarianism, absent from Eikhenbaum's.
29. *Ibid.*, p. 3.
30. I have already referred to Shklovsky's seminal essay. English criticism has by and large taken a different view of the novel tradition, largely because of the influence of Leavis. Such a book as Mendilow's *Time and the Novel*, however, is indebted to Shklovsky.
31. *Ibid.*, p. 1.
32. *Ibid.*, p. 7.
33. Gogol, *The Overcoat*, p. 74.
34. Nabokov, *Gogol*, p. 10. Petersburgers 'gesticulated in undertones' (*Ibid.*).
35. Nabokov, *Gogol*, p. 41.
36. *Ibid.*, p. 44.
37. *Ibid.*, p. 76. It is in this chapter, by the way, that Nabokov calls the U.S.A. 'this wise quiet country', thus demonstrating that everything is as relative as he claims it is.
38. Nowadays we see Tolstoy as a moralist: at the time, he was

accused of moral nihilism. It would be impossible to imagine a novelist morally more relativistic (not to say confused) than Dostoyevsky, the great prophet, as he was once considered.

39. Nabokov, *Gogol*, p. 83.
40. *Ibid*., p. 113. The conclusion of *Dead Souls* has received a lot of attention from apocalyptic exegetes.
41. Henri Bergson, *Laughter*, p. 153.
42. *Pnin*, p. 27.
43. *Ibid*., p. 33.
44. Gogol, *The Overcoat*, p. 71.
45. And from the comic to the cosmic, as Nabokov himself points out in his Gogol book, p. 142, is a distance of one sibilant.
46. *Pnin*, p. 35.
47. *Ibid*.
48. *Ibid*., p. 32.
49. *Ibid*., p. 36.
50. *Ibid*., p. 67.
51. *Ibid*., p. 30. As late as *Lolita* Nabokov turns foreignisms to good effect. Before *Pnin* the solecisms occasionally showed through the artifice.
52. The precise nature of the trick is different, of course: cf. *The Overcoat*, p. 176.
53. There seems no need to reiterate the fundamental understated fact that comedy is humanising. But Nabokov believes (with Bergson) that the human has come to be confused with the humanitarian.
54. The allusion is to Frank Kermode, *The Sense of an Ending* (London: O.U.P., 1969).
55. Cf. Viktor Shklovsky, *Isskustvo kak priyom*, translated Lemon and Reis (op. cit.) as *Art as Technique* (more commonly and accurately, *Art as Device*).
56. Gogol, *The Overcoat*, p. 70.
57. *Pnin*, p. 108. Language is character in action: in Russian Pnin is a precise but original scholar and critic (Nabokov, in fact).
58. Julia Bader (*Crystal Land*) is very good on squirrels.
59. There is no need to call Nabokov an impressionist, as Page Stegner does: yet these passages (pp. 78-82) of *Pnin* recall Chekhov's celebrated letter to his brother, which might be taken as a statement of impresionist theory. I think Nabokov's literature.
60. *Pnin*, p. 82.

61. This image is connected with that of the thirsty squirrel given a drink by Pnin, the creature which is his talisman, the 'shadow' which 'tails' him all the way from his Russian nursery (cf. Kinbote in *Pale Fire*).
62. Central Asian witchdoctor. If the analogy seems inappropriate, it seemed doubtfully apposite in the case of those Russian Futurists who donned the shaministic mantle in order to justify their ritualistic use of language. The point, however, is that it was here that sound and gesture as semantic items entered modern Russian literature and critical theory.

# VIII

## One Character in Search of an Author: **Pale Fire** (1962)

*Pale Fire* has been taken as Nabokov's masterpiece. It is certainly his most ingenious novel, the ingenuities serving here, as always, to point a moral as well as to adorn a tale. Couched as it is in the extraordinary form of a deranged and pedantic commentary appended by a mad Central European (if that is where Zembla is) scholar to a deceptively limpid all-American poem by a notably self-effacing poet (appropriately named Shade), its endless allusiveness tries to trap the reader into aping the professional critic, until he becomes ashamed of the rapt pseudo-creativity he feels at tracing recondite references. What the tone of Shade's poem really demands, with its homage to Robert Frost and its Augustan allusions (Frost is himself a kind of Augustan, and Shade has been writing a book on Pope), is a Johnsonian 'common reader'. No doubt one of the lesser ironies in the novel lies in this contradiction, and I believe that ultimately Kinbote's madness constitutes the final critique of Shade's urbanity. Nevertheless, in contradistinction to certain other critics, I propose to emulate Shade's way with materials which would not lie still in the formal frame of his poem — and destroy them, like those black butterflies spied by Kinbote rising from 'the pale fire of the incinerator'.[1] My comments, therefore, will stop well short of total exegesis.

This quotation is one of the sources of the novel's title. Another is *Timon of Athens*:

> The sun's a thief, and with his great attraction
> Robs the vast sea: the moon's an arrant thief
> And her pale fire she snatches from the sun! [2]

Either context for 'pale fire' reveals that the vexed relationship between Shade and Kinbote is alluded to. Kinbote, a recent immigrant from Zembla, which he has left for political reasons, has got hold of the index cards on which Shade's poem Pale Fire is written, after the poet's sudden tragic death. His brief friendship with the poet had been devoted to the monomaniac exposition of what he delicately refers to as 'the Zemblan theme', that is, the flight (in disguise) of the ex-king of Zembla, Charles the Belovèd, after the revolution in his capital, Onhava, in which he was overthrown, in the confident but futile hope that Shade would use it as the basis of the long poem he was engaged in writing. In point of fact Shade's poem contains one direct reference to Zembla evidently taken not from Kinbote but from the passage of Pope's 'Dunciad' in which he describes the activities of the goddess of Dulness (or maybe from Swift, since Nova Zembla is, in *The Battle of the Books*, the home of Criticism, who lies 'extended in her den upon the spoils of numberless volumes, half devoured'[3]). This of course does not satisfy Kinbote: in fact it drives him to despair and aggravates the paranoia from which he suffers (it is not at once evident that his narrative is addressed to a ghostly interlocutor he calls 'doctor': and while we have no reason to suppose he is writing from an asylum — as Humbert writes from prison — he is clearly on the way there, and the music that breaks in on him may not all come from the fairground outside his motel cabin). What Kinbote therefore does is no more than many other, less tenacious, critics have done: he supplements the 'inadequacies' of his author by means of his momentous commentary.[4]

His crudest device is, at line 12, to fake two 'discarded' lines in which the Zemblan theme is touched upon:

> As, I must not forget to say something
> That my friend told me of a certain king

Their sad ineptitude at once gives them away as wretched forgeries (the discovery adding — with how much justification? — to our sense of Shade's solid worth); and then, to compound the deed, he pathetically owns up to the imposture at line 550:

> Conscience and scholarship have debated the question, and I now think that the two lines given in that note are distorted and tainted by wishful thinking.

The innocence Kinbote manifests here (the helplessness of a character in search of an author confronted by the indifference of the universe and the shadowy god, the Shade who presides over it) is actually very moving, despite his grotesqueness. The pale fire of his commentary is all stolen from the sun; but the sun's a thief too (Shade is hardly a sun of course, but in Kinbote's eyes he lives eternally in Apollo's rays): the poet steals from Time, and Shade's poem is obsessed and shaped by mortality.[6] The creator of the *artistic* universe, the microcosm of the poem, is a shadowy figure whom we know of only through his works (acceptable Deism?). Indeed (and this is the Augustanism dissolved in the arbours and colonnades of pastoral New Wye — Shade lives between Wordsmith and Goldsworth and writes between Goldsmith and Wordsworth) the artist (like God) may be no more than the shadow thrown by his creation. All that is not Shade's poem, everything forbidden to enter the magic circle of the finished work, is a black butterfly a charred scrap caught for a moment in a pale fire: and such is Kinbote and the whole Zemblan dream. Kinbote is to Shade as Shade is to . . . what?

Despite the complexity of the novel, much of its material is familiar. In fact it picks up and elaborates a number of themes from earlier works, especially *Pnin*, another novel devoted to mollifying through comedy the ache of exile.[7] Kinbote, gazing absorbedly at the windows of the nearby Shade house and desperately trying to make his impress on the leathery Frostian poet, may be a different proposition from

Pnin, but the enchanted kingdom conjured up by Pnin's sense of homelessness (a land, perhaps, beyond the frontier of death — off the edge of the page) foreshadows Zembla. Victor is of course the link: the crystal bowl he gives to Pnin and the 'portable world' Pnin's gestures evoke in the sports shop (he is trying to describe a football) point to both the glass factory and endless mirrors of Onhava, and Aunt Maud's paperweight:

> the paperweight
> Of convex glass enclosing a lagoon.[8]

These stand for the autonomous and private world of art which does not reflect reality (is not a mirror held to nature) but encapsulates it; moreover that paperweight begins life in *Pnin* as

> a sad stylized toy, a bauble found in the attic, a crystal globe which you shake to make a soft luminous snowstorm inside over a miniscule firtree and a log cabin of papiermâché.[9]

The harder one gazes into these crystal balls (the snowy garden called by Shade 'that crystal land', his window projecting the room out on to the grass, at once starts Kinbote thinking about Zembla), the more clearly one sees that Kinbote's mirror-crazed fantasy about Zembla (which we have to accept as a 'real' country within the conventions of the fiction — and it is after all a derivation of the familiar cartographic corruption of Russian *zemlya*, or 'land', Nova Zembla being *Novaya Zemlya*, New Territory)[10] originates in an invert's regression to the consoling baubles of childhood — magnified by despair to the dimension of an alternative but lost world and refracted through the realities of the political tyranny which have banished him from it (and it from him) for ever. If we accept for the moment that Kinbote tells the truth, somewhere in Zembla, a country remembered only from childhood games, dressing up, playing at Kings and Queens and soldiers, Charles Kinbote was born, an outsider from the start by virtue of his homosexuality (it is clear that despite his ornate dreams of compliant page-boys his condition gave rise to bitter feelings of guilt and that he was subjected to pressure to become 'normal'). His inversion must serve him as the next best thing to the imaginative vision of the artist. His fantasy life is his creative life, but it is as ephemeral and unjustified as the emotional struggles of Pirandello's six characters unless he finds the author who will give him immortality (he will, of course, have no offspring, so that particular Shakespearian resolution of the problem is not open to him). The form his fantasy takes (the way in which he elects to arrogate the importance he feels adheres by rights to his rich inner life) is a reworking of Victor's fantasy in *Pnin* — which is to say that it is the common dream of the child born into difficult or uncongenial family surroundings, the masculine equivalent of the Cinderella story. Victor's 'real' family is, as we know, highly inadequate; his central European origins, again refracted (like Kinbote's fantasy) through political reality (the rise of Fascism followed by the Sovietization of Eastern Europe — the country bordering Zembla is gigantic Sosed, this being simply the Russian word for 'neighbour') form the basis of a reworking of the romantic tale of Bonnie Prince Charlie forced to flee from tyrannous (and physically unattractive) usurpers. This is history as taught in the school of Sir Walter Scott, a Romantic afterglow of Shakespearian history.

> The King, his father, wearing a very white sports shirt open at the throat and a very black blazer, sat at a spacious desk whose highly polished surface twinned his upper half in reverse, making of him a kind of court card . . . the main city square, where decapitations and folk dances had already started, despite the weather . . . 'Abdication! One-third of the alphabet!' coldly quipped the King, with the trace of an accent. 'The answer is no. I prefer the unknown quantity of exile.'[11]

Exile, that 'unknown quantity', is the Pninian surd that touches the absurd. Victor can call himself back to modern America and will evidently not come to grief — in any case, he is only for a moment the narrator of his own fantasies. But Kinbote is old, tired, and far more out of place in his milieu than Pnin, who, though isolated, can at least talk to his students and throw a party. Moreover, Kinbote is denied the mixed blessing of a creator (hence perhaps his compensatory religious piety concerning the 'other' creator) who might have ousted him as the narrator ousted Pnin but who might have immortalized him — the *real* Kinbote, Charles the Belovèd — in doing so. In fact, of course, Kinbote is actually waiting and hoping to be assassinated (and by the Shadows, at that, who are a short of Shade-substitute) since his surrender to the aggression of the political police would be a confirmation of the reality of his claims to be the exiled king, the *solus rex* of Victor's fantasy,[12] and prove his fitness to be the hero of the fiction which is his own life (Kinbote is a displaced person in more senses than the bureaucratic). A conspiracy in the Glass Works, a strong plot, is in fact his only hope of salvation.[12] But Victor's fantasy-father's tight-lipped joke ('Abdication! One-third of the alphabet!') raises, in *Pnin*, another issue explored in depth in *Pale Fire*. The Bolsheviks reformed the Russian alphabet, expunging unnecessary letters along with those other 'whoreson zeds' their political opponents. The king in exile, refusing to abdicate, takes with him his language, snatched from hands of the philistines, and it forms the substance of his 'portable world'. Other modern artists (Joyce, Kafka, Lawrence among them) have been in this sense 'kings in exile'.[13]

*Pale Fire* is, as I have said, a gift to the explicator (actually a fatal poison wrapped up like a chocolate cream). It explicitly contains its own appropriate critical apparatus, complicated by numerous false clues. Many of these depend on the Russian elements in Zemblan, that charming mixture of Germanic and Slavonic roots. Thus, for example, a *shootka* (note to line 493) is not a little parachute, but the Russian for 'a joke' (even, by a linguistic stretch, a 'small buffoon');[14] the name of the conspirator Izumrudov, who pays a visit to Gradus in the note to line 741, does not mean 'of the Eskimos tribe of the Umruda' but derives from the Russian word *izumrud*, 'emerald', indicating that this stage villain who, Kinbote bitterly supposes, goes off 'to resume his whoring' in the midst of his murderous quest is a paranoid's double of Gerald Emerald, the loathsome green-jacketed instructor at Wordsmith who casually and insultingly refers to the King of Zembla (pictured in an encyclopaedia) as probably homosexual:

> 'Young, handsome, and wearing a fancy uniform,' continued Emerald. 'Quite the fancy pansy, in fact.'
>
> 'And you,' I said quietly, 'are a foul-mouthed pup in a cheap green jacket.'[15]

These are bonuses for the erudite, though Nabokov even here does not make the demands on his reader's scholarship that Joyce does. It is self-destructive, however, to suppose that a total exegesis is the same as an appreciation and evaluation. What *is* clear is that Kinbote's rich interlingua is a derivative of the opacities of literary language that modernism has inherited from Mallarmé's ambition to 'donner un sens plus pur aux mots de la tribu'. As such it is thoroughly European, as intrinsically a product of the estranged artistic sensibility of an ancient conglomeration of distinct nations and cultures as Shade's idiom is the poised and lucid expression of a circumscribed, perhaps slightly philistine, but stable New England (hence the 'Augustanism' which Shade shares with his real-life co-eval Frost[16]). Shade and Kinbote are both wordsmiths: but where Shade has the talent (and the limitations?) to forge the achieved object, Kinbote is trapped in his web of words experiencing in the texture of language itself the hopeless dividedness of his psyche (in this he is like Humbert). He is not only the character in search of an author; he is, like Humbert, the bearer of a whole wasteland of cultural fragments which he has shored against his ruin — myths of a decayed and deposed aristocracy, the ghost of the mind of Europe, an encyclopaedism based on the obscure supposition that painstaking work to extend the frontiers of knowledge will contribute to the advance of humane learning, but expressed in the baroque intricacies, paradoxes, puns of a Joyce — in whose work taxonomic exactitude cohabits with infinite relativism. In his more comic aspects he may be no more than a walking collage in search of a card index; but he is also a tragic figure in his hopeless affirmation of the reality of his dream kingdom and in his quest for redemption.

Human mortality and the power of art to overcome time are the central themes of *Pale Fire*. To say this is not to go very far, since the same could be said of Shakespeare's *Sonnets*. The specific forms in which Nabokov has chosen to embody his theme are, however, rich, beguiling, and highly original. Shade, although he describes the age of Pope as 'preposterous', has sought (and found: the poem, though no masterpiece, is successful) a pastiche equivalent for the Augustan couplet. Frost had of course hit off a kind of Augustan idiom before him; as C. Day Lewis writes in an essay on him:

> When we come across lines such as 'Or highway where the slow wheel pours the sand,' or 'The swamp dilating round the perfect trees', or 'To warm the frozen swamp as best it could/With the slow smokeless burning of decay', we hear the Augustan manner, but sharpened — as Crabbe sharpened it — by close realistic observation, and informed with 'a calm eagerness of emotion'.[17]

And with this careful deliberateness goes an assumption about the moral concern of art and a purity and chastity of language which, though repossessed by Shade deviously and by deliberate choice, does constitute an element of the sensibility we think of as characteristically New England — is, in fact, part of his inheritance as inescapably as translated Shakespeare is part of Kinbote's. Frost's preferred seclusion, like Shade's, did not imply subjectivism, since his most personal poetry shapes itself in relation to a particular landscape and community (the family is a focal point, as for Shade) implying shared and safeguarded moral values together with a New England exclusiveness and hatred of promiscuity. Frost's observation that a poem 'begins in delight and ends in wisdom'[18] is a post-Wordsworthian variant of the classical requirement that poetry shall instruct by pleasing. And although Frost's poetic world contains its share of terrible and incomprehensible things, his own laconicism in the face of them implies a strategy for mastering them and a will equal to it (disaster and sudden death in the well-known *'Out, out'* is handled in a manner similar to that in which Shade treats of the death of his daughter, the central theme of the poem *Pale Fire* which mad Kinbote quite misses). There is nothing excessive or gratuitous in Frost's relationship with his poetic material, and above all (and this is of course a moral as well as an artistic quality) no trace of self-indulgence. In him the rational humanism of the eighteenth century is transmitted in a recognizably New England form, accompanied by a deep-rooted instinct for survival. And although Shade's world has more gloss and gadgetry about it than Frost's, and its pastoralism is as literary as Frost's is homespun, the kinship remains. All this is, of course, achieved by a partial denial of the outside world which is at the same time a rejection of history in favour of pastoral. Pnin's first university was called Waindell. In *Pale Fire* we are in New Wye, another version of pastoral of the kind deemed (though no-one knew why) appropriate for 'older' seats of learning in the New World and newer ones in the old. A campus is still at heart a field, though carefully tonsured. Homage to Wordsworth in this name is echoed by homage to Shakespeare in the proud avenue made up of all the trees mentioned in his plays (a sort of leafy card-index). Shade has an eye for landscape and a love of foliage, is sensitive to the effects of light on a favourite shagbark tree and iridules in the mountains, and echoes Wordsworth's *Ode on Intimations of Immortality* in both sound and sense — though in couplets, and with more than a dash of the late Augustan (Johnson, Goldsmith, Cowper) — throughout the earlier part of his poem — as in the opening of Canto Two:

> There was a time in my demented youth
> When somehow I suspected that the truth
> About survival after death was known
> To every human being: I alone
> Knew nothing, and a great conspiracy
> Of books and people hid the truth from me.

(cf. Wordsworth's 'There was a time when meadow, grove and stream . . .'). In general Shade is closer to Wordsworth, Wordsmith closer to Goldsmith, or indeed to Pope, whose 'Windsor Forest' opens with the conjunction of a Monarch and a Muse

> Thy forests, Windsor! and thy green retreats,
> At once the Monarch's, and the Muse's seats,
> Invite my lays. Be present, sylvan maids!
> Unlock your springs, and open all your shades.[19]

and in lines 41-2 celebrates the English royal family immortalized by colourful exile:

> Rich Industry sits smiling on the plains,
> And peace and plenty tell, a STUART reigns.[20]

We have Kinbote's sad example to remind us that that way madness lies; anyway, there aren't actually any 'sylvan maids' in Kinbote's line of vision, only Sybil Shade (the poem is, to borrow Hopkins's title, spelt from Sybil's leaves) whom he loathes.

Kinbote's rococo fantasies of the Zembla of his youth, the paradise of erotic distractions where kittenish Fleur, who is described as 'pretty but not repellent', has the not uncongenial job of seducing the king and producing an heir while

> beyond the vestibule of his vigil (here he began falling asleep), in the dark cold gallery, lying all over the painted marble and piled three or four deep against the locked door, some dozing, some whimpering, were his new boy pages, a whole mountain of gift boys from Troth, and Tuscany, and Albanoland.[21]

— such fantasies compensate Kinbote for the suffering inflicted by what he (and Nabokov) can only regard as a peculiarly nasty period of history. Between the creation from the void of magical Zembla and the rooted domesticities of New Wye there is an impenetrable divide, and one which Shade is in any case not interested in crossing; and this is not altogether to his credit. Zembla, in other words, is not just the Swiftian home of the dreary goddess of Criticism, nor an allusion in 'The Dunciad'.

It is a chaotic, baroque fairyland of the imagination into which Shade will never be allowed to penetrate. His disciplined art, founded on an acceptance of the limitations of the phenomenal world, is accompanied by a certain failure of sympathy, made manifest in *Pale Fire* through the Johnsonian allusions. The epigraph has an obvious aptness, casting Kinbote as Boswell to Shade's Johnson (a role which the American Augustan enjoys). But beyond this, it evokes the scheme of the novel in microscom: the violent young madman of the epigraph serves economically to allude to the Zemblan theme and its mad inventor, while Johnson's concern for Hodge, greater by far than his interest in the fate of the young man, embodies Shade's unconcern with Kinbote's misery and loneliness. Johnson himself took a more sympathetic interest in disorders of the intellect, which he feared as he feared death, and which he felt to be lying in wait for the scholar, who necessarily cultivates solitude. *Rasselas*[22] has a fine section devoted to this subject, in which the young Prince of Abyssinia meets a mad astronomer who believes he has been entrusted with absolute control over the seasons (he is therefore a kind of artist who, in arrogating a God-like role, comes to believe in the literal reality of his symbolic fictions). Imlac, Rasselas's tutor, thinks the astronomer's ravings worthy of a detailed commentary, and begins by counselling charity:

> 'Ladies,' said Imlac, 'to mock the heaviest of human afflictions is neither charitable nor wise. Few can attain this man's knowledge, and few practise his virtues; but all may suffer his calamity. Of the uncertainties of our present state, the most dreadful and alarming is the uncertain continuance of reason.'[23]

Johnson's approach to what he elsewhere calls 'the invisible riot of the mind' is thoroughly classical. But Imlac manifests here an understanding of the predicament, compared to Kinbote's, and advocates a remedy, unlike Shade, who is too involved in his poetry to do either. Moreover, the 'reign of fancy' acquires a seductive beauty in the process of evocation:

> To indulge the power of fiction and send imagination out upon the wing is often the sport of those who delight too much in silent speculation. When we are alone we are not always busy; the labour of excogitation is too violent to last long; the ardour of inquiry will sometimes give way to idleness or satiety. He who has nothing external that can divert him must find pleasure in his own thoughts, and must conceive himself what he is not; for who is pleased with what he is? He then expatiates in boundless futurity, and culls from all imaginable conditions that which for the present moment he should most desire, amuses his desires with impossible enjoyments, and confers upon his pride unattainable dominion. The mind dances from scene to scene, unites all pleasures in all combinations, and riots in delights which Nature and fortune, with all their bounty, cannot bestow. . . . By degrees the reign of fancy is confirmed; she grows first imperious and in time despotic.[24]

A better description of Kinbote's malady could not be found. Imlac's solution (which works) is frequent feminine company, soothing and civilizing: a remedy not available to poor Kinbote.[25] The allure of Fancy's reign (explicitly set against Nature) insinuates itself unbidden as does the beauty of artifice in the ostensibly derisive passage of 'The Dunciad' in which Zembla is invoked, reminding us that strange creatures inhabit the looking-glass land of art, the distorting mirror held up to misshapen 'natural' phenomena: the queen, Dulness,

> . . . sees a Mob of Metaphors advance,
> Pleas'd with the madness of the mazy dance;
> How Tragedy and Comedy embrace;
> How Farce and Epic get a jumbled race;
> How Time himself stands still at her command,
> Realms shift their place, and Ocean turns to land.
> Here gay Description Egypt glads with show'rs,
> Or gives to Zembla fruits, to Barca flowr's;
> Glitt'ring with ice here hoary hills are seen,
> There painted valleys of eternal green;

In cold December fragrant chaplets blow,
And heavy harvest nod beneath the snow.[26]

The Johnson and Pope passages, both relevant to *Pale Fire*, are instances of inevitable flaws in Augustan order, reminding us that this novel is in toto a romantic fictionalized biography organizing itself in relation to an urbane neoclassical poem: they are inextricably bound together, an interdependence reinforced by the fact that Kinbote's references to Shade's poem are supported by queer hints at Kinbote's commentary in Shade's poem (e.g. at 1.938:

*Man's life as commentary to abstruse*
*Unfinished poem.* Note for further use).

Interpenetrations of this kind in fact abound in the novel, binding together Kinbote's fantasy, Wordsmith University, Shade's life, and Shade's poem into an artefact of immense intricacy won from that void and abyss which haunt the whole rash enterprise of human life and endeavour. Everywhere there is a sense of the fragility of life and the closeness of death: Shade is already in fact dead when the novel opens, after an earlier experience of momentary death produced by a heart attack, and his poem is a Shade's reflection upon death, the death of his daughter, and an affirmation of the goodness of life. Kinbote's stiff piety and Calvinist sense of sin (contrasted with Shade's Enlightenment Deism — 'Personally, I am with the old snuff-takers: L'homme est né bon') is accompanied by a fear of death. Shade's poem is written against despair, or death-in-life; the characteristically off-hand references to Eliot mock 'The Waste Land' by flagrantly borrowing from it:

'If you're not sleeping, let's turn on the light.
I hate that wind! Let's play some chess.' 'All right.'
(11.611-12)

and dismiss the metaphysics of *Four Quartets* in lines 368-79 without deigning to name the poem:

'It does not matter what it was she read
(some phony modern poem that was said
In English Lit. to be a document
'Engazhay and compelling' — what this meant
Nobody cared).[27]

In addition, the poem finds in nature refracted through art and memory those few 'shoots of everlastingness' which we intermittently glimpse through the bars of our artistic cage (cf. line 114).[28] For Kinbote the problem and its solution take on a different form: unbearably lonely, trapped in a sense of alienation and sin reinforced by his homosexuality, he tries to transcend the present altogether, to melt it quite away in his memories and fantasies, which are so densely woven that the facts from which they originate can be only very dimly discerned. His unhappy marriage can just be made out behind the fictions in which he has veiled it. His fear and suspicion of his university colleagues is present momentarily in its own terms, but mostly disguised in the saga of Izumrudov and the Shadows. Odd details of the Zemblan theme reveal their origin in the context from which he writes it, the context of his flight from New Wye (the king still in exile) and of his precarious existence in uncongenial motels. (In the note to line 810 we are told that the owner of his motel, who looks a bit like Shade, sells worms to fishermen. This detail penetrates the saga of the King's flight, since little shops in the Zemblan mountains sell 'worms, ginger bread, and *zhiletka* blades'. Much odder, of course, is the reappearance of this well-known proprietary brand of razor blade, stripped of its Slavonic disguise, in the poem itself — it is the Gillette Shade shaves with — and in the bloody suicide of Shade's killer, who cuts his throat with a safety razor blade.)

Cross-references of this kind have led critics to speculate on the possibility of Shade being the author of both poem and commentary, or of Kinbote having dreamed up Shade as well as Zembla[29]; but one might as well contend that Gloucester created King Lear, or Hamlet Claudius. Nabokov presides over the total structure of *Pale Fire* as commandingly as he does over his Pushkin translation and commentary,[30] from which the novel evidently derives. Kinbote is related to Nabokov: not just because he is a mad exiled exegete, and Nabokov is indulging in light self-mockery, but because in translating and editing Pushkin's poem Nabokov, clearly, not only combed English and French eighteenth-century literature for the sources of many of Pushkin's key locutions and metaphors — the results can be seen in *Pale Fire*'s Augustanisms and the archaisms of the Pushkin translation — but also, by doing so, introduced an historical 'plot' into what he over and over again insists ought to be read as poetry and not as social history or (and he accuses Soviet scholars of this) social criticism of a radical and revolutionary bent. His commentary is a *Gradus ad Parnassum*: a shadowy scholarly schema contrived only to help the reader ascend the heights of a great poem, yet always on the verge of imposing a form of its own, evolving a ghostly anti-hero (Jakob Gradus) with his own 'plot', inimical to the 'real' hero, the poet himself, Pushkin or Shade. Soviet critics, Nabokov claims, are always foisting tawdry historical costume-dramas on to Pushkin (see, for instance, his notes on Pushkin's *Ode to Liberty*[31]). These are easily dealt with; but the scrupulous scholar is still open to the temptation to read too much into the rough drafts and discarded stanzas he turns up in his researches, and to guess at Pushkin's 'intentions' in passages he in fact expunged or omitted. And in the case of *Eugene Onegin* — the first great masterpiece of Russian literature, and incalculably influential on the development of later writers — the temptation to get as close as possible to the author, to penetrate the devices and disguises by means of which he reveals and conceals himself in his own work,[32] is as attractive as comparable intrusions have proved in the case of Shakespeare.

In his commentary, Nabokov stresses among other things the poise and harmony of Pushkin's art.[33] A masterly diagnostician of that spiritual disease of hypochondria which the English eighteenth century liked to abbreviate to 'hyp' and the Russian nineteenth century adopted as *khandra* ('chondria')[34], he never succumbs to it in his art, though in his life he did. Still less does he promote it to the status of a muse and a creative mystery as does Byron (whom Pushkin read avidly, filtered through the sobriety of a French prose translation[35]). The tumult of the imagination fashionable in the period, and associated in Russia with Romantic cults of revolutionary fraternalism promulgated by the Decembrists,[36] doubtless played its part in the shaping of Pushkin's sensibility, but as an artist he presents it only to distance and transcend it. His contemporaries found *Eugene Onegin* cold and uncommitted:[37] noone more so than Küchelbecker, the source of Nabokov's Kinbote. This minor poet and dramatist, who combined a Kinbotian penchant for sub-Shakespearian theatricals with an emotive historicism which led to his part in the Decembrist uprising and consequent exile, passionately admired Pushkin but wanted him always to be a different kind of writer from what he was in actuality.[38] Both he and Pushkin belonged to the modernizing faction (a debate between archaists and modernizers comparable to that satirized in *The Battle of the Books*, and echoed in *Pale Fire*, raged throughout the period[39]); but Küchelbecker's modernism was as turbid as Pushkin's was urbane. His chief critical claim to fame is an essay asserting the merits of the ode against the elegy, specifically criticizing the mundane predictability of Pushkin's elegies. Nabokov comments on this in a long and sympathetic note on Küchelbecker, in the course of which he mentions that Pushkin replied to it by accusing him

> of confusing 'vostorg' (the initial rapture of creative perception) with 'vdohnovenie' (true inspiration, cool and continuous, 'which is necessary in poetry as well as in geometry').[40]

For his part in the uprising Küchelbecker was first sentenced to death; but the sentence was commuted to twenty years' imprisonment and exile to Siberia. He served only half of the sentence, but it was enough to destroy him. In his poetry of exile he projects his own sense of futility and despair into historical personages, seeing himself as King David, or as Ahasuerus, the Wandering Jew, in a Kinbotian effort to find some artistic meaning in a shattered life. Johnson believed that a melancholy madness was always lying in wait for the man of letters; from Nabokov's earlier novels, and from the sympathetic tone of his role on Küchelbecker, we may assume that he shares this view:

> Only at the very end of a singularly sad and futile literary career, and in the twilight of his life, first jeered at by friend and foe alike, then forgotten by all; a sick, blind man, broken by years of exile, Küchelbecker produced a few admirable poems, one of which is a brilliant masterpiece, a production of first-rate genius — the twenty-line-long *Destiny of Russian Poets* (written in the province of Tobolsk, 1845). I quote its last lines:
>
> . . . thrown into a black prison,<br>
> killed by the frost of hopeless banishment;
>
> or sickness overcasts with night and gloom<br>
> the eyes of the inspired, the seers!<br>
> Or else the hand of some vile lady's man<br>
> impels a bullet at their sacred brow;<br>
> Or the deaf rabble rises in revolt —<br>
> and him the rabble will to pieces tear<br>
> whose winged course, ablaze with thunderbolts,<br>
> might drench in radiance the motherland.
>
> The bullet killed Pushkin, the rabble murdered Griboedov.[41]

— to which one might add that the bullet, aimed not by the 'vile ladies' man' Gerald Emerald (Izumrudov) but by mad Jack Grey (Gradus) killed Shade, but not Kinbote, who was denied this classic entry to Parnassus. The status of Shade's poem remains problematic, since it is hardly the work of a latterday Pushkin; but it works well enough within the total context of a novel which, while never losing its point and pathos, seems to be marred only by a certain archness: a more serious flaw in *Ada*, where literary history has become a superior *divertissement*.

## Notes to Chapter 8

1. Vladimir Nabokov, *Pale Fire* (New York: Lancer Books, 1962) p.9.
2. Shakespeare, *Timon of Athens*, Act IV, Scene 3. On pp. 57-8 (notes to lines 39-40) Kinbote quotes an Englished version of Conmal's Zemblan translation of Shakespeare; it contains about fifty per cent of Shakespeare's meaning, and none of his poetry. Timon, in his bitter melancholia, finds that Nature's 'great chain of being' is in fact a great chain of thieving. The case relates to Kinbote's own (cf. his reference to his note to 1.962).
3. The battle between the ancients and the moderns, Swift's theme, is in the largest way relevant to *Pale Fire*. This will emerge later, I think, in my discussion of the relationship between Pushkin and Küchelbecker.
4. Critics have taken a good deal of masochistic pleasure in this spoof, as if afraid of being caught not laughing. The point is that the editor of a text cannot help imposing a schema upon it.
5. Cf. Chapter 7, above.
6. The prevailing philosophy of the book is a late enlightenment mixture of Deism and occultism, as promulgated by (for example) Mozart and Pushkin. Late eighteenth century poetry produced a kind of melancholy madness quite different from Romantic transports. In *Speak, Memory* Nabokov has himself admitted to dabbling in occultism, and the *Eugene Onegin* edition has a long note on Pushkin's odd interest in such matters.
7. There are crucial differences. Zembla is not Russia (though evidently Nurseryland). The Zemblan language, a fusion of Germanic and Slavonic elements (cf. *Bend Sinister*) is a tissue of word-games. It is not, however, self-explanatory, for some of the jokes only make sense if you know Russian.
8. *Pale Fire*, p. 25.
9. *Pnin*, p. 38. Motifs of this kind play a crucial part in *Pnin*: the log-cabin, for example, reappears on p. 49, conjured up (of course) by a squirrel (glossed in the novel as 'shadow-tail'). It is the fate of the emigré to be tailed by shadows and move among shades.
10. In *Speak, Memory* the index entry for Nova Zembla refers us to Novaya Zemlya: we learn that there is a river in Novaya

Zemlya called 'Nabokov's River' after the author's great-grandfather, Nikolay Aleksandrovich Nabokov, who helped map Nova Zembla in 1817 (i.e. during the Romantic period). Cf. *The Refrigerator Awakes, Poems,* 1961.

11. *Pnin,* p. 71. On the loss of a language, its pathos, and at the same time the challenge to be inordinately inventive, see *An Evening of Russian Poetry* (which I have already referred to) in *Poems,* 1961.
12. Enough has been said, I think, to show that Nabokov questions the temporal conventions (and indeed the ontological status) of representational art. 'Plot' is the most strongly marked convention of the realist novel, if one takes the word 'plot' as synonymous with 'story', as it is in common usage. It is a time-bound plot (and a historical one, moreover) that Kinbote wishes to impose upon Shade's poem, thus redeeming history and himself along with it.
13. Mythic languages are to be found in the work of each of these writers, or a concern with the special nature and status of art language: Stephen Daedalus is the fabulous wordsmith, Kafka's *In the Penal Settlement* opposes text-as-machine to text-as-communication, Lawrence creates a synthetic dialect as a medium of 'pure' feeling, etc. In each case, the writer is a refugee whose richest treasure is language.
14. 'Shoot' is in Russian a court jester (Cf. Prokoviev's ballet of this title). Rather than a diminutive, it may actually be just a lower-class variant. In the Pushkin commentary (Vol. 2, p. 106) Nabokov notes that 'before the era of Soviet provincialization' the variant 'zhiletka' for 'zhilet' (Fr. 'gilet', a waistcoat) was thought vulgar. The connection with the well-known brand of razor blade is a fortuitous *trouvaille* of *Pale Fire.*
15. *Pale Fire,* pp. 189-90.
16. . . . my name.
    Was mentioned twice, as usual just behind
    (one oozy footstep) Frost.
    (*Pale Fire,* 11. 424-6 of Shade's poem.)
17. Robert Frost, *Selected Poems* with an introduction by C. Day Lewis (Harmondsworth: Penguin Books, 1955) p. 13.
18. Quoted by Day Lewis, op. cit., p. 15.
19. Alexander Pope, *Windsor Forest,* in *Poetical Works* (London: Macmillan and Co., 1930) p. 31. This is the opening of the poem — one of innumerable texts evidently scrutinized by Nabokov in the quest for a vocabulary in which to translate Pushkin.

20. *Ibid.*
21. *Pale Fire*, p. 81.
22. I am aware of the fact that Nabokov, with an unaccountable error of taste and judgement, describes Johnson's masterpiece as 'insipid' (*Eugene Onegin*, Vol. 3, p. 402).
23. Samuel Johnson, *Rasselas* (London: George Routledge and Sons, n.d.) p. 252.
24. *Ibid.*, p. 255.
25. His homosexuality is represented, against the domesticity of the Shades, as a sad disability.
26. Alexander Pope, *The Dunciad*, Bk. 1, 11.67-78.
27. *Pale Fire*, p. 33. This is Shade's voice, not Nabokov's; but I have noted elsewhere the apparent denigration and actual assimilation of Eliot in Nabokov's work.
28. *Ibid.*, p. 26.
29. It seems to me that such theories (like the theory that *Bend Sinister* is all Krug's dream) are in the end based on a naïve notion of character in fiction.
30. A. S. Pushkin, *Eugene Onegin* (London: Routledge and Kegan Paul, 1964). Cognoscenti may recall the acrimonious debate between Nabokov and Edmund Wilson on the subject of this translation, at the centre of which was the pastiche, synthetic nature of the English into which Nabokov chose to render Pushkin. Nabokov's commentary is almost as vivid as Kinbote's.
31. *Ibid.*, Vol. 3, pp. 336-7.
32. I would like to print here one short note from the *Commentary* in its entirety: it is Vol. 2, p. 78: One, XVII, 9.

    > Onegin poletel k teatru: Onegin has made off for the theater but does not fly fast enough: his fellow hero, Pushkin, outstrips him, and has been at the theater for three stanzas (XVIII, XIX, XX) when Onegin arrives there (XXI). The Pursuit Theme, with its alternate phases of overtaking and lagging behind, will last till XXXVI.

    *Pale Fire*, *Pnin*, and other Nabokov novels have 'pursuit themes' in which there is a complex relationship of this kind between fiction and narrator. In a sense Gradus (Degree, Grey) is in the pay of Nabokov, the plot-maker.
33. Cf. my first chapter.
34. Nabokov, op. cit., Vol. 3, pp. 150-56.
35. Nabokov and Wilson disagreed about the extent of Pushkin's knowledge of English. It seems clear, at any rate, that, like

his contemporaries, he read English literature mostly in French.

36. On the death of Alexander I a group of well-born army officers, in quasi-masonic lodges, organized an abortive uprising. The event is to this day shrouded in romance.
37. The Decembrist poets generally found *Eugene Onegin* a disappointment: cf. V. K. Küchelbecker, *Izbranniye Proizvedeniya v dvukh tomakh* (Moscow-Leningrad: Soviet Writer, 1967) p. 37. The editor (N. Koroleva) suggests plausibly enough that the absence of agitational 'rapture' irked them. The parallel with *Pale Fire* is clear.
38. Cf. *Eugene Onegin*, Vol. 2, pp. 448-50.
39. *Ibid.*, Vol. 2, p. 29.
40. *Ibid.*, Vol. 2, pp. 445-50.
41. *Ibid.*, p. 447.

# IX

## Nabokov's Unreal Estate: **Speak, Memory** (1967), **Ada** (1969) and **Transparent Things** (1972)

In the preface to his revised version of his autobiography (once called *Conclusive Evidence* — evidence, that is, of having existed), Nabokov tells us that he had wanted to retitle it *Speak, Mnemosyne*. It may be just as well that his publisher resisted; yet the reference to the Classical Mother of the Muses was not gratuitous. Memory is to Nabokov what it is to Proust, a rich actuality through the medium of which art discloses the truth of things.[1] It is, however, true that, just as Proust's Time defines itself only in and through his novel, Nabokov's Memory comes into being, is apprehensible, only as the process of writing (and reading) these three late books.[2] In the introduction to *Speak, Memory* he tells us also that he has a bad (or rather an 'anomalous') memory, following this by an excursus upon the difference between the Julian and the Gregorian calendar which foreshadows the relativized time and space of *Ada*. But to hold this vagueness against Nabokov is as misguided as objecting that Proust is imprecise about dates. *Speak, Memory* must be regarded as a work of fiction; which is to say that it is scrupulously truthful to Nabokov's 'real' life (cf. *Sebastian Knight*[3]).

The Proustian note in all three works is explicit, the first paragraph of *Speak, Memory* sounding this keynote clearly. The young chronophobiac (Nabokov's own term) who saw, on family film shot before his birth, the black pram waiting to receive him like a coffin, has in a sense survived his own death[4] (a feat accomplished in more and less legitimate ways by other Nabokov characters: Shade, Smurov — in *The Eye* — Van Veen, Hugh Person, even Hermann in *Despair*), and the fright it gives him is no more than the sense of severance from an earlier (now remembered) 'dead' self, which may also serve (as in Shade's case) to effect a penetration of Proustian time (formerly called eternity). The fragility of human life, everywhere a dominant theme in his work, is here most fully explored: that curious existence of ours which is 'a brief crack of light between two eternities of darkness'. The future we cannot know; the hero of *Ada* even proves (to his own satisfaction, at least) that it does not exist. But our present is a quondam future since we are on the hither side of an existence once ours. To meet up with that strange person we once were (who also contains our might-have-beens), to set him free from the trap of the third person past tense in which he has been caught in so many 'realistic' reworkings of events, is one way of passing through the looking glass.

Nabokov dispenses his facts sparingly in *Speak, Memory*, and there is very little 'historical' information. When he insists that the loss of his family wealth and estates after the Revolution did not trouble him, this rings true: his personal and inward sense of continuity needs no historical or material support (in fact, like his beloved butterflies, it is more typicallv itself in flight than at rest). He is proud of his ancestors, but evokes them by means of their oddities rather than their glories. He enjoyed the spacious freedom of the life of a well-born child of a prominent (though liberal, and once imprisoned) father, but he censures Eliot (with whose *Four Quartets* these three novels have much in common) and Pasternak for conservative myth-making about lost continuities, vanished orders, exhausted and betrayed symbols. 'The Waste Land' and *Four Quartets*, are, as I have said, slighted in *Pale Fire*, though Eliot is not named. In *Ada* we read of the 'old real-estate magnate

Milton Eliot' as well as

> solemn Kithar Sween, a banker who at sixty-five had become an *avant-garde* author; in the course of one miraculous year he had produced *The Waistline*, a satire in free verse on Anglo-American feeding habits, and *Cardinal Grishkin*, an overtly subtle yarn extolling the Roman faith.[5]

Ardis Hall, in *Ada*, is a pastiche mock-up of all the ancestral houses of lost symbolist childhoods from Poe to Eliot; while history, far from being 'now and England', is a sideshow which in *Speak, Memory* intrudes upon the attention only intermittently, and is either comic or nasty (or both). In *Ada* it is the chronicle of another, fallen, world known as Terra (terrifying indeed) where events run oddly parallel at times to those of the 'real' world, Van and Ada's Demonia, but are marked by gratuitous brutality. In *Speak, Memory* the Russo-Japanese War is an edgy incident in a café[6] and some Japanese propaganda pictures of Russian locomotives falling through the ice on Lake Baikal, which merge simultaneously into the toy trains which the young Nabokov tried to run over frozen puddles in Wiesbaden (in the winter of 1904[7]). The point is not that history is bunk, but that one is immersed in it as one is in Time: its metamorphoses can be traced in the microcosm of one's consciousness but its rhetoric need not delay us. It is easy to accuse Nabokov of political indifferentism; but in fact his father's liberalism (it was not easy to be a liberal in Russia; as I have mentioned, some Russian fascists cleared an old score by assassinating him in Berlin after the Revolution) has left a strong mark on his work.[8] His delight in individual liberty, in freedom of movement and of consciousness, is the serious core of the gossamer fantasies of *Ada*, and his sense of his authorial powers over the 'portable worlds' he creates and the characters who dwell in them is qualified by a recurrent urge to break open the structures of the text and set free the creatures caught in the webs of his metaphors.[9] *Speak, Memory* offers a special perspective on this; as he says at the beginning of Chapter Five,

> I have often noticed that after I had bestowed on the characters of my novels some treasured item of my past, it would pine away in the artificial world where I had so abruptly placed it.

The strict thematic coherence of *Speak, Memory* can be seen either as the result of the hand of the novelist imposing a pattern on life, or as life — registered by the seismographic novelistic consciousness — imposing its pattern on events. Oscar Wilde, confronting the materialism and determinism of his time, proclaimed that, far from art imitating nature, nature imitated art (London sunsets producing passable imitations of Turner). Nabokov takes a stricter taxonomic view: the amazing disguises of chrysalis and butterfly exceed the demands of 'the struggle for life', a protective device being

> carried to a point of mimetic subtlety, exuberance and luxury far in excess of a predator's power of appreciation. I discovered in nature the nonutilitarian delights that I sought in art. Both were a form of magic, both were a game of intricate enchantment and deception.[10]

In both there is immanent, though undeclared, the transcendent 'theme' which we half-sense as we half-sense Time (and in pursuit of which Nabokov and his Shade confess to sundry unworthy dallyings with spooks[11]). Motifs wander across the Pacific (like that intrepid butterfly in Chapter Six of *Speak, Memory* which Nabokov pursued in Russia and 'finally' overtook 'after a forty-year race' in Colorado). Nabokovian metaphors (which here might more properly be called conceits) yoke together the most heterogeneous ideas in defiance of laws of time and space, and, as in the Marvell's metaphysical poetry, cited so lovingly in *Ada*,[12] imagination liberates from language the things caught in 'the frozen lake of time' (Nabokov's description of a chess-board in Chapter Fourteen of *Speak, Memory*). The metaphor is like that souvenir of Biarritz (so apt it might have been planted), the 'meerschaum penholder with a tiny peephole of crystal in its ornamental part'[13] which discloses at last the name of Colette's dog. His life is, he says, 'a coloured spiral in a small ball of glass':[14] the same themes keep coming round but each time on a different level (so there is never mere recurrence). The power of metaphor relates one such gyre to another, maybe miles away in time and space (as Colette, in her kingdom by the sea, recurs as Ada and Lolita, among others). Thus this most mellow of Nabokov's books, a perfect blend of sentiment and intelligence, spirals round upon itself to produce the marvellous closing pages in which his son strays into the spacetime vacated by the now middle-aged narrator, in Berlin,

> where, of course, no one could escape familiarity with the ubiquitous picture of the Führer, when we stood, he and I, before a bed of pallid pansies, each of their upturned faces showing a dark mustache-like smudge, and had great fun, at my rather silly prompting, commenting on their resemblance to a crowd of bobbing little Hitlers.[15]

The little girl leading a butterfly on a thread (from which he diverts his son's attention) is both actuality and metaphor — as indeed are all events worth recording. The public parks have 'replaced' the spacious grounds of the Nabokov estates; an old man reading a foreign-language newspaper and picking his nose wanly embodies the reality of exile — but this is one more loop of the spiral, and it, too, has its thematic significance. Experiences resonate simultaneously together as Nabokov's son collects pebbles on the beach where his father played; pieces of majolica he finds continue the pattern in the fragments found by his father in 1903, by his mother (the beach was different, but what does it matter?) in 1882, and by her mother a hundred years before, until

> this assortment of parts, if it had been preserved, might have been put together to make the complete, the absolutely complete, bowl, broken by some Italian child, God knows where and when, and now mended by *these* rivets of bronze.[16]

In *Ada*, Van describes Time as, among other things, 'a fluid medium for the culture of metaphors'. In *Speak, Memory,*

Vivian Bloodmark (the anagram of the author's name signifying intrusive omniscience[17]) is quoted as saying that,

> While the scientist sees everything that happens in one point of space, the poet feels everything that happens in one point of time.

Both generalizations (reminiscent of Eliot) derive from Nabokov's early experience of literary creation, described in *Speak, Memory* and elaborated in the two novels which follow it — which are, indeed, a fluid sequence of writings and rewritings which demand the full participation of the reader in the creative process, even while they (characteristically) mock his witless inflexibility.[19] The 'coloured hearing' leaking from some ideal world which Nabokov describes in Chapter Two of *Speak, Memory* is his earliest aesthetic experience (or rather the first statement of a recurrent theme). Synaesthesia has rich hermetic antecedents, of which Huysmans and the symbolist poets constitute only a small part.[20] At bottom it is deployed as a more extreme form of metaphor which reveals the simultaneous interrelatedness of all our experiences: it is thus a special mode of cognition, part visionary, part taxonomic, and thus crucial to art as a means of knowing reality. There may or may not be some wholly ideal order to which it 'corresponds', but we have no language for apprehending such an order directly. Passing in this way through the looking-glass of a merely denotative use of language the author, taking his properly wonderstruck Alice, the reader, along with him, discovers the White Queen's world in which one grows giddy from living backwards[21] but in which Mnemosyne is uniquely untramelled. Nabokov's adolescent poetry-writing is closely connected with an experience of the fluidity of space:

> So little did ordinary measures of existence mean in that state that I would not have been surprised to come out of its tunnel right in the park of Versailles, or the Tiergarten, or Sequoia National Forest; and, inversely, when the old trance occurs nowadays, I am quite prepared to find myself, when I awaken from it, high up in a certain

> tree, above the dappled bench of my boyhood, my belly pressed against a thick, comfortable branch and one arm hanging down among the leaves upon which the shadows of other leaves move.[22]

Space 'warps into something akin to time', and time into 'something akin to thought', and then 'surely another dimension follows — a special Space maybe'. It is in this special Space that *Ada* is set. The most encyclopaedic of Nabokov's novels, it is also the most *scriptible*[23] (to adopt Barthes' term); though, as is often the case, the rules determining the possible 'combinations' turn out to be as strict as in his earlier chess problems.

*Ada's* material overlaps with that of *Speak, Memory,* though here the epiphane calls the tune, the ecstatic fantasy being interrupted only by the pangs of organic decline in the elderly fantasist (this is quite a substantial 'only', as *Transparent Things* recognizes). The family chronicle novel, with its necessarily historical structure, highly developed sense of place, intricate and leafy family trees[24] forms the framework of the novel, but is parodied from the opening page, where a slightly ponderous joke about translation annihilates national boundaries by running three languages into one. A plethora of place names, and the unfamiliar welter of proper names which the inexperienced English reader is so vexed by in Russian novels, map out an area of consciousness which Nabokov calls a 'dream-bright America' but which incorporates consubstantially Nabokov's 'remembered' (in the sense of *Speak, Memory*) Russia (or rather its civilized and consciously Europeanized element: the rest he brands 'Tartary'[25]). The interpenetration of languages, literatures, history, and geography defines an Antiterra, or alternative world; but whereas in *Speak, Memory* he evoked the 'footpath' running parallel to the highroad of 'fool-made history', Nabokov here reduces Terra (firma) to the status of an unverifiable rumour. The Tolstoy of *Anna Karenina* and the Chekov of the plays (especially *The Cherry Orchard,* set in a twilight of genteel landownerdom, and *The Three Sisters,* with its rage against space and time) merge with James and Faulkner (and of course Proust) to form an encyclopaedic continuum, the unreal estate of Van and his father Dementiy, who borrows his soubriquet and his wings from Lermontov's poem 'The Demon', an ethereal Byronic romance in which the eponymous hero sweeps across the heavens like one of Nabokov's 'jikkers' in search of the innocence and beauty which will assuage his tormenting desire.[26] It is of course a love story, embodying that 'slow-motion, silent explosion of love' which Nabokov describes in *Speak, Memory* as evoking

> the sense of something much vaster, much more enduring and powerful than the accumulation of matter or energy in any imaginable cosmos.[27]

The love is of course incestuous, in the best tradition of Romantic *affaires* between the poet and his muse; thus the determined pattern of causality which regulates the development of the family chronicle is broken, the future is pre-empted.[28]

If transcendence were accomplished so easily, of course, it could only be a conjuring trick; and in this novel as in others, Nabokov attempts to discriminate between the artist and the conjurer by himself pointing to the analogy (Van cheats more successfully at cards than his wretched opponent; as 'Mascodagama', a sort of masker-adventurer, he walks on his hands on a public stage, thus 'performing organically what his figures of speech were to perform later in life' — but his hands bear real scars, stigmata[29]). There is frequent reference to the black shadows on Ada's desirable whiteness; as well as *a, da*! (a Russian expression of joy[30]) she is a hellish shade, a creature from *ad* (Russian Hades). As the embodiment of desire she is the progenitor of pain (longing, loss) as well as the creative drive, and her infidelities (real and imagined) move Van to despair; in this, her relationship to Proust's Albertine is evident.[31] This demonic power is one aspect of her 'ardour'; and Ardis Hall is her proper dwelling place (from Greek *ardis*, an arrow point; French *flèche*, English *flesh*; also the arrow that Zeno used to prove that movement was illusory but which nevertheless landed on Valéry's head — one might go on in this exegetical vein but it merely duplicates work admirably done by Nabokov already as part of his novel, and one only perpetrates what he has called 'middle-aged puns'). The 'despair of desire' (Pt. 1, Chapter 16) killed Aqua who wrote in her suicide note 'ya teper' iz ada' (I have now quit hell[32]). Ada's infidelities and marriage threaten to destroy for ever the marvellous garden (sic) of childhood love — and Van himself, whose despair at aging is checked only by a fortunate kink in the plot, a lifebelt held out to him by his creator (as to Krug in *Bend Sinister*), in order to save him for the task he is uniquely equipped to carry out.[33] There was no such lifebelt for Lucette, destroyed by the madness of Van's frustration.

This is the supreme act of anamnesis,[34] the relation of 'the dubious reality of the present to the unquestionable one of remembrance'. In Part Three, Chapter Five, shortly before Lucette's suicide, he calls up the image of Ada in association with 'a series of sixty-year-old actions which I can grind into extinction only by working on a succession of words until the rhythm is right'.[35] The mass of bogus circumstantial detail of Parts One and Two gives way (the parts get shorter and shorter) to the laconic phenomenology of Part Four and the lucid intensity of Part Five; it is a curious process of diminution (pointing to the very spare *Transparent Things*), and since Nabokov is so close to his hero (who is conceived, in fact, as a device for repossessing 'things' incarcerated in the third persons and past tenses of earlier novels), we can see this as part of the Nabokovian myth of the consubstantiality of life and art: the image shrinks to a point of concentrated light.[36] The analysis of space and time propounded in Part Four is of course not new; Bergson and Proust have been there before. It is a commonplace that we habitually translate Time into Space in order to apprehend it (time is long and short, and we even talk of a 'space of time') and that the sequential nature of discourse (and the act of writing from left to right, or even vice versa) conspire with the monstrous temporal conventions of the so-called 'realist' novel to impose a constricting horological carapace on Time. In Part Four, in the form of a kind of public lecture which slides unobtrusively into the logbook of a journey[37] (maybe this is why the God of Antiterra is called Log), Nabokov appropriates the spatial metaphors of sequence and progress we habitually use to describe time and works them into the texture of his exposition.

The trick is ingenious. As he loses his way in his argument, the 'imaginary' car he is driving (which is taking Van to Mont Roux and Ada, to indulge in the 'simulacrum of possession' which is the communion with time he desires) runs into a muddy patch, or up a blind alley. Thus the spatial metaphor of the journey, which traditionally structures passing time, is an actuality within the metaphoric system of the novel, and instead of 'Space, the comedy villain, returning by the back door with the pendulum he peddles',[38] he is made to play his part in Nabokov's conceits, dissolved in the fluid medium of metaphor. In fact Nabokov is quite as concerned with Space as with Time, as indeed the whole novel has revealed, directed as it is towards exploring interlingual consubstantiality, interpenetration, the synthetic and simultaneous occupation of one territory by two — or more — ideas. Van quotes Shade (*Pale Fire*) to the effect that 'Space is a swarming in the eyes, and Time a singing in the ears',[39] and uses common non-verbal symbols (like those traffic signs along the road he is following, a nice touch) to demonstrate our ability to relate diverse shapes in 'no time'. It is all very dextrous, an extension (as Nabokov admits) of symbolist synaesthesia ('to which I am inordinately prone'[40]) but of course 'works' not as philosophy but as part of a novel, if at all. Any possible objection that it is only a trick, Nabokov has characteristically pre-empted. And yet one feels that one has been sold short, at the end of it all.

*Transparent Things* is the coda to Nabokov's time-trilogy, and its tone is quite different. Extraordinarily compressed (by contrast with the mannerist flourishes of *Ada*), it is imbued with an acute consciousness of aging[41] (which intruded into *Ada* as well, but which was dismissed in Van's lecture on Time as an irrelevant objection to the claim that Time is not linear). Van had remarked that 'we build models of the past and use them spatiologically to reify and measure Time'.[42] The universal truth of this is self-evident, but it also has a special truth for Nabokov as a writer, a truth explored in *Transparent Things*, wherein an old man tours the unreal estates of his life, enumerating the 'transparent things through which the past shines' much as Beckett's characters do. And all the time 'things' (the word is used over and over again, and objects named and enumerated) threaten to become opaque, no more than themselves; or to disintegrate, leaving only infinite, inhuman space. Eliot said that 'only through time, time is conquered';[43] here we have the proposition that only through memory is matter transcended. It was all foretold in *Speak, Memory*, life and work thus once again enacting that characteristic spiral.

The novelist makes art out of his experience: meaningful objects from his life are scattered liberally about the houses and landscapes of his fiction (thus in *Speak, Memory* we find the pedometer used by the young Charles the Belovèd in *Pale Fire*[44]). Moreover Nabokov distributes himself throughout his works to such an extent that author and hero, subject and object are no longer distinct. Where he differs from many authors of 'high' modernism however, is in his sense that the work, which is the justifying life-activity 'redeeming' mere material existence, may also be a kind of prison, the maze made to trap the maze-maker in which Daedalus unwittingly forfeits his freedom. *Transparent Things* combines a Beckettian scepticism about the activity of writing, perhaps better than in any other Nabokov novel, with a conviction that only the concrete word can unlock the door of the prison, and in this lies its pathos. Nabokov's narrators characteristically peer at us from behind the frame of the canvas, climbing in and out of the picture as in Gogol's 'The Portrait'.[45] In earlier novels this serves to break open the clichetic forms in which automatic ways of seeing things become embodied (as, for example, in *Pnin*) so that life, though revealed only through art, is at the same time greater than art. Comedy, especially as Bergson defines it, was Nabokov's habitual mode of defamiliarization. But if the 'spatiological' novel, what Van calls a 'model of the past', reifies Time, the author of *Transparent Things* has resolved not only that this shall not be a spatiological novel but that it shall be the counterspell that releases 'things' of his own from the sclerosis that has turned them to stone like the victims of a magic spell. The task is an impossible one and the tone of this novel — seemingly a farewell to art — far from comic.

The narrative introducing the 'hero' (who is pure possibility, Hugh Person, created as it were by chance) is preceded by a chapter lying outside the 'frame' of the novel in which this 'Person' tries not to hear the voice of the narrator, whom he suspects of waiting to accost and 'reify' him: the puppets are in revolt. Person, however, sets out on his own quest in past time, trying to avoid sinking into its irrelevant causalities. The narrative is concerned with Person's attempts to enter Time as Van had done, but the old man finds the task much harder. He is dogged by disappointment, and the enchanted artifices of *Ada* fade, like Prospero's dream-kingdom, into thin air. Memory and actuality refuse to coincide; the Ascot hotel has red shutters, not green (as he had remembered), the hotel management has changed, the records of guests have been destroyed (the manager having committed suicide — an equivalent of faking accounts[46]) and Person cannot remember the number of the room in which he stayed and where he was visited by Armande. The ghostly presence of excavating machines outside his window and Villa Nastia (nastier than what?), while underlining the theme of Person's own 'excavation', suggest the inexorable change that defeats and destroys him, and perhaps also something mechanical in his own makeup and way of proceeding. New roads and houses have grown, 'crowding out the meager landmarks he remembered or thought he remembered'.[47] His own aging is itself seen as a process of degradation to the status of a mere object, an 'opaque' thing.

This process was always latent in the cluster of themes which constitute Hugh's destiny. The serene succession of generations evoked by the closing pages of *Speak, Memory* is here strangely mocked. Hugh's search for a drawer in which to put his 'things' in Chapter Three (in the course of which he dislodges a pencil, a 'thing' which threatens to merge back into its constituent materials as the narrator contemplates it, and is held on to by a stratagem) gives way, by a backward flip of time, to his memories of a visit to Switzerland with his father eighteen years before, during which his father, vexed by objects in the way the old are, fumbling for 'things' as if 'in the bath-water of space', had suddenly and unreasonably turned into a thing himself: had died in the shop changing-room among his 'things' (trousers, umbrella, hat[48]). At that time things had not bothered Hugh. The narrator of his own plot (a prerogative of youth), he had unwittingly glimpsed his destiny in the things in a shop window; they are all, for him, 'coincident symbols', though he cannot know (as the novelist does) that the green figurine of a skier prefigures Armande, that its maker pre-echoes his own disaster, least of all that he will find it again in room 313 ('a convict between two guards') in which he dies. Only at the point of death do things become transparent again for Hugh as they were in his youth (his room, up to then occupied by a Chekhovian lady with a little dog, acquires the permeability of the earliest of his sexual experiences, the encounter with the prostitute in the same room, which had formerly been occupied by a Russian novelist).

The reification of Hugh's world (including the murder of Armande — real or imagined) is partly, of course, a moral correlative to his arrogance. He suffers from a kind of moral sclerosis which is underlined in his attitude to Julia, for instance; he welcomes the fact that his affair with her was hidden in the secrecy of 'the Past Tense'. Yet his desperate sense of the impermeability of things, growing upon him in the course of the novel (his assault on his bedside table in Chapter Seven prepares for his assault on Armande in Chapter Twenty — the cold object of his fantasies, he reduces her literally to inert matter), is seen as disproportionate to his own shortcomings. He dies in a fire which was kindled in Armande's imagination (as a function of the frigidity that made her perverse and promiscuous[49]), and this at the hoped-for moment of ghostly consummation in Room 313; his past has proved irredeemable, the mountains as daunting as they always were, his boots too heavy for an old man to climb in, the rain falling like 'a kiss on his bald spot'. Perhaps this is why Hugh tried, in Chapter One, not to hear the narrator's summons: he may have foreseen that in his case only death would render 'things' transparent.

Nabokov enters this novel as he does others, but with a difference. One part of him is Hugh. The publisher's representative proof-reading the novels of Baron R. (he read them twice, 'once for the defects of the type and once for the virtues of the text'[50]) is the judicious and critical author casting his eye over his life's work, novels as 'things' with which he feels no necessary connection although they live with his life. His other self is the author Baron R., an emigré writing in English with whom Hugh has shared the same mistress, a liaison complicated by a mother-daughter relationship (incorporated in one of R.'s novels) which recalls *Lolita* (as does a motif in one of R.'s novels). Some of R.'s devices, though he is a 'master stylist', do not accord with Nabokov's own. But when he refers to R. as 'touchy, unpleasant and rude', and refers to 'the streak of nasty inventiveness so conspicuous in his writings', it is as if Nabokov were placing his less attractive traits (or unfavourable reviews) within this narrative structure in order that they should be made into 'things' — while we know all the time that it is *this* novel that Nabokov is writing: or being written by.[51] Thus he is in on his own death: among the different runthroughs of death in the novel (Person senior's metamorphosis into a thing, Armande's sticky end, the flames of unsatisfiable desire that consume Hugh's material being) there is also the intercalated farewell letter from R. to his publisher Phil, in which (and it fits the epistolary style) he plays like Richardson on the epistolary mode's strange freedom — the absence of a framework which permits the correspondent's rich ambiguities ('I am leaving you for another even greater Publisher'). The fact that the publisher has taken over the role of God (a role usually reserved, since Joyce at least, for the author) contributes to one's sense that this novel enacts a kind of breaking of the magic staff. R. is dying of a liver complaint, lying, inoperable, in a Bologna hospital; 'my wretched liver is as heavy as a rejected manuscript', he writes, acknowledging his impotence to fuse self, the world, and death in a concrete visionary moment. Things fall apart and yet he sees himself — as an object, from without — growing more and more material. R. dies but the narrator survives — to tell the tale, as they say.

The landscape of Time in this novel is much more chill, then, than in the earlier time novels, and it has very much the air of a 'last word', although it is not. Doubtless the portraits of the author on the dustjackets of these novels are intended to contribute to the meaning: if this is so, then while the face on *Speak, Memory* suggests an author urbane and aloof, and that on *Ada* one knowing and sportive, the face on *Transparent Things* reveals strain and anxiety. It is not at all sure that things can be transparent for long, holding their surface tension while the past shines through them; they harden or disintegrate, consciousness is stranded among mere objects (and is no more than an object itself) or sinks through the thin layer of materiality into an abyss. Robbe-Grillet's *Nouveau Roman* haunts *Transparent Things* threateningly (a novel, that is, stripped of the anthropomorphic deceptions which we foist on to the neutral universe in our fruitless quest for significance).[52] The neutral ground of Switzerland becomes an arduous and hostile mountain terrain; the French language, instead of combining with English and Russian (as in *Ada*) to form a rich synthetic interlingua, is characterized by its impersonal locutions ('And now one is going to make love,' says Armande; and M. Wilde notes that, in the magazine he picks up, 'one talks here of a man who murdered his spouse', the receptionist breaking in to remark that at the all-important hotel in Stresa 'one does not reply'). Hugh (or 'you') Person might, of course, be anyone. A significant hiatus in the 'manuscript' (of the kind the 'editor' of *Ada* does not trouble to tidy up) lays bare a 'thing' which seems to epitomize the novel. At the end of Chapter Eleven we read:

> We now see a torn piece of *La Stampa* and an empty wine bottle. A lot of construction work was going on

This marks the end of the affair with Julia and the beginning of Hugh's love for Armande. But Chapter Twelve begins

> A lot of construction work was going on around Witt, scarring and muddying the entire hillside . . . some litter had already been left, such as a workman's empty bottle and an Italian newspaper.

The ambivalence of this, the scepticism it reveals about the power of language to create order through symbol and metaphor, seems characteristic of the novel. The old newspaper and bottle unmistakably invoke paintings of Braque and Picasso where 'things' usurp the privileged realm of art.

# Notes to Chapter 9

1. As Nabokov has become less Russian, so Proust has become more and more his principal inspiration.
2. It is essentially a way of writing: reduced to its basic concepts it compares pretty unfavourably with Bergson.
3. Nabokov could hardly have treated his own life differently from that of Sebastian Knight, or indeed of Gogol — which is essentially Gogol's 'life in art' (to borrow the phrase Field applies to Nabokov), and avoids stereotyped chronology, in Nabokov's evocation of it.
4. Proust's Marcel operates similarly. The comparison with Proust suggests — I think rightly — that Nabokov's work has become more metaphysical. This does not necessarily mean that it has improved.
5. Vladimir Nabokov, *Ada* (Weidenfeld and Nicolson, 1969), p. 459.
6. Valdimir Nabokov, *Speak, Memory: An Autobiography Revisited* (London: Weidenfeld and Nicolson, 1967) p. 26.
7. *Ibid.*, pp. 7-8.
8. I have tried elsewhere to show that Nabokov's formal devices are not the refuge from the world they have sometimes been taken for.
9. This is itself only a very qualified kind of aestheticism.
10. *Speak, Memory,* pp. 124-5. This parallels passages in (for example) *The Gift*, but although consistent with Nabokov's earlier ideas about art, clearly belongs to his later phase by reason of its special lyricism.
11. Both share with Pushkin a 'concern with the fatidic'. (*Eugene Onegin*, Vol. 2, p. 128).
12. Marvell crops up several times in the Pushkin commentary. In Kinbote's note to 1.678 (*Pale Fire*, pp. 171-2) there is some very nice material on translating Marvell, including two lines in 'our magic Zemblan', called by the poet Conmal 'the tongue of the mirrors':

    Id wodo bin, war id lev lan,
    Indran iz lil ut roz nitran.
13. *Speak, Memory*, p. 151.
14. *Speak, Memory*, passim. I think the first mention of this motif is on p. 152. It is probably entirely coincidental that Patrick White makes a marble of this type the symbol of a secret knowledge in the novel named from the marble *The Solid*

*Mandala*. The quasi-philosophical implications of the thing are gone into on p. 275 of *Speak, Memory*.

15. *Speak, Memory*, p. 305.
16. This beautiful Jamesian image occurs on pp. 308-9 of *Speak, Memory*: which is to say that it immediately precedes Nabokov's departure for America.
17. This is his 'philosophical' manifestation.
18. T. S. Eliot, *Selected Essays*, p. 287.
19. Some readers find this offensive: but Nabokov's mockery is without malice.
20. Maybe the best-known statement of the phenomenon Nabokov here describes is Rimbaud's famous sonnet *Voyelles*.
21. Lewis Carroll, *Through the Looking Glass*, p. 253.
22. *Speak, Memory*, pp. 223 et. seq.
23. This term is glossed in Chapter 1, note 3. If a novel is analogous to a chess game (a comparison which will not, of course, hold up for very long), then although the rules of the game are fixed, the actual conduct of play on the part of author and reader is infinitely varied, and different strategies may be equally valid. Death and the devil habitually played chess and other games with mortal opponents.
24. *Ada* borrows even more than the other novels from Nabokov's store of lost property.
25. Behind this fanciful nomenclature lies (as often with Nabokov) a substantial actuality: Russian criticism — and the sociology of which it was a branch — was split throughout the nineteenth century between those who urged Russia to adopt Western European institutions and technology, and those who saw the possibility of a finer alternative society founded upon orthodoxy and the peasant commune. Nabokov, a 'Westerner' through and through, is not the first to suggest that Soviet Communism represents the triumph of the Slavophiles — traduced here as 'Tartars'.
26. Mikhail Lermontov (1814-1841) was the greatest of the Russian Byronists. His highly original novel, *A Hero of Our Time*, was translated by Nabokov in collaboration with his son (see Chapter 5 above).
27. The whole passage from which this is taken is very fine (*Speak, Memory*, pp. 296-7).
28. Nabokov, who grew used to living without a future, dismisses any such phenomenon as an irrelevance in many of his novels.
29. There is a faint echo here of Nabokov's first novel, *Mary*,

where the hero does some such trick when in good spirits. Van's act is more complex, since it involves him walking on his hands in the costume of a man walking upright — who thereupon stands on his hands, thus turning Van right way up. This game with court cards is an analogue of the artist.

30. *Da* means simply 'yes'. The conjunctive 'a', however, meaning obligingly 'and' or 'but' according to context, adds an emotional colouring.
31. Including the hint of sexual ambivalence.
32. *Ada*, p. 29. Evidently she was one of those who could not bear very much 'reality' (i.e. the world of Van and Ada).
33. One is left with a doubt about the validity of the undertaking. V. V. Nabokov's life's work is after all much more substantial than the other V.V.'s.
34. This term is a favourite of David Jones's, though it also (stripped of its mythic element) fits Nabokov.
35. *Ada*, p. 490. It is worth remarking that in this chapter Lucette drowns herself for love of Van, who is quite indifferent to her.
36. Cf. *Pale Fire* (the poem), 11.472-4.
37. Van is driving and lecturing simultaneously.
38. *Ada*, p. 538.
39. *Ibid.*, p. 541.
40. Cf. n. 20.
41. In this matter *Transparent Things* is Nabokov's *Temps Retrouvé.*
42. *Ada*, p. 544. This is not a new insight: cf. for instance, A. A. Mendilow, *Time and the Novel* (New York: Humanities Press, 1972).
43. T. S. Eliot, *Burnt Norton.*
44. There is nothing very unusual in this, except that Nabokov reassembles his transparent things in *Speak, Memory.*
45. See, for instance, *Tales of Good and Evil* (New York: Doubleday Anchor, 1957), translated by David Magarshack.
46. Vladimir Nabokov, *Transparent Things* (London: Weidenfeld and Nicholson, 1973), p. 4.
47. *Ibid.*, p. 87.
48. *Ibid.*, p. 15
49. *Ibid.*, pp. 80-81.
50. *Ibid.*, p. 74.
51. In this, the novel contrasts sharply with his warmest comedy, *Pnin*, where the author exercises full control.
52. In the interview with Alfred Appel, Nabokov dismisses Robbe-

Grillet's theories as 'preposterous', while expressing admiration for his 'magnificently poetical and original' fiction (L. S. Dembo, op. cit., p. 34).

# X

## Positively last performance: **Look at the Harlequins** (1974)

Proust's hero in *A La Recherche*, by becoming the chronicler of his own life, emerges at the hither side of the succession of deaths that time and oblivion force human experience to undergo. By entering the plenitude of his own subjectivity, writing the fiction of himself, he sees as much of eternity as man can apprehend. He is, as it were, the God of his own universe, rescuing events from oblivion and contingency by an act of total recall. The act of writing must be coterminous with the transcendence of time, so that the 'plot' shall be seen as nothing other than an act of redemption. For this to occur, there can be no disjunction between subjective and objective reality, and this is the essence of the harlequinade. Proust's way of resolving the problem that has obsessed literature since the Renaissance, when it supplanted religion as man's explanation of his place in the cosmos, has, as we have seen, left its imprint on Nabokov's work. Conventionally, the work was immortal, and the writer immortal in his work: so that in talking of the immortality of Shakespeare we know that we mean his *oeuvre*. In talking of the immortality of Proust (if we do) or of Joyce or of Lawrence or of Mann we must mean something different: immortality in this case consists not so much in the classic status of their work as in the kinds of mythic orders they construct so as to displace the sequentiality of narrative and the 'stability' (Lawrence's term) of the character such narrative posits as objectively 'real'. Fictions enact the redemption of lost time.[1]

*Look at the Harlequins* takes the form of the autobiography of a novelist, liberally interspersed with detailed allusions to the works which have made him famous. The chronicle of events and literary works constitutes the plot of the novel. There are a number of well-marked recurrent themes, the most striking of which is perhaps the narrator's obsession with his inability to imagine himself changing direction, doubling back on himself, so that the landscape he can easily envisage before him could become (again in the projective imagination) behind him.[2] This difficulty is presented as a kind of nervous disease from which the narrator suffers, and which is marked by other symptoms. Another recurrent theme is that contained in the title of the novel, which derives from a grand-aunt's command to 'invent reality' and 'look at the harlequins' —

> Trees are harlequins, words are harlequins. So are situations and sums. Put two things together — jokes, images — and you get a triple harlequin. Come on! Play! Invent the world! Invent reality!

Thus the narrator refers at one point to what he calls 'the most authentic and faithful joys of my life',

> the coloured phrase in my mind under the drizzle, the white page under the desk lamp awaiting me in my humble home.

— from the 'humblest' reality one can create, or invent, harlequins of glittering fiction. This fictional world, called into being by the conjuror's wand (or 'lath' — the initial letters of the words of the title compose the magic instrument) oddly combines, like all narrated worlds, the sequentiality of time-bound language arts[3] with the dispositional freedom or 'spatiality' of a symbolic ordering of sensations and impressions. One small example may serve, drawn from the large range of erotic motifs deployed as wittily and poignantly in this novel as in his others: leaving his academic post the narrator remarks:

> In the name of moral hygiene I had got rid long ago of my Bechstein desk.

The desk in his office is the locus of his 'trite' coupling with Dolly Borg thirteen years after; his 'ribald neighbour', Professor King, had remarked that it 'slept two'; the Bechstein, otherwise unrelated to the desk, is the white 'iceberg' on which Louise was 'laid at eighteen' by Aldy Landover, and not unrelated to the piano being played in Iris's house in Chapter Six: all pianos everywhere, real and imaginary, being linked by the fact that Kanner the butterfly-collector and circus-ringmaster (cf. harlequins with laths) is also a great pianist, as Iris mentions a little earlier in the same chapter. They are, in other words, props in Nabokov's magic circus (or more strictly the narrator's). Steeped in memory and desire they reveal the pattern of significance which validates their thematic status.[4] Yet one does not cease to be aware of them *as* 'props'.

And this is the crux: the relationship between the factual record of the life and loves (especially loves) of the writer Ivor calls 'McNab', the maker of fictions, and the fictionalized record of the career of Nabokov himself which the novel transparently is. Vadim Vadimich's published works are weird transpositions of Nabokov's own, just as his life story (flight from Russia, emigré literary world, American academia, sudden wealth — after the publication of *A Kingdom by the Sea* — followed by Switzerland) parallels Nabokov's. Autobiographical fragments — many of them rescued from among earlier novels — are scattered more liberally than ever before. There is, of course, one significant event in Vadim's life which Nabokov's own lacks to date: the return to Russia predicted long ago in *Podvig* (English *Glory*) wherein the wheel comes full circle. Moreover, Vadim seems to be more than just the author of these shadowy distortions of Nabokov's own novel. His life story seems to be actually made up of extracts from them, extracts which skilfully evoke the mood or pattern of images of the books concerned while carefully scrambling a few allusions, or transposing them from another context, so as to give the complete Nabokovian the joy of unmasking the deception. Entering the novel as the superfluous man, the *lishny chelovek* (cf. *The Eye*) he exits along the slanting ray (*naklonny luch*) that leads Krug to the refuge of imbecility in *Bend Sinister* (where he metamorphoses at last into the free, blind moth). Moreover it does not go unnoticed, by Vadim or by others, that his novels are preternaturally close to those of another author, or that he might be

> permanently impersonating somebody living as a real being beyond the constellation of my tears and asterisks

and that his work might be

> an unconscious imitation of another's unearthly art.[5]

Evidently McNab is, in some sense, as his name indicates, the son of Nabokov; direct allusions to *The Government Inspector*, where Khlestakov plays the part of another man, the 'real' inspector, and this performance is all his reality, accompanied by a discussion of whether or not the whole play is Mayor's nightmare (it isn't), inaugurate the shadow-play of the plot, which moves towards the disclosure of the 'reality' behind it.

Vadim is not the first of Nabokov's characters to sense that his life has, or is, a plot: it is a common device in Nabokov's work. But the degree of self-consciousness is here heightened by a special kind of urgency, reflected in the structure of the novel, a kind of gyre diminishing to vanishing point. *Transparent Things* had the air of an epilogue: this novel is a kind of fictionalized index to Nabokov's work.[6] The self-consciousness here is more than that of the artist who lets us into some of the secrets of his art only in order that we shall find more baffling the tricks which we cannot fathom, a habit which creates the sense of wonder that surrounds Nabokov's best work; it is the self-consciousness of an author immensely over-exposed to publicity yet shunning it, insisting that, in Vadim's words, 'his only real identity papers' are his novels (cf. *The Real Life of Sebastian Knight*; or, as this novel has it, *See Under Real*). Nabokov has lived two lives in so many senses of the phrase that the split personality has become his most characteristic theme.[7] A Russian novelist and an American novelist, and a two-in-one (in *Pale Fire* and *Ada* especially) for whom style becomes an endless act of translation, he is additionally a writer projecting habitually his doubled selves into his narratives — as all novelists no doubt have done — but with a jealous sense of rivalry controlling the relationship between the narrative self and the narrated anti-self. He has also become, as this novel reveals, anxiously aware of himself as creator (seer of harlequins) and as object of study, and therefore in some way 'created' by his critics: and it is indeed striking how much critical and scholarly energy has gone into the elucidation of the hermetic elements in his work. It is a plot: and he, V. V., cannot change direction. He must spiral down to nothingness in order that the whole life-history discloses its shapely logic, being himself no more than one element in a sequence of fictions pressed hard for their autobiographical content, forced by a demon, as V. V. says, to impersonate another man.

But this, as I have already suggested, is not the whole story. McNab has a protector. Professor Moody, 'the London specialist', may confuse him with 'a Mr. V. S.' (Sirin, Nabokov's pen-name, was his first double), but his 'complaint' (marked by insomnia and panic) reveals glimpses of 'Being' beyond his own precarious identity, 'states' neither before nor after but 'definitely out of bounds, mortally speaking'.[8] These can be disclosed by no other means than the contrivance of some kind of formulaic equivalence between V. V. and the great original (the Being who created him, Nabokov himself) as an eccentric allegory of man's curious sense that his life has a plot and its own recurrent themes and symbols, tending to operate at odds with the irreversible movement through space (or is it through time, and a gyre?) that is the story of a life, externally represented.[9] V. V. may well wonder about the nationality

> of the bronzed old man with the hoary chest hair who was wading out of the low surf preceded by his bedraggled dog

whose face he thinks he recognizes, for Kanner, 'the great pianist and butterfly hunter' cannot be altogether distinct from the Kanner who runs 'Kanner's Circus' (in which, no doubt, V. V.'s 'dear bespangled mimes and their wands of painted lath' perform). Shifts and rifts in clock-time and automated perception reveal things 'unchanged by eternity, disfigured by time' in the world of the 'other' (cf. Rimbaud's 'je est un autre' which started the whole thing going) which is the homeland of art.[10] Nabokov is not the first writer to discover that love discloses this world, its own native territory. When first he makes love to Iris, V. V. describes it as if he were still the small boy who climbed a ladder to spy on a great-uncle and his bride in bed. V. V.'s shirt ('Your tum is as pink as your shirt', says Iris) is the link:

> A superhuman effort afforded me the sight of a salmon-pink shirt over the back of a chair. He, the enraptured beast, doomed to die one day as so many are, was now repeating her name with ever-increasing urgency, and by the time my foot slipped he was in full cry, thus drowning the noise of my sudden descent into a crackle of twigs and a snowstorm of petals.

Proust has not equalled this vision of the opening of the gates of paradise. Yet V. V. too is betrayed, by a grotesque double not unrelated to his benefactor, and Iris dies a victim of the 'plot' she longed to contrive for the detective story she was doomed not to write. There is always, beyond what V. V. calls the 'secret struggle with the wrong shape of things', the possibility that there is somewhere a 'real' being, and indeed 'Being' itself, in a kind of interlinear world (cf. *Ada*) outside of time which art intermittently reveals, presided over by the great sly artist who may in the end agree to deliver his characters from the plots he has contrived for them when once they have confirmed to themselves beyond all dispute that they cannot of their own volition change the direction in which they are moving. It is the villains like Starov who are condemned to travel round and round for ever in that hellish pleasure-park train (twice invoked as an analogue of damnation) while the hero pursues his journey through the plenitude of Time.

Perhaps the most curious section of the novel is the one covering the visit to the USSR undertaken by V. V. in disguise. This journey rounds off the fictional career of V. V. and resolves the longing of the emigré to return again to his origins; but the graphic details of the journey, drawn with malice not from first-hand experience but from accounts by Nabokov's scholarly admirers, do not make up the record of a revelation, since even the house on Hertzen St. which any reader of *Speak, Memory* will recognize as the Nabokov family house seems at the most faintly and unaccountably suggestive (did he go to a children's party there once?) to the narrator. When Oleg, the noxious agent, levels against him the accusation of betraying 'his compatriots' by concocting

> this obscene novelette about little Lola or Lotte, whom some Austrian Jew or reformed pederast rapes after murdering her mother — no, excuse me — *marrying* mam first before murdering her

the travesty of the plot of *Lolita* angers Vadim even while he protests that the novel he wrote — a copy of which is in his hand — has a quite different plot and is called *A Kingdom by the Sea.*[11] The punch on the nose Vadim gives Oleg makes his watch 'tick like mad' and he accelerates out of the historical 'reality' of modern Russia (there was never so little mirth in Nabokov's wilful travesties of Soviet life and letters as there is here). The episode is followed closely by the last sequence of the novel, the 'fall' (cf. the amorous fall into the snowstorm of petals quoted above) into the accelerating void of madness, or death, which the surface of things had barely concealed.

Despite its wit and charm, *Look at the Harlequins* is, however, a disappointing follow-up to the acerbities of *Transparent Things*. It is as if Nabokov had recoiled from what promised to become a new direction in his art, contained in what I briefly alluded to as its 'Cubist' material, its confrontation of contingency and the limits of subjectivity.[12] But at the same time one should not underestimate the importance of the issues it presents. It is the work of a deeply isolated man, whose wealth and success have done little to temper this isolation. It is also the work of a man whose richest subject matter is himself, yet who feels estranged from his life's work — as if it were the work of someone else. The fantasy of return to Russia could perhaps be taken as marking the failure of the 'extraterritorial' principle[13] to provide deliverance from increasing commercialization and trivializing of Western culture, not to mention the virtual extinction of Russian emigré writing.[14] It may be that Nabokov espoused too readily the fame that latterly came to him and the mythology assiduously manufactured by his admirers. But I think the real point to be made here is not in essence a point about a particular kind of personal failure, because Nabokov's creative gifts seem undiminished. We are dealing rather with a failure that is symptomatic. Of Picasso's painting *The Race* (1922) John Berger[15] observes that it is 'a painting that cancels itself', adding that 'It is like seeing a candle blow itself out'. So too with Nabokov's new novel, and perhaps for similar reasons. The problem was implicit already in *Ada*. Parody and pastiche have formed a substantial part of his work (as with Picasso and Stravinsky),[16] and these modes have been richly productive; but they are dependent upon the accepted values, the traditional methods, or even simply the unthinking orthodoxies, which they travesty. *The Gift*, for instance, works so well because the audience at which it was directed (the Russian emigration) could see itself as the focus of a definable culture, a culture which an English reader has to work to understand, but which he is assisted in understanding precisely through the novel itself. *Lolita* is less particular in its cultural referents but is a major novel by virtue of the awareness it projects through Humbert's consciousness of the provisional and relativized cultural attitudes of our age, the age of America's apogee and deliquescence. It is also a love story of great power. In both works one is conscious of a deep insight into a historical moment: in the case of *Lolita* it would not be an exaggeration to say that the novel did not simply reflect a moment with profound truth, it materially assisted in creating it. To have survived — or outlived — such an achievement — the writing of a best-seller which brought wealth and fame and was at the same time unquestionably one of the handful of masterpieces of our age — might be expected to have taken its toll of any artist. In Nabokov's case the price of success has been particularly high. *The Gift* is the work of a Russian novelist in exile; *Lolita* is the work of a novelist delighting in his freedom of cultural cross-reference between America and Russia, though troubled, at the same time, by the relativity of cultural values. The later work has situated itself nowhere, and by doing so has renounced content, or tried to make a virtue of solipsism. I would not for a moment suggest that such an undertaking is irrelevant to our age; but if it springs from it, it does not go very far towards understanding it. Despite the gestures of finality in the last two novels there will surely be others, and the last word has not been said. Stravinsky, the arch-eclectic, after half a lifetime of opposition to it, came to terms with Schoenberg's 'method', a systematic reformulation of the dialectic of symphonic form, which gave him a new lease of musical life. For the writer, whose art is inevitably closer to the everyday world, the task of confronting the void of our culture is harder. But if anyone succeeds in doing so, it ought to be a Russian: for has not Nabokov himself, writing of Gogol, identified

> the remarkable creative faculty of Russians, so beautifully disclosed by Gogol's own inspiration, of working in a void?[17]

# Notes to Chapter 10

1. Cf. Frank Kermode, *The Sense of an Ending*.
2. It seems as if the linear sequentiality of narrative, exploded in modernist writing, is always threatening to assert itself again in each individual life.
3. The original distinction is in Lessing's *Laocoon*.
4. *Look at the Harlequins* shows beyond doubt that all Nabokov's works are really one work.
5. As in the case of *Pale Fire*, one is put in mind of Pirandello.
6. The whole career is therefore represented under the guise of a sustained literary work, and not just all the novels (i.e. the *life* is incorporated as well into the supreme fiction).
7. See Chapter 5, above.
8. Cf. Shade in *Pale Fire*.
9. This draws unpleasantly close to the mystifications of certain Russian Symbolist poets.
10. Again, this seems too easy, after *Transparent Things*.
11. Cf. Chapter 5 (on the place of Poe in *Lolita*).
12. 'Cubist' is only shorthand, of course, although the specific materials named do evoke Cubist paintings. What I wanted to allude to here is the collage techniques of Cubism, which break down the privileged status of the work of art in a way quite unlike Nabokov's in all novels but this.
13. My allusion is to George Steiner's book *Extraterritorial* (and his later *After Babel*) which seem to me to overstate the virtues of rootlessness.
14. There has, of course, been in recent years a 'new wave' of Russian emigré writing, but it is the reverse of cosmopolitan.
15. John Berger, *The Success and Failure of Picasso* (Harmondsworth: Penguin Books, 1965) p. 143.
16. It would be instructive to compare the careers of Stravinsky and Nabokov in greater detail.
17. Cf. Chapter 7.

# BIBLIOGRAPHY

A. Works by Vladimir Nabokov.

(No adequate bibliography of Nabokov writings exists; reference is to the edition cited in the text.)

1. *Mary* (Harmondsworth: Penguin Books, 1973).
2. *King, Queen, Knave* (London: Weidenfeld and Nicolson, 1968).
3. *The Defence* (London: Panther Books, 1971).
4. *The Eye* (London: Panther Books, 1968).
5. *Glory* (London: Weidenfeld and Nicolson, 1972).
6. *Laughter in the Dark* (Harmondsworth: Penguin Books, 1969).
7. *Despair* (London: Panther Books, 1969).
8. *Invitation to a Beheading* (Harmondsworth: Penguin Books, 1969).
9. *The Gift* (London: Panther Books, 1966).
10. *The Real Life of Sebastian Knight* (Harmondsworth: Penguin Books, 1971).
11. *Nikolai Gogol* (New York: New Directions, 1961).
12. *Bend Sinister* (London: Weidenfeld and Nicolson, 1961).
13. *Pnin* (Harmondsworth: Penguin Books, 1971).
14. *Lolita* (London: Weidenfeld and Nicolson, 1959).
15. *Pale Fire* (New York: Lancer Books, 1963).
16. *Speak, Memory* (London: Weidenfeld and Nicolson, 1967).
17. *Ada* (London: Weidenfeld and Nicolson, 1969).
18. *Transparent Things* (London: Weidenfeld and Nicolson, 1972).
19. *Look at the Harlequins* (London: Weidenfeld and Nicolson, 1974).

Volumes of short stories include:

1. *Nabokov's Dozen* (Harmondsworth: Penguin Books, 1971).
2. *Nabokov's Quartet* (London: Panther Books, 1972).
3. *A Russian Beauty* (New York: McGraw-Hill, 1973).

Other publications consulted:

1. *Poems* (London: Weidenfeld and Nicolson, 1961).
2. *Eugene Onegin*, by Alexander Pushkin, translated from the Russian with a commentary by Vladimir Nabokov (London: Routledge and Kegan Paul, 1964).
3. *Pushkin, Lermontov, Tyutchev: Poems*, translated by Vladimir Nabokov (London: Lindsay Drummond Ltd., 1947).

4. *The Waltz Invention: A Play in Three Acts* (New York: Phaedra, 1966).
5. *A Hero of Our Time*, by Mihail Lermontov, translated from the Russian by Vladimir Nabokov in collaboration with Dmitri Nabokov (New York: Doubleday Anchor, 1958).

B. Critical studies of Nabokov's work:

Appel, A., and Newman, C., eds., *Nabokov: criticism, reminiscences, translations and tributes* (London: Weidenfeld and Nicolson, 1970).

Appel, A., *Nabokov's Dark Cinema* (New York, O.U.P., 1974).

Bader, J., *Crystal Land: artifice in Nabokov's English novels*, (Berkeley, California U.P., 1972).

Dembo, L. S., *Nabokov: the man and the work* (Madison, Wisconsin U.P., 1967).

Field, A., *Nabokov: his life in art. A critical narrative* (London, Hodder and Stoughton, 1967).

Fowler, D., *Reading Nabokov* (Ithaca, New York, Cornell U.P., 1974).

Mason, B. A., *Nabokov's Garden: a guide to Ada* (Ann Arbor, Ardis, 1974).

Moynahan, J., *Vladimir Nabokov* (Minneapolis, Minnesota U.P., 1971).

Proffer, C. R., ed., *A book of things about Nabokov* (Ann Arbor, Ardis, 1974).

Proffer, C. R., *Keys to Lolita* (Bloomington, Indiana U.P., 1968).

Stark, J. O., *The Literature of Exhaustion: Borges, Nabokov and Barth* (Durham, N.C., Duke University Press, 1974).

Stegner, P., *Escape into aesthetics: the art of Vladimir Nabokov* (London, Eyre and Spottiswoode, 1967).

C. Other primary material referred to:

1. Bely, Andrey, *St. Petersburg* (New York, Grove Press, 1959) tr. John Cournos.
2. Bergson, Henri, *Matter and Memory* (London: Allen and Unwin, 1950).
3. Bergson, Henri, *Laughter*, in Sypher, Wylie, *Comedy* (New York: Doubleday Anchor, 1956).
4. Chekhov, Anton, *Letters on the short story, the drama, and other literary topics by Anton Chekhov*, ed. L. S. Friedland (London: Vision Press, 1965).
5. Carroll, Lewis, *Alice's Adventures in Wonderland and*

*Through the Looking Glass* (Harmondsworth: Penguin Books, 1970).

6. Conquest, Robert, *The Great Terror* (Harmondsworth: Penguin Books, 1971).
7. Dostoyevsky, Fyodor, *Notes from Underground* (Harmondsworth: Penguin Books, 1972) tr. J. Coulson.
8. Eimermacher, Karl (ed.), *Teksty sovetskogo literaturovedcheskogo strukturalizma* (Munchen: Fink Verlag, 1971).
9. Eliot, T. S., *Selected Essays* (London: Faber, 1958).
10. Eliot, T. S., *The Complete Poems and Plays* (London: Faber, 1969).
11. Fitzgerald, F. Scott, *The Great Gatsby* (Harmondsworth: Penguin Books, 1971).
12. Frost, Robert, *Selected Poems* (Harmondsworth: Penguin Books, 1955).
13. Gogol, Nikolai, *The Diary of a Madman and other stories* (New York and London: Signet Books, 1960) tr. R. MacAndrew.
14. Golombek, H., *The Game of Chess* (Harmondsworth: Penguin Books, 1963).
15. Goncharov, Ivan, *Oblomov* (Harmondsworth, Penguin Books, 1954) tr. David Magarshack.
16. Küchelbecker, V. K., *Izbranniye Proizvedeniya v dvukh tomakh* (Moscow-Leningrad: Soviet Writer, 1967).
17. Joyce, James, *Ulysses* (London: The Bodley Head, 1955).
18. Laing, R. D., *The Divided Self* (Harmondsworth: Penguin Books, 1965).
19. Lemon, L. T., and Reis, M. J., *Russian Formalist Criticism: Four Essays* (University of Nebraska Press, 1965).
20. Lawrence, D. H., *Studies in Classic American Literature* (New York: Doubleday Anchor, 1955).
21. Matlaw, Ralph, *Belinsky, Chernyshevsky and Dobrolyubov: Selected Criticism* (New York: E. P. Dutton, 1962).
22. Mendel, Arthur, and Makanowitzky, Barbara, *The Short Stories of Leo Tolstoy* (New York: Bantam Books, 1960).
23. Mayakovsky, Vladimir, *The Bedbug and Selected Poetry* (London: Weidenfeld and Nicolson, 1961) tr. Reavey and Hayward.
24. Mayakovsky, Vladimir, *Poetry and Prose* translated by Herbert Marshall (London, Dennis Dobson, 1965).
25. Musil, Robert, *The Man without Qualities* (London: Panther Books, 1968).

26. Obolensky, Dimitri, ed., *The Penguin Book of Russian Verse* (Harmondsworth: Penguin Books, 1962).
27. Poe, Edgar Allan, *Tales, Poems, Essays* (London, Collins, 1952).
28. Pushkin, A. S., *Sochineniya* (Moscow: State Publishing House for Literature, 1962).
29. Racine, Jean, *Théâtre Complet* (Paris: Librairie Garnier Frères, n.d.).
30. Sartre, J.-P., *Being and Nothingness* (London, Methuen, 1956).
31. Sartre, J.-P., *Nausea* (Harmondsworth: Penguin Books, 1965) tr. R. Baldick.
32. Saussure, Ferdinand de, *Cours de Linguistique Générale* (Paris: Payot, 1949).
33. Schopenhauer, A., *The World at Will and Idea* (London: Routledge and Kegan Paul, 1964).
34. Shklovsky, Victor, *Khod Konya* (Moscow-Berlin, 1923).
35. Trotsky, Leon, *Literature and Revolution* (Michigan: Ann Arbor, 1968).
36. Todorov, Tsvetan (ed.), *Théorie de la Littérature* (Paris: Editions du Seuil, 1965).
37. Tolstoy, Leo, *Anna Karenina* (Moscow: Pravda Press, 1962).
38. Striedter, Jurij, *Texte der Russischen Formalisten*, vol. 1 (Munchen: Fink Verlag, 1969).
39. Turgenev, I. S., *Rudin* (London: Heinemann, 1911) tr. Constance Garnett.
40. Wilson, Edmund, *The Triple Thinkers* (Harmondsworth: Penguin Books, 1962).
41. Berger, John, *The Success and Failure of Picasso* (Harmondsworth, Penguin Books, 1965).

D. Additional critical material consulted:

1. Barthes, Roland, S/Z (Paris: Editions du Seuil, 1970).
2. Clive, Geoffrey, *The Broken Icon: Intuitive Existentialism in Classical Russian Fiction* (London: Collier-Macmillan, 1972).
3. Erlich, Victor, *Russian Formalism: History, Doctrine* (The Hague: Mouton, 1969).
4. Harkins, William E., *Dictionary of Russian Literature* (Paterson, New Jersey: Littlefield, Adams and Co., 1959).
5. Kermode, Frank, *The Sense of an Ending* (London: O.U.P.,

1969).
6. Mendilow, A. A., *Time and the Novel* (New York: Humanities Press, 1972).
7. Steiner, George, *Extraterritorial* (London: Faber, 1972).
8. Simmons, E. J., *Pushkin* (New York: Vintage Books, 1964).
9. Tanner, Tony, *City of Words: American Fiction 1950-70* (London: Joanthan Cape, 1971).

# INDEX